Isaiah and Imperial Context

Isaiah and Imperial Context

The Book of Isaiah in the Times of Empire

Edited by
Andrew T. Abernethy,
Mark G. Brett,
Tim Bulkeley,
and Tim Meadowcroft

PICKWICK *Publications* · Eugene, Oregon

ISAIAH AND IMPERIAL CONTEXT
The Book of Isaiah in the Times of Empire

Some scripture quotations are taken from *Holy Bible: New International Version*®. NIV®. Copyright© 1973, 1978, 1984 by International Bible Society.

Some scripture quotations are taken from *New Revised Standard Version Bible*, copyright© 1989, Division of Christian Education of the National Council of the Churches of Christ in the United States of America.

Pickwick Publications
An Imprint of Wipf and Stock Publishers
199 W. 8th Ave., Suite 3
Eugene, OR 97401

www.wipfandstock.com

ISBN 13: 978-1-4982-6558-4

Cataloguing-in-Publication data:

Isaiah and imperial context : the book of Isaiah in the times of empire / edited by Andrew T. Abernethy, Mark G. Brett, Tim Bulkeley, and Tim Meadowcroft.

xii + 236 pp. ; 23 cm. Includes bibliographical references.

ISBN 13: 978-1-4982-6558-4

1. Bible. Isaiah—Criticism, interpretation, etc. 2. Assyria in the Bible. 3. Bible—Postcolonial criticism. 4. Imperialism—Biblical teaching. 5. Bible and Politics.
I. Abernethy, Andrew T. II. Brett, Mark G. III. Bulkeley, Tim. IV. Meadowcroft, Tim. V. Title.

BS1515.52 A127 2013

Manufactured in the U.S.A.

Contents

Illustrations

Contributors

Andrew T. Abernethy is Old Testament Lecturer, Ridley Melbourne Mission and Ministry College

Mark G. Brett is Professor of Hebrew Bible, Whitley College, MCD University of Divinity.

Tim Bulkeley is recently retired from Carey Baptist College, Auckland, and is now a freelance Old Testament scholar teaching both in Auckland and overseas.

John Goldingay is David Allan Hubbard Professor of Old Testament, Fuller Theological Seminary, Pasadena

Christopher B. Hays is D. Wilson Moore Associate Professor of Ancient Near Eastern Studies, Fuller Theological Seminary, Pasadena

Joy Hooker is Internship Dean, Ministry Training College, Auckland

Malcolm Mac MacDonald is a former Postgraduate Student, Laidlaw-Carey Graduate School, Auckland

Judith E. McKinlay is former Senior Lecturer in Old Testament Studies, University of Otago, Dunedin

Tim Meadowcroft is Senior Lecturer in Biblical Studies, Laidlaw College, Auckland

Lena-Sofia Tiemeyer is Senior Lecturer in Hebrew Bible, University of Aberdeen

David Ussishkin is Professor-Emeritus of Archaeology, Tel Aviv University

Preface

EMPIRE IS A DOMINANT factor throughout the book of Isaiah, be it Assyrian, Babylonian, Persian, and/or YHWH's kingdom. It is surprising, then, that no book-length treatment of the topic in Isaiah exists. While the essays in *Isaiah and Imperial Context* by no means exhaust the issue, our hope is that they will stimulate further investigation on how empire is a helpful avenue for engaging with the book.

These essays are the result of a colloquium, "Isaiah and Empire," hosted by Laidlaw-Carey Graduate School in Auckland on February 14–15, 2011, under the leadership of Tim Meadowcroft and Tim Bulkeley, and with Mark Brett as keynote speaker and respondent. The group consisted of scholars and students from Australia, Israel, New Zealand, the United Kingdom, and the United States of America. In addition to these participants, John Goldingay accepted our invitation to participate in this volume. We are grateful to Laidlaw-Carey Graduate School for funding the initial colloquium, and also for a contribution by Laidlaw Graduate School of Theology towards the costs of preparing this set of essays for publication.

The contents of *Isaiah and Imperial Context* reflect a rich variety of interests from the various eras and sections of Isaiah. From an archaeological angle, David Ussishkin offers a sketch, along with a myriad of illustrations, of Sennacherib's campaign into Judah, with a particular focus on Lachish and Jerusalem. Sharing this interest in Assyria, Andrew T. Abernethy explores how the book of Isaiah uses Assyria's imperial tactics of food confiscation and provision to endorse YHWH's kingship. Drawing upon post-colonial African poets Frantz Fanon and Ngugi wa Thiong'o, Christopher B. Hays casts Isaiah as a prophet of death amidst colonized reality. More broadly, Tim Bulkeley, in his study on assertions of divine sovereignty, and Joy Hooker, in her exploration of Zion symbolism, bring their topics to bear on the question of empire within Isaiah as a whole. Focusing on Isaiah 40–55, Judith E. McKinlay utilizes the concept of "hidden transcripts" to explore how Daughter Zion alludes to Lamentations to deal with devastation at the hands of empire. In the same corpus, Lena-Sofia Tiemeyer makes the case that there is no linguistic data to support an often presumed Babylonian provenance for Isaiah 40–55. Tim Meadowcroft offers a theological exposition of "the word of God" in Isaiah 55 as an agent in transformation, even in the imperial realm. Shifting attention to Isaiah 56–66, John Goldingay offers a theological reading of it by considering Isa 56:1 within the entire book and by drawing upon post-colonial theory. Mark G. Brett also examines Isaiah 56–66, but focuses on how the communities behind this text are attempting to navigate life in the Persian era as they wait for YHWH to establish his rule. This is followed by a creative, lyrical essay by Malcolm Mac MacDonald that casts Isaiah as a folk-singing bard bringing hope to despondent exiles through envisioning creation's redemption. The volume concludes with responses from Mark G. Brett and John Goldingay.

Empire, in the unfolding of Isaiah, is unavoidable and inevitable. Under YHWH's rule it is desirable; under most rulers, it is devastating, and God's people need prophetic imagination to survive the journey. May this volume be of assistance today in navigating the tides of empire.

Sennacherib's Campaign to Judah

The Events at Lachish and Jerusalem

David Ussishkin

A. The Assyrian Campaign

LACHISH AND JERUSALEM WERE the most important cities which were militarily challenged by Sennacherib during his campaign to Judah in 701 B.C.E. The events that transpired in these cities are documented in the historical chronicles, and their material remains have systematically been studied by archaeologists. In the case of both cities an analysis of the archaeological data helps in interpreting the written sources and in understanding better the events of 701 B.C.E.

In 705 B.C.E. Sennacherib ascended to the throne of Assyria, which at that time was the largest and most powerful kingdom in the Near East. The young king was soon faced with a revolt organized by Hezekiah king of Judah. An alliance against Assyria was formed between Judah, Egypt and the Philistine cities in the Coastal Plain, possibly with Babylonian support. Sennacherib met the challenge. In 701 B.C.E. he marched to Phoenicia, Philistia, and Judah, and succeeded in reestablishing Assyrian supremacy in those regions (see map in Fig. 1).

Based on the detailed information in the Old Testament and the Assyrian records it seems that the main course of the campaign can be reconstructed in different ways. The following reconstruction seems to us the most plausible. Sennacherib and his powerful army marched on foot from Nineveh, the capital of Assyria to the Phoenician cities situated along the Mediterranean coast (see map in Fig. 1). Sennacherib received there the tribute of various vassal kings and continued his advance southwards to Philistia. He then defeated in open battle a large Egyptian expeditionary force, and reestablished Assyrian rule in Philistia.

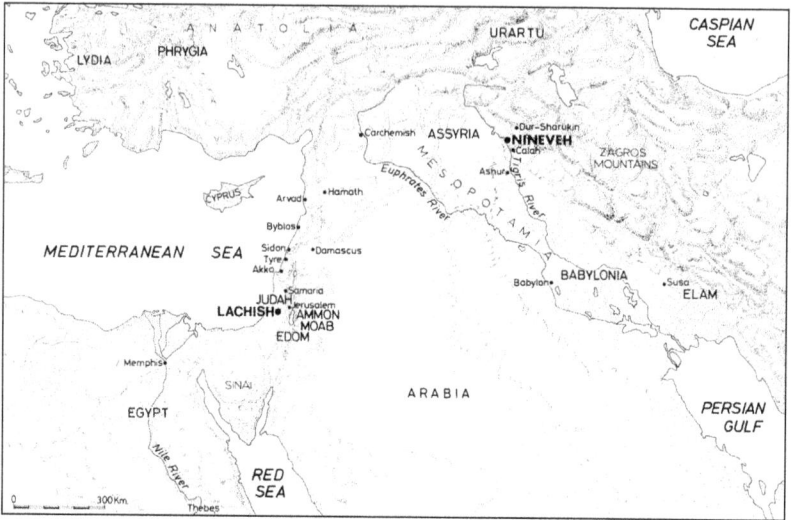

Fig. 1. The ancient Near East at the end of the eighth century B.C.E.

At this point Sennacherib turned against Judah and its ruler Hezekiah (see map in Fig. 2). It is clear that upon arriving in Judah, Sennacherib's attention was focused primarily on the city of Lachish rather than on the capital Jerusalem. Lachish was the most formidable fortress city in Judah, and its conquest and destruction were the paramount task facing Sennacherib when he came to crush the military powers of Hezekiah. In fact, the conquest of Lachish was of singular importance and a great Assyrian military achievement as indicated by the Lachish reliefs (see below).

The Old Testament informs us that Sennacherib encamped at Lachish and established his headquarters there during his campaign in Judah (2 Kgs 18:14, 17; Isa 36:2; 2 Chr 32:9). He conquered and destroyed forty-six Judean cities, and from Lachish he sent a task force to challenge Hezekiah in Jerusalem. Eventually, as related in both the Old Testament and the Assyrian annals, Jerusalem was spared, and Hezekiah, who came to terms with Sennacherib, continued to rule Judah as an Assyrian vassal, and paid heavy tribute to the Assyrian king.

A detailed account of the Assyrian campaign in Judah is given in the biblical texts, focusing on the events in Jerusalem (2 Kgs 18–19; Isa 36–37; 2 Chr 32). It should be noted that the prophet Isaiah played a significant moral and political role in solving this acute crisis, the most difficult one during the reign of Hezekiah.

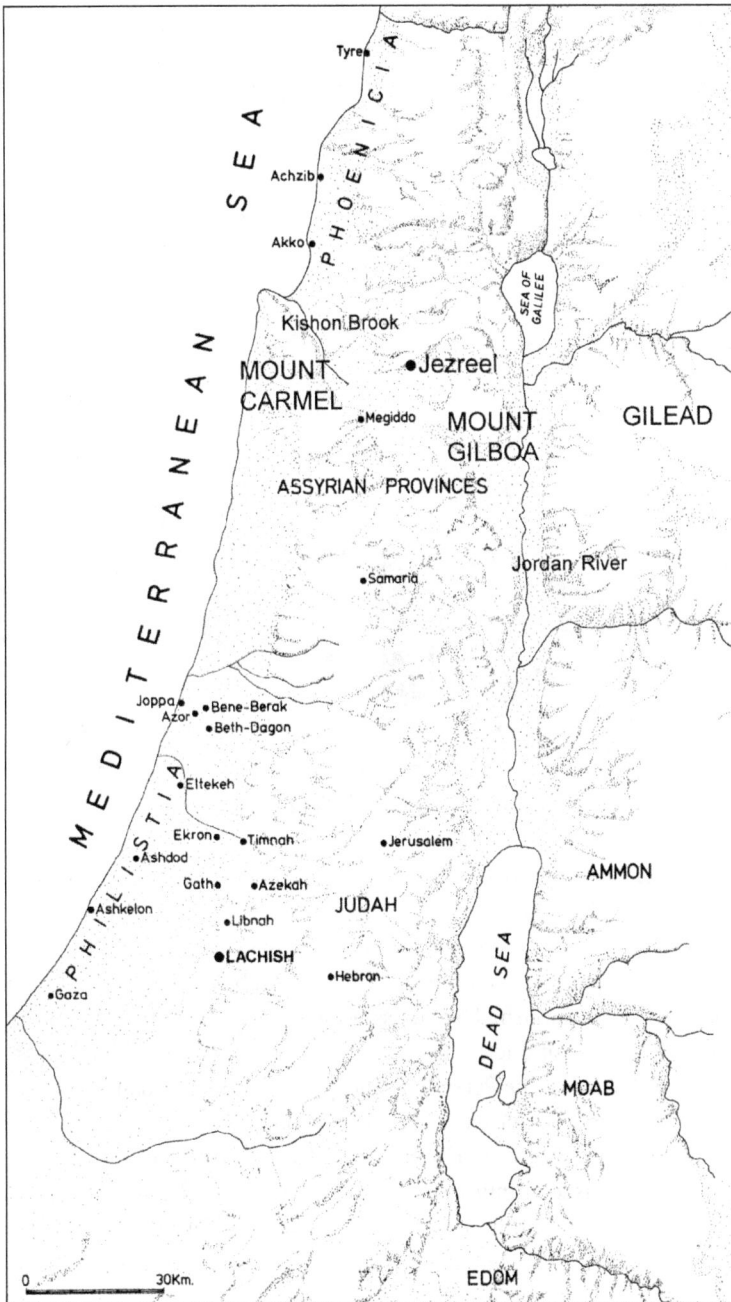

Fig. 2. The Land of Israel at the end of the eighth century B.C.E.

B. Biblical Lachish: The Judean Fortress City

Turning to Tel Lachish, the site of the biblical city, we see that it is one of the largest and most prominent mounds in southern Israel (Fig. 3). The mound is nearly rectangular, its flat summit covering about eighteen acres. The slopes of the mound are very steep due to the massive fortifications of the ancient city constructed here.

Fig. 3. Tel Lachish, the site of biblical Lachish, from the north.

Extensive excavations were carried out at Lachish by three expeditions. The first excavations were conducted on a large scale by a British expedition, directed by James Starkey, between 1932 and 1938. The excavation came to end in 1938 when Starkey was murdered by Arab bandits. The excavation reports were later published by his assistant, Olga Tufnell.[1] In 1966 and 1968 Yohanan Aharoni conducted a small excavation, limited in scope and scale, in the Solar Shrine of the Persian period (Fig. 4 no. 11).[2] Finally, systematic, long-term and large-scale excavations were directed by me on behalf of the Institute of Archaeology of Tel Aviv University between 1972 and 1993.[3]

Lachish was continuously settled between the Chalcolithic period in the fourth millennium and the Hellenistic period in the third century

---

1 Tufnell, Inge, and Harding, *Lachish II*; Tufnell, *Lachish III*; Tufnell et al., *Lachish IV*.

2. Aharoni, *Investigations at Lachish*.

3. Ussishkin, *The Renewed Archaeological Excavations at Lachish (1973–1994)*.

B.C.E.[4] Our concern here, however, is the city of Levels IV and III, dated to the ninth and eighth centuries B.C.E. respectively.

At the beginning of the ninth century B.C.E. one of the kings of Judah constructed here a formidable fortress city, turning Lachish into the most important city in Judah after Jerusalem. With the lack of inscriptions it is not known who is the king who built the city and at what date. The fortress city continued to serve as the main royal fortress of the kings of Judah until its destruction by Sennacherib in 701 B.C.E. In archaeological terminology this fortress city is divided into two successive strata, labeled Level IV and Level III.

The plan in Fig. 4 shows the outlines of the fortress city, and the illustration in Fig. 5 portrays a reconstruction of Lachish from the west on the eve of Sennacherib's conquest in 701 B.C.E.

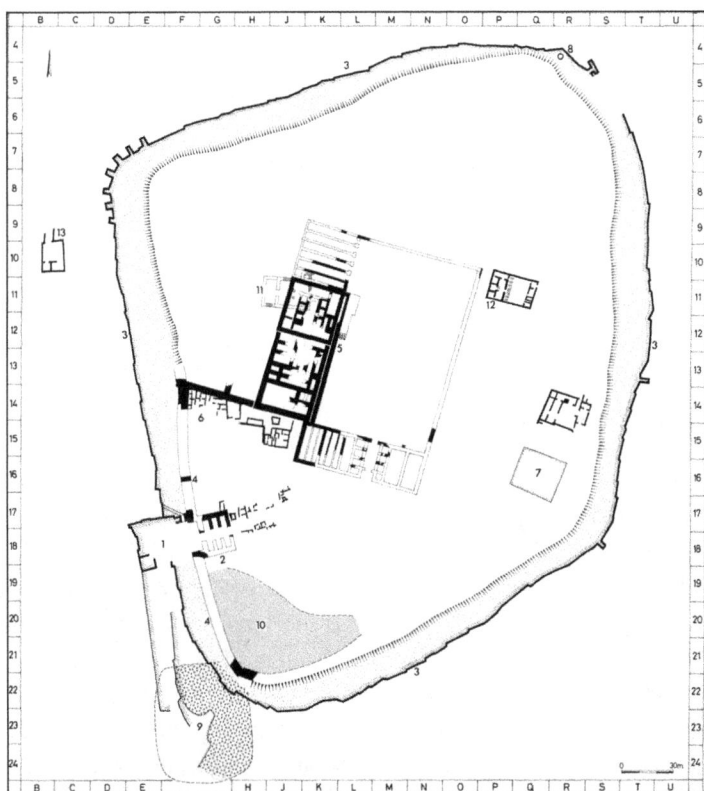

Fig. 4. Plan of Tel Lachish: (1) Outer city-gate; (2) Inner city-gate; (3) Outer revetment; (4) Main city-wall; (5) Judean palace-fort complex; (6) Area S—the main excavation trench; (7) The Great Shaft; (8) The well; (9) Assyrian siege-ramp; (10) The counter-ramp; (11) Acropolis Temple; (12) Solar Shrine; (13) Fosse Temple.

4. See summary in Ussishkin, "Lachish."

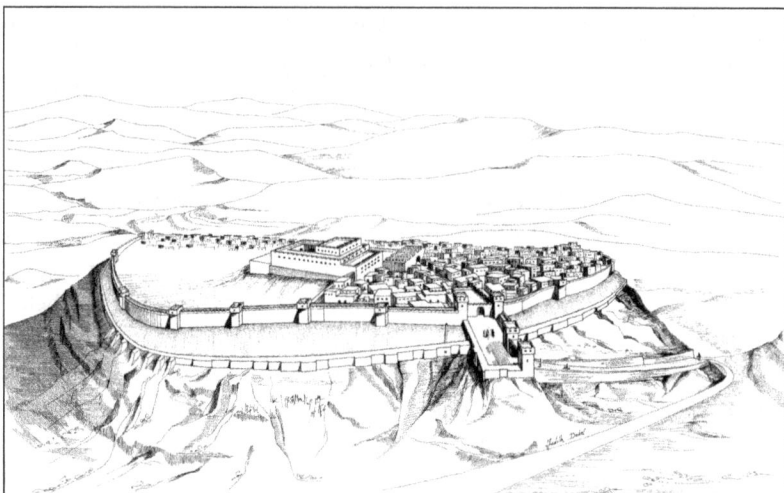

Fig. 5. Reconstruction of Lachish on the eve of Sennacherib's siege, from west; prepared by Judith Dekel from a sketch by H. H. McWilliams in 1933, supplemented by newly excavated data.

The nearly rectangular fortress city was protected by two city-walls —an outer revetment surrounding the site at mid-slope (Fig. 4 no. 3), and the main city-wall, extending along the upper periphery of the site (Fig. 4 no. 4). The massive outer revetment was uncovered in its entirety by the British expedition. Only its lower part, built of stones, was preserved. It probably served mainly to support a rampart or glacis, which in turn reached the bottom of the main city-wall. The main city-wall was built of mud-brick on stone foundations. It was a massive wall. Being more than 6 m or about 20 ft thick, its top provided sufficient, spacious room for the defenders to stand and fight.

A roadway led from the south-west corner of the site to the gate. The city-gate complex included in fact two gates: the outer gate (Fig. 4 no. 1), connected to the outer revetment, and the inner gate (Fig. 4 no. 2), connected to the main city-wall, and an open, spacious courtyard between the two gates.

The city-gate is the largest, strongest and most massive city-gate known today in the Land of Israel (Fig. 6). We started at the time to reconstruct the gate but this project was stopped for the time being due to lack of funds. Most impressive is the back corner of the gate complex, now partly restored. The massive corner, built of huge stone blocks, originally rose to a height of nearly 10 m or 30 ft.

Fig. 6. The Judean city-gate, partly reconstructed.

From the inner gate a roadway led the way to the huge palace-fort complex which crowned the centre of the summit (Fig. 4 no. 5). The palace-fort served as the residence of the royal Judean governor and as the base for the garrison.

The palace-fort is undoubtedly the largest and most massive edifice known today in Judah (Fig. 7). Very little is known about the building proper as only its foundations below floor level have been preserved. The structure of the foundations resembles a big box rising above the surrounding surface. Some parts of the exterior walls of the foundation structure were exposed in the excavations. These walls are about 3 m or 9 ft thick. The spaces between the foundation walls were filled with earth and the exterior walls were supported by an earth rampart.

Fig. 7. The Judean palace-fort, from south; a group of people stand on the floor of the edifice.

The floor of the building extended at the top of the foundations, and nothing of the superstructure remains today. We can safely assume that a magnificent, monumental edifice rose at the time above these foundations.

A deep well, which formed the main water source of the settlement, was located near the city-wall in the north-east corner of the site (Fig. 4 no. 8). Apparently it provided sufficient quantities of water during times of peace and siege alike. The upper part of the well was lined by stone blocks and the lower part was hewn in the rock (Fig. 8). It was 44 m or 130 ft deep and still contained water when the British expedition uncovered it. Significantly, in the earlier part of the twentieth century C.E., as in the past, Arab villagers in the Lachish region still drew their water from similar wells.

Fig. 8. The well—the main water source of ancient Lachish.

The city of Level III was completely destroyed by fire in 701 B.C.E. when Lachish was conquered by the Assyrian army. Apparently, following the successful conquest, Assyrian soldiers holding burning torches in their hands walked systematically from house to house and set everything on fire. The remains of the destruction have been encountered wherever the excavations reached the houses of Level III. The domestic houses were largely built of mud-brick, and the fire was so intense that the sun-dried mud-bricks were nearly baked and colored, and in some cases it can in fact be observed how the walls of the houses collapsed. The floors of the houses were found covered with a layer of ashes, smashed pottery, and various household utensils—all buried under the collapse.

An impressive assemblage of pottery was retrieved in the houses of Level III. Many vessels could be restored from the fragments dispersed on the floors of the houses. Sometimes the broken vessels still kept their shape when smashed, thus making the restoration work much easier.

One group of pottery vessels—the royal Judean or *lmlk* storage jars—is of special importance (Fig. 9a). These are large storage jars, uniform in shape and size, which were manufactured in one production centre by the Judean government, apparently as part of the military preparations made before the Assyrian invasion. These jars were used to store oil or wine. They are known from various sites in Judah, including Jerusalem, but mainly from Lachish. Their handles were stamped. The stamps included a four-winged or a two-winged emblem—apparently royal Judean emblems—and an inscription in ancient Hebrew characters (Fig. 9b). It reads "*lmlk*" that is "belonging to the king" and the name of one of four towns in Judah: Hebron, Sochoh, Ziph or *mmšt*. These towns must have been associated with the manufacture or distribution of the storage jars, or with the produce stored in them. Some of the jars were also stamped with a "private" stamp bearing the name of the potter or an official, like the one in Fig. 9c, stamped with the name "Meshulam son of Ahimelekh."

Fig. 9. Royal Judean or *lmlk* storage jars: (a) Restored storage jars; (b) *lmlk hbrn* seal impression; (c) "Private" seal impression "Meshulam (son of) Ahimelekh."

C. Lachish: The Remains of the Assyrian Siege

When Sennacherib arrived at the head of his army in Lachish, he did not have to deliberate at length on where to direct the main attack on the city. The obvious answer was dictated by the topography of the site and the surrounding terrain. The city was enveloped by deep valleys on nearly all sides, and only at the south-west corner did a topographical saddle connect the mound with the neighboring hillock (Fig. 10). The fortifications at this corner were especially strong, but nevertheless, the south-west corner of the site as well as the nearby city-gate were the most vulnerable and most logical points to assault.

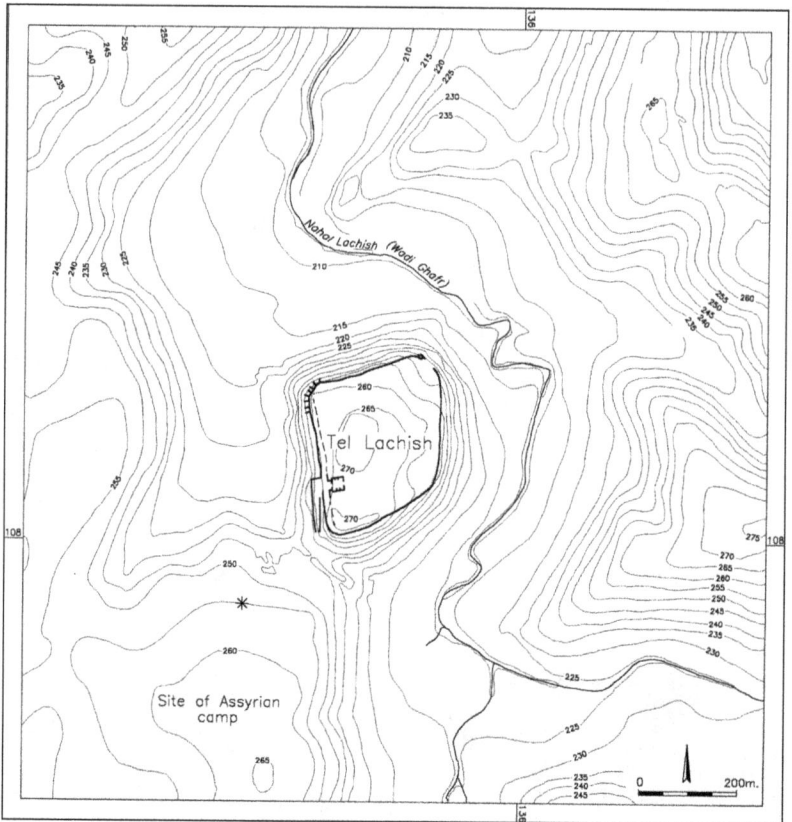

Fig. 10. Topographical map of Lachish and its surroundings.

Upon arrival at Lachish the Assyrian army must have pitched its camp, as was the practice in the Assyrian campaigns. It must have been a large camp, providing facilities for the expeditionary force, and accommodating the king's retinue and headquarters. I assume that the site of the camp, which is also portrayed on the Lachish relief, can be fixed with much certainty on the hillock to the south-west of the mound, where the modern Israeli village Moshav Lachish is now located (Fig. 10). This hillock is situated a short distance from the mound exactly opposite the place where the main attack was to take place. It is situated not far from the city-wall but beyond the range of fire of the defenders. This hillock is relatively high and its summit broad and flat. Unfortunately, all remains of such a camp, if still preserved, would have been completely eradicated when the houses and farms of Moshav Lachish were constructed about sixty years ago.

The excavations in the south-west corner were started in 1932, when Starkey cleared the face of the outer revetment around the entire mound.

Large amounts of stones were uncovered at this spot, and the digging extended down the slope as more stones were removed. As the excavations developed, the saddle area at the foot of the south-west corner and the roadway leading up to the city-gate were cleared of many thousand tons of fallen masonry. Starkey believed that these stones collapsed from above, from the strong fortifications of the south-west corner destroyed during the Assyrian attack.

We resumed the excavation of the south-west corner in 1983. It soon appeared that the stones encountered by Starkey were irregularly heaped against the slope of the mound rather than fallen from above, and hence it became clear that they form the remains of the Assyrian siege-ramp. The excavations at our trench enabled us to reconstruct the Assyrian attack to a large degree.[5]

A general picture of the area which shows the features discussed above is shown in Fig. 11. On the left the roadway leading to the city-gate can be seen, and in the center our trench. In the lower center the siege-ramp can be seen, with Starkey's excavation looking in the picture like a disused quarry.

Fig. 11. The excavation in the south-west corner of the site.

At the bottom of the slope the siege-ramp was studied (Figs. 4 no. 9; 12). Although removed to a large degree by Starkey it could still be studied and reconstructed. At its bottom, the siege-ramp was about 70 m or 210 ft wide, and about 50 m or about 150 ft long. The core of the siege-ramp was

5. Ussishkin, "The Assyrian Attack on Lachish"; Ussishkin, *The Renewed Archaeological Excavations at Lachish (1973–1994)*, 695–767.

made entirely of heaped boulders which must have been collected in the fields around. We estimated that the stones invested in the construction of the ramp weighed 13,000 to 19,000 tons.

The stones of the upper layer of the siege-ramp were found stuck together by hard mortar, forming a kind of stone-and-mortar conglomerate, which was preserved at a few points. This layer was the mantle of the ramp, added on top of the loose boulders in order to create a compact surface which was necessary to enable the attacking soldiers and their siege machines to move on solid ground. The top of the siege-ramp was crowned by a horizontal platform; it was made of red soil and was sufficiently wide, thus providing even ground for the siege-machines to stand upon.

To end the discussion of the siege-ramp it has to be emphasized that the siege-ramp of Lachish is, first, the earliest siege-ramp so far uncovered in archaeological excavations, and second, the only Assyrian siege-ramp which is known today.

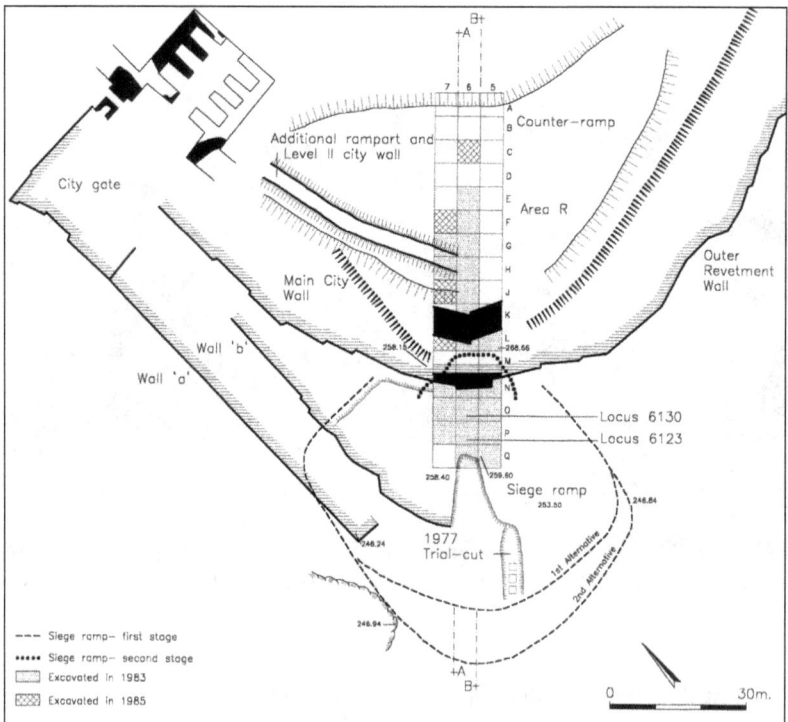

Fig. 12. The south-west corner of the site.

Above the siege-ramp were uncovered the fortifications of the south-west corner which were especially massive and strong at this vulnerable point (Fig. 12). The outer revetment formed here a kind of tower; it was built of mud-brick on stone foundations and stood about 6 m or 18 ft high, preserved nearly to its original height. The tower was topped by a kind of balcony, protected by a mud-brick parapet, on which the defenders could stand and fight.

The main city-wall extended above and behind the balcony of the tower of the outer revetment. The main city-wall was preserved at this point nearly to its original height—almost 5 m or 15 ft. A stone glacis, well preserved, covered the façade of the wall (Fig. 13).

Fig. 13. The façade of the main city-wall exposed at the south-west corner.

Once the defenders of the city saw that the Assyrians were building a siege-ramp in preparation for storming the city-walls, they started to lay down a counter-ramp inside the main city-wall (Figs. 4 no. 10; 12). They dumped here large amounts of mound debris taken from earlier levels, which they brought from the north-east side of the mound, and constructed a large ramp, higher than the main city-wall, which provided them with a second, inner new line of defense.

As a result of the construction of the counter-ramp, the south-west corner became the highest part of the mound. It undoubtedly was a very impressive rampart, its apex rising about 3 m or 10 ft above the top of the main city-wall. Some makeshift fence or wall, perhaps made of wood, must have crowned the rampart, but its remains were not preserved. Our soundings in the core of the counter-ramp revealed accumulation of mound debris containing much earlier pottery, as well as limestone chips, which was dumped in diagonal layers.

Significantly, once the Assyrians reached the walls and overcame the defense, they extended the siege-ramp over the ruined city-wall—we called it the "second stage" of the siege-ramp—to enable the attack on the newly-formed, higher defense line on the counter-ramp. The boulders of the second stage of the siege-ramp can be seen in the picture in Fig. 13, in the section at the side of the trench, dumped against the façade of the main city-wall.

Turning to weapons and ammunition used in the battle I shall first introduce the siege-machine, the formidable weapon used by the Assyrians to destroy the defense line on the walls. No less than seven siege-machines arrayed for battle on top of the siege-ramp and near the city-gate are portrayed in the Lachish reliefs (Fig. 14). The South-African artist Gert le Grange who took part in our excavations, prepared an excellent, detailed reconstruction of such a siege-machine (Fig. 15). It is largely based on details of the Assyrian relief, shown here at left. The machine moves on four wheels, partly protected by its body, which is made in six or more separate sections for easy dismantling and reassembling. The ram, made of wooden beam reinforced with a sharp metal point, is suspended from one or more ropes, like a pendulum, and several crouching soldiers are moving it backwards and forwards. The defenders standing on the wall are throwing flaming torches on the siege-machine. As a counter measure, an Assyrian soldier is pouring water from a long ladle on the façade of the machine to prevent it from catching fire. The artist did not forget to add a cauldron containing water beside this soldier.

Fig. 14. The Lachish reliefs: an Assyrian siege machine attacking the city-gate.

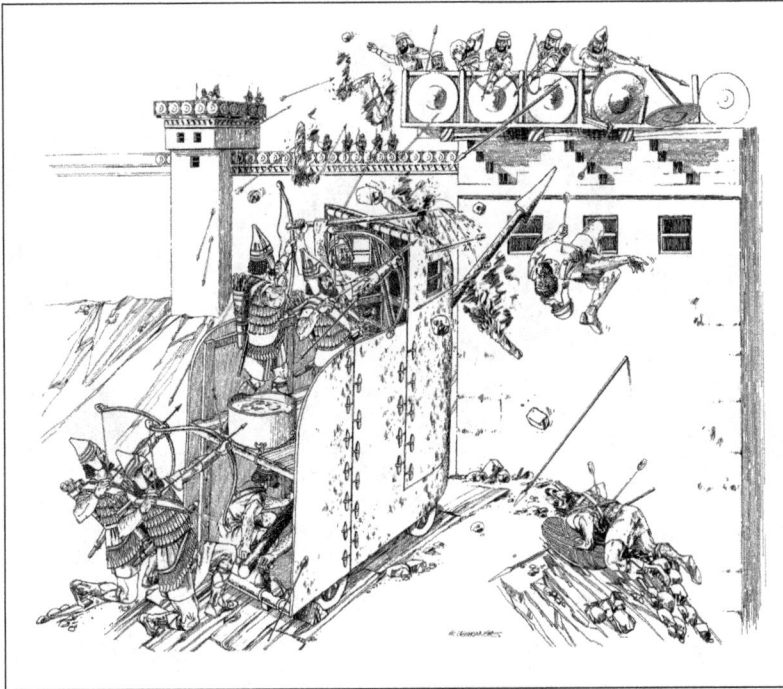

Fig. 15. The attack on the city-wall: a reconstruction by Gert le Grange.

Significantly, this reconstruction emphasizes the fact that the fight between the two sides took place at very close quarters, something very difficult for us to imagine at the present time when long-range guns and missiles form the main weapons.

Two more unique finds are apparently associated with the attempts of the defenders to destroy the siege-machines. The first one includes twelve "perforated stones" which were discovered at the foot of both city-walls (Fig. 16). These are large perforated stone blocks, with a flat top, straight sides, and an irregular bottom. Each of them is nearly 60 cm or 2 ft in diameter and weighs about 100 to 200 kg. Remains of burnt, relatively thin ropes were found in the holes of two of the stones.

Fig. 16. "Perforated stones" found at the foot of the city-wall.

Fig. 17. Iron chain found at the foot of the city-wall.

It seems that the "perforated stones" formed part of the weaponry of the defenders. As indicated by the remains of the ropes, the stones were tied to ropes and lowered from the wall. I assume that these stones were lowered from some makeshift installation, such as a thick wooden beam projecting from the line of the wall. The defenders probably used the stones in an attempt to damage the siege-machines and prevent the rams from hitting the wall; they must have dropped the stones on the siege-machines and moved them to and fro like a pendulum.

The second find is a fragment of an iron chain, being 37 cm long and containing four long, narrow links, which was uncovered in the burnt mud-brick debris in front of the outer revetment (Fig. 17). The defenders probably used the iron chain to unbalance the siege-machines; we can assume that they lowered the chain below the point of thrust of the ram, in order to catch the shaft of the ram when it reaches the wall, and raise it up.

Some of the ammunition used in the battle was also found. The Lachish reliefs displays slingers shooting at the walls as well as defenders shooting sling stones at the attackers, and many sling stones were indeed found in the excavations (Fig. 18). These are round balls of flint or limestone, shaped like tennis balls, each weighing about 250 grams or even more.

Fig. 18. Assyrian slinger shown on the Lachish reliefs and sling stones found at Lachish.

The Lachish reliefs display Assyrian archers supporting the attack on the walls, and indeed close to one thousand arrowheads were discovered in the excavation of the south-west corner (Fig. 19). The arrowheads are not uniform in size or shape, and different types are represented. Almost all of them were made of iron, and a few were made of bronze or carved of bone. In some cases ashes, the remains of the wooden shafts of the arrows could still be discerned when exposed in the excavation. Most of the arrowheads were uncovered in the burnt mud-brick debris in front of the city-walls. Apparently these arrows were shot by Assyrian archers at warriors standing on the balconies on top of the walls. The discovery of so many arrowheads in such a small area shows how concentrated the Assyrian fire power was. Many arrowheads were found bent—an indication that they were shot at the walls with powerful bows from close range.

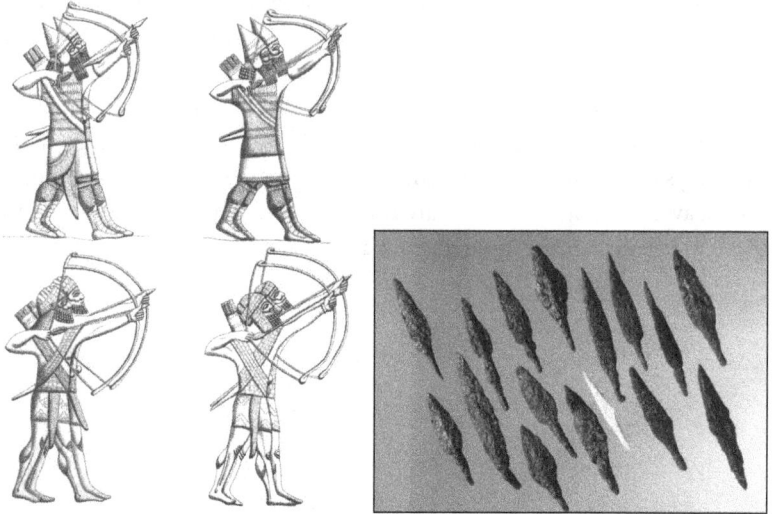

Fig. 19. Assyrian archers shown on the Lachish reliefs and arrowheads found at Lachish.

D. The Lachish Reliefs

A few years after the campaign in the Levant and the subjugation of Judah Sennacherib constructed his royal palace in Nineveh, at that time the capital of Assyria (see map in Fig. 1). The palace is known today as the South-west palace. This extravagant edifice, its construction, size, magnificence, and beauty are recorded in detail in Sennacherib's inscriptions; he proudly called it the "Palace without a rival." The palace was largely excavated in 1850 C.E. by Sir Henry Layard on behalf of the British Museum in London. Layard prepared a plan of the building and uncovered a large number of reliefs cut on slabs of alabaster stone which adorned the walls.

The stone slabs depicting in relief the conquest of Lachish were erected in a special room, known as Room XXXVI, located at the back of a central ceremonial suite in the palace. It seems that the whole room—and perhaps also the entire suite —was intended to commemorate the conquest of Judah and the victory at Lachish.[6]

According to Layard, the Lachish room (no. XXXVI) was 38 ft wide and 18 ft long (Fig. 20). Its walls were probably entirely covered by the Lachish reliefs. The stone slabs of the relief on the left side of the room were left by Layard on the site and were thus lost, while the rest of the series, comprising twelve slabs, was transferred by him to the British museum in London and is presently exhibited there. The length of the preserved series is about 19 m or 57 ft. It seems that the missing part of the series was about 8 m or 24 ft long. Accordingly, the entire series depicting the conquest of Lachish must have been about 27 m or 81 ft long. This is the longest and most detailed series of Assyrian reliefs depicting the storming and conquest of a single fortress city.

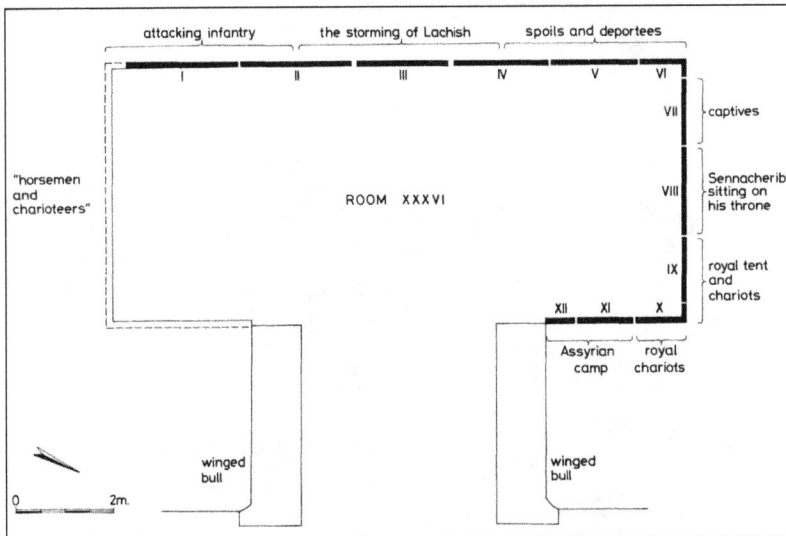

Fig. 20. Plan of the room (no. XXXVI) in which the Lachish reliefs were exhibited.

The missing relief slabs were not documented, and the only hint as to their content is Layard's remark that "the reserve consisted of large bodies of horsemen and charioteers." Further along, in consecutive order from left to right, are shown the attacking infantry, the storming of the city, the transfer of booty, captives and families going into exile, Sennacherib sitting on his throne, the royal tent and chariot, and finally the Assyrian military camp.

Significantly, the section portraying the storming of the city was placed exactly in the center of the rear wall of the room, opposite the monumental

---

6. Ussishkin, "The 'Lachish Reliefs' and the City of Lachish"; Ussishkin, *The Conquest of Lachish by Sennacherib*, 59–126.

entrance. Given good lighting conditions, anyone who passed through the entrance could see the storming of Lachish facing him as he entered the room.

Surveying some details of the relief series from left to right, we first see the infantry, composed of slingers and archers, attacking the walls of the besieged city (Fig. 21). The soldiers are shown against a uniform background resembling scale armor or fish scales, the same background that characterizes the entire series. It is possibly meant to represent a stony landscape, like the rocky small hillocks typical of the Lachish region. Two grape vines and a fig tree can be seen at the top, easily recognizable by their typical leaves and fruits.

Fig. 21. The Lachish reliefs: Assyrian soldiers shooting at the walls of the city.

Next is shown the central scene, the attack on the city-walls, schematically portrayed on three adjoining stone slabs (Fig. 22). The city-gate is shown in the centre, being attacked by a siege machine (also Fig. 14). Refugees are shown carrying their belongings and leaving the city through the gate. On both sides of the besieged city are depicted the city-walls. Judean warriors stand on the walls and on the balcony on the roof of the gate

and shoot at the attacking Assyrians. The siege-ramp is shown to the right
of the gatehouse. Altogether, as mentioned above, seven siege-machines are
attacking the walls—five on top of the siege-ramp, and two attacking the
city-gate, possibly placed on an additional siege-ramp built against the gatehouse. The royal Assyrian reliefs usually portray one, and in a few cases two
siege-machines attacking the walls of a besieged city. The relief portraying
the siege of Lachish is unique in showing no less than seven siege-machines
taking active part in the battle.

Fig. 22. The Lachish reliefs: The city under attack—the central part of the scene.

A very interesting detail is shown above the right side of the siege-
ramp. Three burning chariots or carts are being thrown down from the
city-wall on the attacking Assyrians and their siege-machines. Additional
vehicles were possibly portrayed above the left side of the siege-ramp, in
that part of the relief which is missing today. The vehicles are rendered in an
identical though schematic manner, each represented by one wheel with a
thick felloe and six spokes, and a yoke with attachments for harnessing two
animals. Tongues of flame indicate that the vehicles were set on fire before
being thrown over the parapets. The fact that several identical vehicles are
shown here suggests that these were chariots of the Judean garrison. Since

these chariots could not be used as such in the besieged city, they were set afire and hurled down by the defenders in a desperate attempt to repulse the enemy and burn down the siege-machines.

Further to the right are shown Assyrian soldiers carrying booty (Fig. 23) as well as the deported or punished inhabitants of the city. The portrayed booty probably contains the symbols of state that formed part of the Judean governor's official equipment and were stored in the palace-fort. The first soldier holds a scepter with its round top pointing downwards, no doubt deliberately. The second and third soldiers each carry a large ceremonial chalice or incense burner which is probably made of copper or bronze. The fourth soldier bears a chair, most likely the governor's throne. The following two soldiers pull a chariot which must have been the official vehicle of the governor, this being the only Judean chariot from the biblical era known today. Finally, three soldiers carry spears, shields and swords.

Fig. 23. The Lachish reliefs: Assyrian soldiers carrying booty from the city.

The artist makes a clear distinction between most of the inhabitants of Lachish, which were deported, and some which were severely punished. A few of those are being stabbed by the Assyrian soldiers or flayed alive and three prisoners are impaled on long sticks near the roadway leading down from the city-gate (Fig. 24). This particular site of execution was probably chosen so that all captives and deportees leaving the city would be forced to see them. The three impaled captives are naked and their heads sag forwards indicating that they are already dead. In my view, the prisoner on the right is wearing a plumed helmet, an indication that he was the Judean governor. If so, he was impaled wearing his official helmet, together with his two deputies, in front of the city-gate.

Fig. 24. The Lachish reliefs: Impaled prisoners near the city-gate.

The inhabitants of Lachish are shown leaving the destroyed city to exile, taking their belongings with them, a tragic picture of entire families forced out of their homes (Fig. 25). The family shown here consists of two women, followed by two girls and a man leading a cart harnessed to two oxen. The cart is laden with household goods and tied-up bundles on which two small children, a boy and a girl, are sitting. The ribs of the oxen are emphasized, possibly to point out that they suffer from malnutrition.

Fig. 25. The Lachish reliefs: Judean family deported from the conquered city.

More families are shown in the continuation of the relief. The most impressive scene is the picture of the father who walks with his two little children and carries his belongings on his shoulders (Fig. 26).

The deportees are distinguishable by their appearance and dress. The women wear a long, simple garment. A long shawl covers their head, shoulders and back, reaching to the bottom of the dress. The men have a short beard and their heads are wound with scarves whose fringed ends hang down. Their garment has a fringed tassel hanging between the legs. Both men and women are barefooted.

The two processions, the one of Assyrian soldiers carrying booty, and the other of the deported inhabitants, face the Assyrian monarch sitting on his throne (Fig. 27). The cuneiform inscription, carved in the background of the relief, identifies the assaulted city as Lachish. The beautiful throne is richly ornamented and is specifically mentioned in the inscription; it was almost certainly brought to Lachish from Assyria. The throne has very high legs, enabling the sitting monarch to look down from above at the people standing in front of him. The feet of the king rest on a high footstool. Both the throne and the stool were decorated with beautifully carved ivories.

Fig. 26. The Lachish reliefs: Judean family deported from the conquered city.

Facing the king stands a high official, possibly the Tartan, the commander-in-chief. He is followed by commanders of lesser rank, and two eunuchs holding fans stand behind them.

Behind Sennacherib's throne is pitched the royal tent, identified as Sennacherib's tent by a short cuneiform inscription. Beneath it is parked the ceremonial chariot of Sennacherib, its royal ownership attested by the soldier holding a canopy behind it. Further to the right is portrayed the king's retinue—dismounted cavalrymen and the king's battle chariot.

The Assyrian fortified camp marks the end of the relief series at the right-hand side. Elliptical in shape, it is depicted in the schematic Assyrian style, which combines a bird's-eye view of the fortifications with a frontal view of the pavilions and other elements inside the camp. The camp is surrounded by a protective wall with towers, and a wide thoroughfare crosses the camp from end to end.

Fig. 27. The Lachish reliefs: Sennacherib sitting on his throne facing Lachish.

Lachish provides us with a unique opportunity of comparing an Assyrian stone relief depicting in detail an ancient city with the site of the same city whose topography and fortifications are well known to us. Strange as this may sound, this is an unprecedented opportunity. Although many enemy cities are shown in the Assyrian stone reliefs found in various Assyrian royal palaces, only a handful of them can be identified by name, and even fewer can be associated with places of known location and nature. In the case of Lachish, however, not only are we well acquainted with the topographical setting, but we have identified the city level that was attacked by the Assyrians and uncovered the remains of the attack on the city.

It seems to me, following the initial study of the British scholar Richard Barnett,[7] that the relief series portrays the city from one particular spot. In the relief the various features of the city are depicted according to the usual rigid and schematic conventions of the Assyrian artists, but they are shown in certain perspective, roughly maintaining the proportions and relationships of the various elements as they would appear to the onlooker standing at one specific point.[8]

In the reliefs the city-gate complex is shown in the center of the mound. The onlooker faces the outer gate, while the roadway leading to the bottom of the mound extends to the right. The palace-fort, which was the most imposing building on the site, probably looms above the gatehouse. The main siege-ramp is shown to the right of the city-gate and the palace-fort. It is the largest feature in the scene, and its top is higher than that of the city-walls shown on both sides of the city.

In my view the particular vantage point from which Lachish is portrayed in the relief is located south-west of the site, on the slope of the neighboring hillock (Fig. 10). At this particular spot, as in the relief, we see the façade of the city-gate in the centre, with the roadway leading to the right. The palace-fort looms above the city-gate. The siege-ramp, being just in front and near this point looks much higher and much larger than the other features.

This theory was contested by several scholars who claim that the city is shown in the relief in a schematic, meaningless manner.[9] However, I hold to my view, although I cannot prove this case. This spot is located just in front of the presumed site of the Assyrian camp, between it and the city, and facing the main point of attack. I believe that this is the very spot where Sennacherib, the supreme commander, sat on his throne, conducted the battle, and later reviewed the booty bearers and the deportees (Fig. 27). Consequently, I believe that the relief presents the besieged city as seen through the eyes of Sennacherib himself at his command post.

E. Biblical Jerusalem At the Time of Hezekiah

Biblical Jerusalem extended on several hills which are still densely settled today (Fig. 28). In fact the city has been continuously settled since biblical times. The black line in the map in Fig. 28 marks the present massive wall of the Old

7. Barnett, "The Siege of Lachish."

8. Ussishkin, "The 'Lachish Reliefs' and the City of Lachish"; Ussishkin, *The Conquest of Lachish by Sennacherib*, 118–26.

9. Jacoby, "The Representation and Identification of Cities on Assyrian Reliefs"; Uehlinger, "Clio in a World of Pictures."

City, which was built by the Ottoman Sultan Suleiman the Magnificent in the sixteenth century C.E. and still stands complete today. The dotted line in the map marks the borders of Jerusalem during the reign of Hezekiah, on the eve of Sennacherib's campaign. The rectangular compound of the Temple Mount can clearly be seen in the map and in the photograph in Fig. 29.

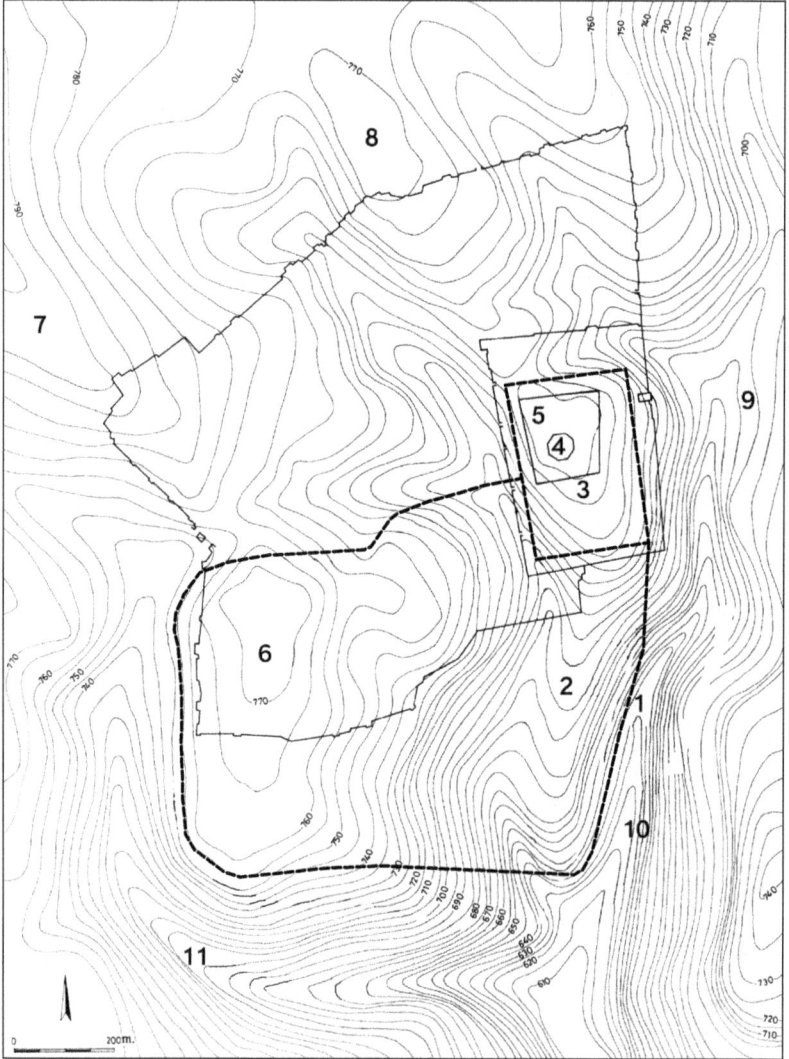

Fig. 28. A topographical map of biblical Jerusalem: (1) Spring Gihon; (2) City of David; (3) Temple Mount; (4) Dome of the Rock where the temple stood; (5) Assumed place of the royal palace; (6) South-West Hill; (7) North-West Hill; (8) North-East Hill—the place of The Camp of the Assyrians: (9) Kidron Valley; (10) Silwan necropolis on slope of Kidron Valley; (11) Hinnom Valley.

Fig. 29. Jerusalem: The Temple Mount; air view from the south-east.

Archaeological research started in Jerusalem 160 years ago, in 1850 C.E. It extensively continues to this day. In fact, at this very time there are several on-going excavations taking place in different parts of the ancient city. The same places have been investigated again and again. Looking at the list of the excavators one finds scholars from many nations. In the earlier period they were mostly Europeans—British, French, Italian, and German scholars predominating. Many of them were biblical scholars, theologians, and monks from the local monasteries, whose interest in the history of Jerusalem was inspired by their religious beliefs. Some of them were travelers or British army officers. In more recent years most of the excavations have been carried out by Israeli scholars. Many of the excavations in recent years are salvage excavations, resulting from development and construction work in the modern, fast growing city.

The literature on the archaeology and ancient history of Jerusalem is enormous. A few summarizing works, which might be useful for further study are noted.[10]

10. Avigad, *Discovering Jerusalem*; Ben-Dov, *Historical Atlas of Jerusalem*; Kenyon, *Digging Up Jerusalem*; Mazar, Shiloh, and Geva, "Jerusalem"; Reich, *Excavating the City of David*; Shanks, *Jerusalem*; Simons, *Jerusalem in the Old Testament*; Vaughn and Killebrew, *Jerusalem in Bible and Archaeology*; Wightman, *The Walls of Jerusalem*.

The kingdom of Judah under King Hezekiah was very strong and powerful during the latter part of the eighth century B.C.E. Jerusalem became the largest city in the kingdom, in fact a huge city in proportion to other cities in Judah. This development was probably due partly to large migration from the northern kingdom of Israel which had been destroyed and annexed to Assyria in 720 B.C.E., and partly due to a process of development and economic and social changes in Judah. Jerusalem now extended over the entire City of David and the Temple Mount, as well as on the large hill to the west, known as the South-West hill (Fig. 28 no. 6). Here was built a domestic quarter known as the *Mishneh*.[11] Jerusalem now covered an area of about 110 acres, and it is estimated that several thousand people lived there. The large city continued to exist in the seventh century, and was finally totally destroyed—the temple and palace included—by the Babylonian king Nebuchadnezzar in 588/6 B.C.E.

Jerusalem of that time was also a heavily fortified city. Segments of its massive fortifications—all walls built with large, roughly-cut blocks—have been uncovered in different parts of the city. On the eastern side, segments of walls were found along the eastern slope of the City of David and immediately to the south of the Temple Mount. On the western side several segments of massive walls and towers were found in the South-West Hill (Fig. 30).[12]

Fig. 30. Jerusalem: A massive tower— part of the eighth-century B.C.E. fortifications in the South-West hill.

11. Avigad, *Discovering Jerusalem*.

12. Ibid.

The fortified royal acropolis, crowning the large city, was built on the Temple Mount (Fig. 28 no. 3). It contained the temple and the royal palace of the kings of Judah. Presently, the Temple Mount is a rectangular compound, a Moslem holy place, known in Arabic as *Haram al-sharif* (Fig. 29). It is the third most important Moslem holy place, after Mecca and Medina. In the middle of the compound stands the beautiful mosque known as Dome of the Rock and in its southern side is situated the large al-Aqsa Mosque. This huge compound—its flat surface and the massive walls surrounding it—was constructed by Herod the Great in the 1st century B.C.E., and in its center stood the Second Temple. The Second Temple was destroyed by the Romans in 70 C.E. but the surrounding compound remained standing till the present day. Since its destruction the enclosing wall of the compound on the western side has become the holiest place for the Jews, known as the Western Wall, where Jews pray and lament the destruction of the temple.

Several superficial surveys were conducted on the Temple Mount in the nineteenth century C.E., but in general it is out of bounds for any archaeological study. In any case, no remains of the First Temple and the nearby royal palace have been discerned there, and it seems that the large-scale building activities of Herod must have obliterated or covered all the earlier remains.

Therefore—from the perspective of the archaeologist—whatever we can say is to a large degree a matter of theory. We can try and reconstruct the Temple Mount but this is based solely on topographical data, circumstantial evidence, comparable finds from other places, and the data presented in the biblical text. Unfortunately—and this indeed is very frustrating—we cannot verify the theories in field work on the ground.

Assuming that the temple stood on the summit of the hill, exactly at the spot where the Dome of the Rock is presently situated (Figs. 28 no. 4; 29), scholars generally reconstruct the royal palace to the south of the temple, where the ground is lower. In my view, however, it is reasonable to assume that the palace stood on the lower ground to the north of the temple, an area sufficiently spacious to accommodate such a large complex (Fig. 28 no. 5). If located to the north of the temple, the royal palace of Jerusalem would have been ideally situated: the royal acropolis of Jerusalem was at the north-east edge of the city and the palace at the northern end of the acropolis, adjacent to the edge of the fortified city. This way the palace would have been more secure and isolated, while if located to the south of the temple everybody approaching the temple from the direction of the City of David would have had to pass near it.

The fortified royal acropolis on the Temple Mount was surrounded on three sides by a steep slope, but on the north-west side it was connected by a topographical saddle to the hill running farther to the north-west, known as the North-East Hill (Fig. 28 no. 8). This saddle constituted the topographical weak point in the defense of the Temple Mount. Based on a survey of the exposed rock-surface in this area it seems possible that a deep ditch or moat was cut into the rock at this point.

F. Jerusalem: The Assyrian Campaign

After the storming and the destruction of Lachish Sennacherib remained encamped near the ruined fortress city (2 Kgs 18:17; Isa 36:2; 2 Chr 32:9). From there Sennacherib sent a strong task force to Jerusalem, headed by three top officials—the Tartan, Rabsaris and Rabshakeh (the commander-in-chief, the chief eunuch, and the chief officer)—who conducted the negotiations with Hezekiah and came to terms with him. Hezekiah—being under heavy pressure—agreed to pay a heavy tribute and became a vassal of the Assyrian king. The story of these events and the salvation of Jerusalem is told in detail in both the Assyrian inscriptions and the Old Testament (2 Kgs 18–19; Isa 36–37; 2 Chr 32).

The government of Hezekiah made thorough preparations to meet the Assyrian invasion. We are informed that changes were made in the water systems of Jerusalem and that buildings were demolished in the city in order to provide building stones for strengthening the city-walls (Isa 22:9–11; 2 Chr 32). Also, hundreds of *lmlk* stamped handles of storage jars, which—as discussed above—had probably been manufactured by the Judean government as part of the preparations to meet the Assyrian invasion, were discovered in Jerusalem.

The location of the camp of the Assyrian army in Jerusalem can apparently be identified with much certainty. The story of the Roman siege of Jerusalem in 70 C.E.—nearly eight hundred years after Sennacherib's campaign to Judah—is related in detail by the Jewish historian Josephus Flavius in his book *The Jewish War*. Josephus twice mentions a place known at that time as "The Camp of the Assyrians." The topographical data presented by Josephus is sufficient to identify the site of the "Camp of the Assyrians" on the North-East Hill, to the north-west of the Temple Mount (Fig. 28 no. 8). We can safely assume that this place marks the very place where the Assyrian task force sent by Sennacherib to Jerusalem in 701 B.C.E. pitched its camp. A schematic view of such a camp is portrayed in the Assyrian stone reliefs describing the siege of Lachish (see above). Apparently, the appearance of the Assyrian army at the gates of Jerusalem left its strong impact on the population of the city, and hence the site of the camp retained its name for nearly eight hundred years.

From the Assyrian point of view, the North-East Hill was the optimal place for pitching the camp. Camping on the spacious summit of the hill, where the Rockefeller Museum now stands, the Assyrian task force faced the Temple Mount which extended on lower ground. The presence of the Assyrian army at this place directly threatened the centre of the Judean government—the royal compound, and in particular the royal palace located, as assumed above, at its northern side. The saddle and the area of the assumed rock-cut moat—apparently known as the "conduit of the Upper Pool on the causeway leading to the Fuller's Field" (2 Kgs 18:17)—was the most suitable place for conducting the negotiations between the Assyrian ministers and Hezekiah as described in detail in the Old Testament.

G. Concluding Remarks

The conquest of Lachish in 701 B.C.E. was an event of unique importance. The historical sources, the archaeological excavations, and the Assyrian relief series combine to present us with a picture unparalleled in the study of the ancient East and the period of the Old Testament. It gives us a unique picture of a biblical city, the Assyrian warfare methods, and the appearance of the people at the time of the Judean kingdom.

A large Assyrian task force arrived in Jerusalem—"a strong force," as the biblical story tells us—and was arrayed for immediate and forceful attack on the walls. However, unlike the case of Lachish (and other towns in Judah) there is no archaeological evidence indicating that a battle, siege, or conquest ever took place in Jerusalem. On the contrary, the archaeological data indicate a continuation of settlement until the Babylonian destruction in 588/6 B.C.E. The archaeological data support the historical evidence, indicating that Sennacherib came to terms with Hezekiah.

Both Lachish and Jerusalem were heavily fortified and formed pivotal strongholds of Hezekiah. However, in each city Sennacherib settled his business in a different fashion, apparently acting according to a preconceived plan. This difference can be explained, in my view, in the following way.

It seems that Sennacherib, given the choice, did not intend to conquer Jerusalem by force. We can assume that he pre-planned to bring the rebellion to an end, to crush Hezekiah's military force, to weaken his kingdom, and eventually to turn Hezekiah into a loyal Assyrian vassal. In his view it was preferable to come to terms with the king of Judah and turn him into an Assyrian vassal rather than to conquer and destroy Jerusalem, and annex Judah to Assyria.

Sennacherib turned first to destroy Lachish, the main military stronghold of Judah. By doing so, he intended to cripple Hezekiah's ability to fight, and to demonstrate the terrible might of the Assyrian army. Both his aims were fully achieved. The destruction of Lachish was indeed a terrible military and moral blow inflicted on Hezekiah, and a vivid example of the determination and ability of Sennacherib and his army. This "message" was clearly understood by Hezekiah. The Assyrian task force then arrived in Jerusalem, ready to attack the city-walls. Not surprisingly, this fact and the harsh, aggressive speech of the Assyrian emissaries sufficed to convince Hezekiah that he should come to terms with Sennacherib.

Finally it has to be noted that the above reconstructions of the Assyrian campaign are primarily based on interpretations of the archaeological data. There are other ways of interpreting the evidence. Significantly, the biblical texts, which emphasized the pivotal role of the prophet Isaiah in the events in Jerusalem, state that Sennacherib intended to conquer the city. The biblical texts present the tradition that the campaign came to an end when the Assyrian army was smitten in a miracle.[13]

13. The illustrations are reproduced by the kind permission of the Institute of Archaeology of Tel Aviv University and the Israel Exploration Society. The reconstruction in Fig. 5 is by Judith Dekel and that in Fig. 15 by Gert le Grange.

2

Eating, Assyrian Imperialism, and God's Kingdom in Isaiah

Andrew T. Abernethy

EATING IS FUNDAMENTAL TO life and society. For this reason, food and drink always have been at the center of imperial policy. If a kingdom convinces a weaker society that aligning with it is their only hope for sustenance, the empire gains both new territory and an opportunity to orient the new community around its ideology. Since Isaiah is a "prophetic interpretation" of life under the shadow of empires,[1] it is not a surprise that eating and empire intersect in the book. Employing a synchronic approach, this essay argues that Isa 1–39 uses Assyria's imperial tactics in the realms of food and drink to promote allegiance to YHWH's kingdom, an alternative to the empires of the day. As an exhaustive study of the topic is not possible here, an analysis of Isa 1 and 36–37 will provide an entry point for approaching the intertwining of eating, Assyrian imperialism, and God's kingdom in Isa 1–39. As structurally strategic chapters, the framework provided by Isa 1 and 36–37 will then be briefly employed to reflect upon several passages from Isa 1–39.

Eating and Assyria in Isaiah and Research

There are nearly 150 verses spread throughout fifty-one chapters of Isaiah that associate with a broad definition of eating.[2] Despite this prevalence, there are only a few scholars who bring eating in Isaiah as a whole to the

---

1. Watts, "Jerusalem," 210. For a recent study of empires in Isaiah, see Eidevall, *Prophecy and Propaganda*, 23–75.

2. For a more thorough treatment of eating in Isaiah, see Abernethy, "'My Servants.'"

foreground for analysis.[3] The three most significant contributors are Patricia Tull, Michelle Stinson, and R. P. Carroll. Indirectly, Tull contributes in her essay on vegetation in Isaiah where she argues that plant life functions both as "metaphors for human life and as necessities upon which we quite literally depend."[4] Michelle Stinson more directly considers the role of food in Isaiah as she organizes Isaiah's use of eating as a triptych of rebellion, judgment, and restoration.[5] In his essay on food and drink in prophetic discourses, Carroll calls for "a special focus on the Isaiah material" amidst the prominence of food and drink within the prophetic corpus.[6] He then devotes several pages to a "spectrum of food and drink discourses" in Isaiah.[7] Of note for our essay, he briefly indicates that some passages in Isaiah reflect a backdrop "that invading forces take over and displace local peoples in the consumption of food and drink."[8] He does not, however, pursue this line of thought. While all three of these works are helpful, the intersection between Assyrian imperialism and the theme of eating has not been examined in much detail.

The prominence of Assyria in Isa 1–39 has attracted the attention of scholars with a variety of interests. With historical foci, many consider if and how Isaiah contributes to reconstructing the Assyrian activities under Tiglath-pileser III, Sargon II, and Sennacherib.[9] From a comparative-literary angle, many also attempt to show how passages in Isaiah utilize Assyrian ideology in conveying its message.[10] Others draw upon both historical and comparative-literary studies as they consider the function of Assyria in the

---

3. There are essays published on eating in individual chapters or portions of Isaiah. For example, see Asen, "The Garlands of Ephraim," 73–87; Clifford, "Isaiah 55," 27–35; Hagelia, "Meal on Mount Zion," 73–95; Rice, "Dining with Deutero-Isaiah," 23–30. Additionally, several scholars focus on select eating passages in Isaiah within larger works on food. See Claassens, *The God Who Provides*, 72–75, 86–90; Davis, *Scripture, Culture, and Agriculture*, 163; MacDonald, *Not Bread Alone*, 193–95. In his structural analysis of Isaiah, Lack briefly notes the recurrence of agricultural fertility in Isaiah but does not pursue the significance. *La symbolique*, 13.

4. Tull, "Persistent Vegetative States," 21.

5. Stinson, "A Triptych of the Table."

6. Carroll, "YHWH's Sour Grapes," 115, 118.

7. Ibid., 118–21.

8. Ibid., 118.

9. See for example, Sweeney, "Sargon's Threat," 457–70; Younger, "Sargon's Campaign," 108–10. For a thorough listing and evaluation of passages associated with the Assyrian context, see Childs, *Isaiah and the Assyrian Crisis*.

10. See Chan, "Rhetorical Reversal and Usurpation," 717–33; Cohen, "Neo-Assyrian Elements," 32–48; Levine, "Assyrian Ideology," 419–21; Machinist, "Assyria," 719–37.

final form of Isaiah.[11] Despite the great deal of attention on Assyria in Isaiah, I have yet to come across a study that foregrounds the intersection between eating and Assyrian imperialism. While our interest below is in the literary function of Assyria and eating in Isa 1–39, historical data will be incorporated at appropriate junctures.

Eating and Empire in Isaiah 1 and Isaiah 36–37

Isaiah 1 and Isa 36–37 are prominent chapters where eating and Assyria intersect. An analysis of these chapters individually and in association with one another will serve as an entry point for understanding the significance of this interface in the whole of Isa 1–39.

Isaiah 1

There is growing recognition that Isa 1 introduces both Isa 1–39 and the entire book of Isaiah.[12] Surprisingly, scholars continually overlook how Isa 1 introduces an eating motif that resonates with other passages throughout Isaiah.[13] Most agree that the purpose of Isa 1 is to invite the reader to repent as it emphasizes God's quest for a faithful Zion through judgment and salvation. The role of eating in this call to repentance, especially in verses 7 and 19–20, will occupy our attention.

After summoning heaven and earth to witness the ignorance and rebellion of YHWH's children (1:2–4), there is a rhetorical question: "Why will you be struck again? Will you again commit apostasy?" (1:5a).[14] This question implies that the audience has already "been struck" due to apostasy. Will they continue in their ways to be struck again? Isaiah then employs the image of an untreated sick and wounded person to depict the "stricken" nature of this audience (1:5b–6). The reality of this metaphor surfaces in 1:7:

> 7a your land *is* desolate (*shemamah*),
> your cities *are* burnt with fire
> 7b your cultivated land (*'admatekem*) before you,

11. Eidevall, *Prophecy and Propaganda*; Hom, "The Characterization of the Assyrians," 316–18.

12. Fohrer, "Jesaja 1," 251–68; Liebreich, "The Compilation (Part I)," 259–77; "The Compilation (Part II)," 114–38; Tomasino, "Isaiah 1:1—2:4 and 63–66," 46–62; Sweeney, *Form and Intertextuality*, 46–62.

13. Roy Melugin suggests eating shapes the message of Isa 1 as an introductory chapter but does not pursue this thought further. "Figurative Speech," 8–9.

14. All translations are my own unless otherwise noted.

> foreigners (*zarim*) are devouring (*'okelim*) it,
> it is desolate (*shemamah*), as overthrown by foreigners (*zarim*).

Several poetic observations provide us with an initial understanding of this verse. The use of *shemamah* at the beginning (7aα) and end (7bγ) establishes a focus on desolation. The parallelism between land, cities, and cultivated land in 7a–b conveys the totality of this destruction.[15] With the four-fold reiteration of the second person plural suffix (*kem*), the message personalizes for a psychological impact. "*Your* land," "*your* cities," and "*your* cultivated land" are desolate "before *you*." Furthermore, the repeated use of *zarim* in 7bβ and 7bγ identifies foreigners as key figures in this destruction. The clauses "burnt with fire" and "foreigners are devouring it" syntagmatically advance the portrayal of destruction by providing specifics regarding how the devastation was carried out. Thus, the "striking" that the audience had experienced for rebellion (1:5) centers upon the destruction of Judah's land by foreigners (1:7).

Two questions arise in verse 7 that we will seek to answer. Who are the *zarim*? Isa 1 does not identify these foreigners. Some argue then that the identity of the *zarim* is ambiguous so that the passage can serve as a pattern that applies to all future foreign enemies.[16] While I agree that Isa 1:7 is a pattern for future enemies, the broader context of Isa 1–39 invites a reader to associate the *zarim* in 1:7 with Assyrian campaigns in the southern Levant. In particular, Zion's remnant status portrayed in 1:7–9 resembles the narration of YHWH's (37:16, 32; cf. 1:9) preservation of Zion amidst Sennacherib's campaign in chapters 36–37. With Isa 1 and Isa 36–39 as part of the scaffolding of Isa 1–39,[17] the association between these chapters invites a reader to understand the *zarim* in Isa 1:7 as the Assyrians.[18] While alluding to a historical referent, the passage also functions as a pattern for future foreign nations in the final form of the book.

The second question relates to food and drink. Does Isa 1:7 bring to mind the destruction of food sources by the foreigners? The obvious starting place for answering this question is the expression "the foreigners are devouring (*'okelim*) it" (1:7bβ). While the verb *'akal* typically conveys the idea of eating food, this is only certain when the object of the verb is a food

---

15. Lack, *La symbolique*, 33.

16. Watts, *Isaiah 1–33*, 17; Ben Zvi, "Isaiah 1:4–9," 18.

17. The metaphor of scaffolding for the structure of a prophetical book comes from Kessler, "The Scaffolding," 57–66.

18. Among many others, see Willis, "An Important Passage," 158–62; and Seitz, *Isaiah 1–39*, 30–38.

item.[19] *'akal* can also describe destruction, especially when it combines with fire or sword. The common English translation "devouring" retains the ambiguity of the Hebrew verb since it can mean destruction and/or eating in 1:7.[20] Nevertheless, we will now consider some evidence for construing this verb in its more literal sense.

Several indications do suggest that "food" should come to mind when reading Isa 1:7. First of all, even if *'akal* is ambiguous, it is hard to imagine that a description of foreigners devouring the *'adamah* does not connote the destruction of food sources.[21] While *'adamah* is more than just a food source, its destruction certainly includes the desolation of agriculture and storehouses. Second, the literary context of Isaiah within the canon presents evidence that the confiscation of food sources is a reality and expectation. In fact, the book of Isaiah hopes for a time when YHWH "will never again give your grain as food to your enemies, and the sons of the foreigner (*nekar*) shall not drink your sweet-wine for which you labored" (62:8; cf. 65:21–22; Mic 6:14–15).[22] The Torah also presents expectations of foreign armies eating the produce of the land due to Israel's disobedience (Lev 26:16; Deut 28:33, 51). If Torah traditions loom in the backdrop, Isaiah may be interpreting the Assyrian destruction of food sources in light of covenantal expectations for punishing disobedience.

The final indication that food should come to mind when reading Isa 1:7 stems from Assyrian epigraphic and iconographic sources. The confiscation, blockade, and destruction of food and drink sources are prominent in Assyrian imperial practice. While overlapping, two categories will help us conceptualize such Assyrian actions: (i) feeding troops and (ii) battle tactics.[23]

Feeding Troops. Any sustained military effort requires feeding an army and its war animals. It is for this reason that Assyrian military campaigns often took place during seasons of harvest. It is common for kings to begin their campaigns during the harvest season of Iyyar (April/May) or Sivan (May/June).[24] This corresponds with the many references to Assyrian armies

---

19. Claassen, "Linguistic Arguments," 13.

20. See ESV; NAB; NAS; NKJV; RSV; Oswalt, *Chapters 1–39*, 84; Williamson, *Isaiah 1–5*, 47; Blenkinsopp, *Isaiah 1–39*, 3; Willis, "An Important Passage," 152; Delitzsch, *Isaiah*, 67.

21. For *'adamah* as cultivated ground, see for example Gen 2:5; 4:2; Deut 28:33, 51; 2 Sam 9:10.

22. Koole, *Isaiah*, 317–18.

23. K. Lawson Younger suggested these two categories to me in a conversation.

24. For examples of campaigns in Iyyar in Grayson, *Assyrian Rulers*, see from Assur-bel-kala II (1073–1056 B.C.E.) A.0.89.7.iii.3b, 8b; from Assur-nasirpal II (883–59 B.C.E.), A.O.101.1 iii.56, 92b. For campaigns in Sivan, from Assur-bal-kala II,

reaping the harvest of those they were invading.[25] This is documented best in Assur-nasirpal II's (883–59 B.C.E.) stone reliefs from the Ninurta temple at Calah.[26] For example,

> I reaped the barley and straw of Luḫutu (and) stored it inside
> [the city of Lubarna].[27]
> I reaped the harvest of their land (and) stored the barley and
> straw in the city of Tušḫa.[28]

These instances of harvesting the crops of those they were invading and then establishing store-cities in north-western Syria and the upper Tigris region seem to be the norm.[29]

One hundred and fifty years later during the reign of Sennacherib we see a similar practice. In Sennacherib's depiction of his campaign against Merodoch-baladan (703–2 B.C.E.), he states the following:

> I provisioned my troops with barley and
> the dates of their groves, (and) their produce from
> outlying regions. I destroyed, devastated and
> burned (their towns) and turned them into forgotten
> tells. I took out the Aramean and Chaldean elite
> forces who were in Uruk, Nippur, Kish and Hursagkalamma,
> together with their rebel inhabitants
> and counted (them) as spoil. I provisioned my
> troops with barley and dates of their groves, from
> the field which they had worked, (and) the produce.[30]

Since this statement follows a general overview of his tour through Mesopotamia, there is the sense that it is the norm for Sennacherib's troops to gather and eat the produce of those they were campaigning against.[31] Prior

---

A.0.89.7 ii. 13, iii. 106; from Adad-narari II, A.0.9.2.91–93, 98; from Assur-nasirpal II, A.0.101.1.ii.50, iii.26b–33; A.0.101.17.iii.30; from Tukulti-ninurta II (890–884 B.C.E.), A.0.100.5.11–15. The campaigns of Tukulti-ninurta II (A.0.100.5.11–15), Adad-narari II (A.0.99.2.91–93), and Assur-nasirpal II (A.0.101.1.iii.26–33) link these Sivan campaigns with harvesting the grain and barley of those they were invading.

25. Grayson, *Assyrian Rulers*, A.0.101.19 83–84, 94–95. During the reign of Adad-narari, there are similar expressions in A.0.99.2 43, 92; A.0.101.17 101–2.

26. For background on this, see Grayson, *Assyrian Rulers*, 191.

27. Grayson, *Assyrian Rulers*, A.O. 101.1 iii. 81.

28. Grayson, *Assyrian Rulers*, A.0.101.1 ii. 116; cf. also 101.1 ii. 6; 101. 17 iv. 101; 101. 19 i. 83, 94–95 where Tušḫa is a store city.

29. Bagg, *Die Orts- und Gewässernamen*, 7:159.

30. Cogan, "Sennacherib's First Campaign," 2:302.

31. See Cole, "The Destruction of Orchards," 34 n45.

to Sennarcherib, Sargon II also describes his troops eating the post-harvest food of those they were attacking. He states, "I opened up their well-filled granaries. And food beyond counting I let my army devour (*ú-šá-a-kil*)."[32] These descriptions from several eras of the Assyrian empire give a sense of Assyria's practice of harvesting the crops of those they were invading and establishing cities for storage. As campaigns stretch beyond harvest time, they would draw upon food from storage cities to feed the troops.

Battle Tactics. Feeding troops by harvesting enemy fields accomplishes more than nourishment; it is also a battle tactic. It is hard to imagine that any society would enjoy having foreign empires harvest their crops. Since the goal of siege warfare is to get the enemy to submit, seeing your crops gathered by invading foreigners has a psychological impact as cities grow anxious from thirst and starvation amidst a siege.[33] Not only did the Assyrians harvest food from these lands, their tactics included destroying food sources. From the time of Tiglath-pileser I (late second-millennium B.C.E.) through the time of Sennacherib, there are written descriptions of Assyrian armies destroying the orchards and grain fields of those they were invading.[34] There are also iconographic portraits of Assyrian armies cutting down orchards.[35] Many of these date to the time of Sennacherib.[36] Baruch Halpern suggests that this destruction of food may have been to bait a city to come out from behind their walls to do battle.[37] While the destruction of food sources may seem counter-intuitive for an empire that re-settles conquered areas, Assyrian kings regularly assign deportees to destroyed areas to re-cultivate such lands.

In summary, there are strong literary and historical reasons for understanding Isa 1:7 as a portrayal of destruction wrought by Assyrian campaigns in the southern Levant that includes the confiscation and destruction

---

32. Younger, *Ancient Conquest Accounts*, 117–18. For other examples of Sargon providing food for his troops, see a summary by Hasel, *Military Practice and Polemic*, 63.

33. Cole, "The Destruction of Orchards," 34–36; Eph'al, "Ways and Means," 51. Halpern finds support for this military mentality in Pericles, Polybius, and Thucydides. See "Jerusalem," 28 n1.

34. See Hasel, *Military Practice and Polemic*, 60–65, for a helpful collection of written sources describing the destruction of food supplies in Assyrian battle tactics. Helpful collections of Assyrian iconography as it depicts the destruction of trees can be found in Cole, "Destruction of Orchards," 31–34; Hasel, *Military Practice and Polemic*, 60–65.

35. Eph'al favors iconography for understanding warfare in Assyria stating, "Reliefs provide richer and more realistic information about siege warfare." "Ways and Means," 50.

36. These reliefs are found in rooms III and XLV of Sennacherib's palace. See Cole, "Destruction of Orchards," 37–40; Hasel, *Military Practice and Polemic*, 66–75.

37. Halpern, "Jerusalem," 28. He points to evidence for the "Assyrian policy to denude the countryside when conditions forbade access to the ruler in revolt."

of Judah's food and drink sources. Theologically, it is a mistake, however, to infer that Isaiah blames foreigners for this desolation. God's hand lay behind the Assyrian invasion as punishment for his people. Rhetorically, Isa 1:5–9 seeks to convince the reader to repent as they consider whether they are on the same road of rebellion that led to devastation before.

Eating again appears in Isa 1:19–20. Following Isa 1:5–9's depiction of the audience's desolation, there is a call for genuine Yahwistic worship that manifests itself in ethical living (Isa 1:10–17). In other words, their sacrificial feasts (1:11–13) were repugnant to God apart from social justice. YHWH then reasons with his people to further convince them to repent (1:18–20). Along with promising forgiveness (1:18), YHWH offers two contrasting destinies for those who do and do not respond positively to YHWH's message.

> 19 If you are willing and will listen, the good of the land you will eat (*to'klu*).
> 20 If you refuse and are obstinate, by the sword you will be devoured (*te'ukelu*).
> For the mouth of YHWH has spoken.

The play on the verb *'akal* is obvious between these verses. The audience has an option: to eat or to be eaten. The use of *'akal* and *'erets* (land) in 1:19 hearkens back to 1:7. This is the first time since 1:7 that either of these terms occurs. Through this association, the offer to eat the good of the land in Isa 1:19 is a reversal of the desolation of the food of the land in 1:7.[38] The expression *tub ha'arets* occurs only here and in Ezra 9:12, where the prospect of eating the good of the land is understood as a central motivation for obedience among the first generation in the land of Canaan.[39] While the terse expression "you shall eat the good of the land" does not occur in the Pentateuch, it relates conceptually with admonitions in Deuteronomy that prospective land fertility stems from YHWH's blessing for covenant faithfulness.[40] With a backdrop of biblical allusions, Isa 1:19 associates with covenantal and conquest traditions to announce to the audience that a promised land of bountiful eating awaits the obedient.

While Isa 1 employs other themes to evoke repentance, the concept of eating is an important element in this introductory chapter. The prophet

---

38. Williamson, *Isaiah 1–5*, 118–19.

39. Ibid. See also Gen 45:18; Neh 9:25, 35–36.

40. E.g., Deut 6:11; 11:11–17; 26:15; 28:12, 23–24; Lev 26:5, 10. So Kaiser, *Das Buch*, 50; Smith, *Isaiah 1–39*, 110–11; Sweeney, *Isaiah 1–39*, 83; Wildberger, *Isaiah 1–12*, 57. Contra Williamson, *Isaiah 1–5*, 108–11, 118–19; Brekelmans, "Deuteronomistic Influence," 172–74.

presents a structural schema where YHWH uses Assyrian policy to punish disobedience through the destruction of food sources, yet he promises a season of abundant food for those who respond to YHWH's message. The following diagram illustrates this schema (Fig. 31).

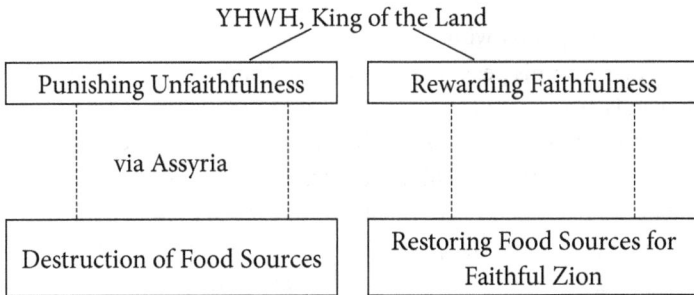

YHWH, King of the Land

Punishing Unfaithfulness	Rewarding Faithfulness
via Assyria	
Destruction of Food Sources	Restoring Food Sources for Faithful Zion

Fig. 31. YHWH, King of the Land in Isaiah 1.

This schema likely counters Assyrian ideology that places the Assyrian King as sovereign over land and food sources.[41] Isaiah 1 then presents YHWH as sovereignly using Assyria's imperial tactics of food confiscation and destruction (1:7) to punish the people, while also asserting himself as the one who can provide them with food if they obey. This abundance of eating will occur within the context of a new, faithful Zion (1:21–26). Thus, imperial and covenantal ideals intersect here in the use of food to motivate repentance.

Isaiah 36–37

Isaiah 36–39 serves as a narrative bridge between Isa 1–35 and Isa 40–66. With Christopher Seitz, many scholars recognize that Isa 36–38 depicts God's *Heil* of Zion and David within history and gives hope for beyond the *Unheil* that Isa 39 anticipates.[42] These chapters, although derived from Kings, have the effect of bringing together the major threads of judgment and salvation in Isa 1–35 and pointing forward to Isa 40–66. While eating plays a notable role in Isa 36–37, its role in these united chapters receives very little attention.[43] As in Isa 1, the intersection between Assyria, eating, and God's kingdom is evident.

41 Postgate, "Ownership," 149.

42. See especially Seitz, *Zion's Final Destiny*. See also Sweeney, *Isaiah 1–4*, 96–97; Clements, "Unity," 117–29; Webb, "Zion in Transformation," 69–71; Blenkinsopp, *Isaiah 1–39*, 82–83; Conrad, *Reading Isaiah*, 34–51.

43. On approaching Isa 36–37 as a literary unit, see Smelik, "Distortion," 74–85;

In Isa 36, the Rabshakeh proclaims to those in Jerusalem that if they do not acquiesce to Sennacherib's demands they will eat (*'akal*) their own refuse and drink their own urine amidst the siege (36:12). If they surrender, they will eat (*'akal*) from their own vine and drink from their own well (36:16) until the Rabshakeh "takes them to a land like your land, a land of grain and sweet wine, a land of bread and vineyards (*keramim*)" (36:17). This offer corresponds with biblical traditions where God promises such food and drink for his people in the promised land.[44] In a context where the Rabshakeh is already undermining the merit of trusting in Egypt (36:6, 9) or YHWH (36:7, 10), the Rabshakeh's "offer of a new promised land" with abundant food (36:17; cf. 36:8) is highly theological.[45] His offer of food utilizes language from Israel's covenantal traditions to present Sennacherib as a replacement for YHWH. As Smelik puts it, "The Assyrian king will act as God; he will give Israel a new land."[46] Accepting the Rabshakeh's invitation amounts to replacing YHWH with empire.

From a historical perspective, the Rabshakeh's promise that King Sennacherib will grant them food and land is not a complete fabrication.[47] As "principal landowner" in Assyrian ideology,[48] the king has the power to determine who receives land. When allotting parcels of land, a chief concern is with "revitalizing agriculture."[49] Assyria often then resettles deportees in desolate areas for the purpose of re-cultivating desolate land.[50] The following excerpts from royal letters illustrate this.

> Insofar as you are a servant of the king, I will assign fields and gardens in the land of Iasubuqu to you.[51]
> Let him move them out, settle them in the town of Argitu, and give them fields and orchards.[52]

Beuken, *Isaiah 28–39*, 2:341; Seitz, *Zion's Final Destiny*, 66–96; Sweeney, *Isaiah 1–39*, 465–71.

44. Lev 19:10; 25:3–4; Deut 6:11; 7:13; 8:8; 11:14; 12:17; 14:23; 18:4; 28:51.

45. Ackroyd, *Israel's Prophetic Tradition*, 111. See also Beuken, *Isaiah 28–39*, 2:354.

46. Smelik, "Distortion," 80. See also Blenkinsopp *Isaiah 1–39*, 472, who likens the Rabshakeh to a travel agent who is making an appealing offer to the oppressed people.

47. For a broad summary of parallels between the Rabshakeh's speech and Assyrian texts, see Cohen, "Neo-Assyrian Elements."

48. Postgate, "Ownership," 149.

49. Ibid., 148.

50. Ibid., 148, 152. K. L. Younger identifies the less important deportees as those who receive the task of land re-cultivation. "'Give Us Our Daily Bread,'" 278–84.

51. State Archives of Assyria I, 179, cited in Fales, "The Rural Landscape," 115.

52. State Archives of Assyria I, 177, 13–16 cited in Fales, "The Rural Landscape," 115.

It is true then, as the Rabshakeh says, that the deportees may receive provisions, plots of land, and even vineyards if they submit to Assyria. Historical records reveal, however, that these provisions were often meager. One text indicates that only 1–2 *qas* of grain per day was given to deportees.[53] Furthermore, the allotted lands were typically under state control and "on the desert margins" that produced the bare minimum for survival.[54] Thus, the Rabshakeh's speech contains elements of truth that are exaggerated for rhetorical purposes. Even if they are deported to cultivatable land, the deportees will likely not have the privilege of enjoying the best of that land.

It is important to detect the imperial ideology undergirding the Rabshakeh's speech as conveyed through Isaiah. Through ideology and other power plays, it becomes possible for a citizen of another society to accept a life of inequality where kings have lavish banquets and deportees live on the bare minimum.[55] As M. Liverani eloquently states,

> Ideology has . . . the aim of facilitating the action, of overcoming the resistance; in the case of imperialism it has the aim of bringing about the exploitation of man by man, by providing the motivation to receive the situation of inequality as "right," as based on qualitative differences, as entrusted to the "right" people for the good of all.[56]

In the Rabshakeh's speech, he seeks to undermine all other powers—Egypt, Hezekiah, YHWH, and the gods of other nations—in order to persuade Jerusalem that life under Sennacherib's dominion is better than life outside of it. As the only positive promise that the Rabshakeh presents to the submissive,[57] the offer of food and cultivatable land is a maneuver to convert the allegiance of the audience to Sennacherib as king and provider. Accepting his offer amounts to rejecting YHWH's and Hezekiah's governance (36:15, 18). This is imperial rhetoric with the ultimate aim of winning "converts" to the Assyrian empire, the provider of protection and food.

In chapter 37, Hezekiah does not respond to the Rabshakeh. Instead, he turns to Isaiah to intercede before YHWH on Jerusalem's behalf (37:1–4). This creates a showdown between King Sennacherib and YHWH. Similar to YHWH's advice through Isaiah to Ahaz (7:4), he commands Hezekiah not to fear (37:6) promising that he will return the king of Assyria to "his own

---

53. Fales, "Grain Reserves," 28–34.

54. Postgate, "Ownership," 152; Younger, "Give Us Our Daily Bread," 279.

55. Grayson, *Assyrian Rulers*, A.0.101.30 102–54.

56. Liverani, "Ideology," 298.

57. This presupposes that Isa 36:8 is not a genuine offer. See Beuken, *Isaiah 28–39*, 2:350–51; Oswalt, *Chapters 1–39*, 636.

land" (37:7–8). After the Assyrian armies focus their attention toward Cush (37:8–9), Sennacherib offers a taunt reiterating the supremacy of Assyria in comparison to other kings and gods (37:10–13). YHWH counters Sennacherib's rhetoric with two poetic oracles that assert YHWH's protection of Jerusalem from Assyria (37:22–29; 33–35). Between these two oracles, YHWH offers a sign (37:30; cf. 7:11) that will occupy our attention.

The sign that YHWH presents in Isa 37:30 centers on agricultural abundance.

> 37:30 This to you is the sign:
> eat (*ʾakol*) this year after growth,
> and in the second year what grows from that,
> and in the third year:
> > sow, harvest, plant vineyards (*keramim*), and eat (*ʾiklu*) their fruit.

The disjunctive waw that begins this verse sets it in contrast with the taunt of Sennacherib where lady Zion mocks Sennacherib, "a rejected seducer."[58] The inclusio of the root to eat (*ʾakal*) in this verse fortifies the importance of eating as a sign of Hezekiah's and Zion's deliverance from Assyria.[59] Furthermore, the prospect of eating from vineyards alludes to traditions depicting the ideal life of blessing in the Promised Land (Deut 6:11). These imperatives then aim to embolden the listener that YHWH will surely provide, just as he promised.

Amidst plenty of debate over how to understand the three year schema,[60] scholars overlook a more obvious rhetorical function of this sign within Isa 36–37. YHWH's sign links back to the Rabshakeh's promise as both share covenantal terminology pertaining to food (*ʾakal* and *keramim*). Just as the Rabshakeh uses the prospect of eating to typify blessing upon submission to the Assyrian king, YHWH's sign counters this by using the promise of food to signal blessing in Zion upon Assyria's fall. This correspondence between Assyria's imperial rhetoric and YHWH's sign contributes to the larger aim of these chapters of asserting YHWH's supremacy over Sennacherib. The following table summarizes the main elements that parallel YHWH with Sennacherib (Fig. 32).

---

58. Eidevall, *Prophecy and Propaganda*, 69.

59. Beuken, *Isaiah 28–39*, 2:369.

60. For a range of opinions on 37:30, see Beuken, *Isaiah 28–39*, 2:369; Blenkinsopp, *Isaiah 1–39*, 477–78; Oswalt, *Chapters 1–39*, 664–65; Sweeney, *Isaiah 1–39*, 475.

Sennacherib	YHWH
Messenger (the Rabshakeh) delivers the words of Sennacherib (36:4, 14, 16; *koh 'amar hamelek*)	Messenger (Isaiah) delivers the words of YHWH (37:6, 10, 21, 33; *koh 'amar YHWH*)
First words try to sway the trust of the audience (36:4–10; 37:10; root *btkh* eight times)	First words try to sway the trust of the audience (36:6; *'al-tira'*)
Claim of supremacy over all enemies—nations, kings, and gods (36:14–20; 37:11–13)	Claim of supremacy over the enemy—Assyria and Sennacherib (37:6–8, 22–29, 33–35)
Believes "the city" (*ha'ir*) will be under his control (36:15; 37:10)	Believes "the city" (*ha'ir*) will be under his control (37:33–34)
Promises eating and cultivatable land (incl. *keramim*) for the submissive (36:17)	Promises eating and cultivatable land (incl. *keramim*) for his people (37:30)

Fig. 32. YHWH versus Sennacherib in Isaiah 36–37.

Within the message of Isa 36–37, the theme of eating contributes to the construal of imperial allegiance. Sennacherib and YHWH both offer food and drink. The ultimate question for a reader is: whose kingdom should I side with?

Associating Isaiah 1 and Isaiah 36–37

The analyses above show that both Isa 1 and 36–37 draw upon the role of food and drink in Assyrian imperialism to highlight YHWH's supremacy. There is reason to believe these chapters associate with one another in the final form of Isaiah to serve as a guide for *"how the Book of Isaiah should be read,"*[61] particularly Isa 1–39.[62] When reading these chapters together something striking arises. While Isa 36–37 anticipates a season of agricultural bounty following Zion's deliverance from Assyria through the unconditional sign of 37:30, Isa 1 alters this by showing that eating has not been taking place as expected (1:7), and in fact more destruction may come, because obedience is requisite for prospective eating (1:19).[63] Isaiah 1 then announces that Assyria's devastation of Judah and Zion's deliverance recounted in chapters 36–37 did not fulfill God's purposes for creating a

61. Laato, "About Zion," 78–79. Italics in original. See also Seitz, *Isaiah 1–39*, 33.

62. Most focus on how Isa 36–37 relates to Isa 7. See Ackroyd, *Israel's Prophetic Tradition*, 117–19; Conrad, *Reading Isaiah*, 38–46.

63. See Laato, "About Zion," 78–79; Seitz, *Isaiah 1–39*, 33.

faithful people. Further judgment will come through future empires due to a lack of repentance (1:5; cf. Isa 39). This impacts the reading of Isa 1–39 as sequentially one would then understand the oracles from Isa 2–35 set within the Assyrian context as "types" for future eras of judgment by empires until an obedient community arises.[64] In other words, Isa 1 in conjunction with Isa 36–37 leads to the expectation that the judgment anticipated and experienced under Assyria in Isa 2–35 will be recycled through other empires. Destruction of food sources will continue until obedience arises.

Along with establishing a historical-hermeneutical orientation for Isa 1–39, Isa 1 and 36–37 coordinate to provide a theological orientation to the book. Zion's future is the chief concern of these chapters.[65] In Isa 1, the concern is with Zion's moral nature. In Isa 36–37, the focus is on Zion's security and the accompanying characteristic of trust. Within this focus on Zion, the theme of eating in these chapters occurs in response to Assyria. Isaiah 1 interprets Assyria's destruction of Judah's food sources as YHWH's means of refining Zion. It also counters such destruction by promising food for those who obey YHWH. In Isa 36–37, YHWH offers the sign of food for those in Zion as a signal of his supremacy over the Rabshakeh who offers a similar future. It is possible then that Isa 1 and 36–37 grant an orientation for approaching the use of food and drink in the rhetoric of Isa 1–39. An imperial-covenantal orientation to eating that asserts YHWH's supremacy in his quest to establish Zion arises in light of Isa 1 and 36–37. This invites a reader to consider the role of food and drink in this light in Isa 1–39.

Reading in Light of Isaiah 1 and 36–37

The argument above is that Isa 1 and 36–37 utilizes Assyrian imperial practices involving food and drink to promote YHWH's greatness as he establishes Zion. Two passages (Isa 3–4 and 30) from Isa 1–39 that correspond with the usage in Isa 1 and 36–37 will be considered briefly.

In the final form of the book, Isa 3:1—4:1 and 4:2–6 offer a unified development of thought as it relates to Zion's destruction (3:1—4:1) and restoration (4:2–6).[66] The intersection between Zion, imperialism, and food is apparent in one of the most obvious reversals between these chapters. Chapter 3 opens with YHWH of Hosts engaging in siege warfare against Jerusalem that involves turning back "every support of food (*lechem*) and every support of water" (3:1). Even those nominated for leadership will have

---

64. Laato, "*About Zion*," 78–85.

65. Webb, "Zion in Transformation," 68–71; Seitz, *Isaiah 1–39*, 31–38.

66. See Sweeney, *Isaiah 1–39*, 107.

no food (*lechem* 3:7; cf. 4:1), an ironic turn of events for a people who burnt the vineyards (*keramim*) of the poor (3:14). The broader context of Isaiah suggests that Assyria is God's agent in Zion's blockade.[67]

The pronouncement of Zion's future lack of food in chapter 3 finds reversal in Isa 4:2. In the realization of Isa 3:10's promise that the righteous will eat (*'akal*) the fruit (*peri*) of their deeds (cf. 1:19),[68] Isa 4:2 announces an era where Zion's remnant will boast in the "branch of the Lord" and the "fruit (*peri*) of the land." While there are various interpretations of Isa 4:2,[69] the literary context suggests that Isa 4:2 announces an era of agricultural abundance, reversing the reality of Isa 3. In this way, Isa 3–4 offers a prophetic perspective on Assyrian sieges to declare that YHWH is using them to punish Zion for sin. Destruction is not the final word, however, as under YHWH's rule the righteous remnant in Zion will enjoy abundant food supply.[70] The role of food in these chapters corresponds with Isa 1 and 36–37 as they capitalize on Assyrian imperial practices to highlight God's sovereignty as the true king who uses these practices to refine his city and also promises food for those who side with him.

Another instance where food, Assyria, and Zion intersect is in Isa 30. In Isa 30:18–26, the prophet depicts a coming era of God's grace (18–19) in Zion for those waiting for him. The particulars and implications of this are spelled out in 30:20–26. Within these verses, the verb *natan* ("to give") occurs twice with YHWH as the subject, both relating to the food theme (20a, 23a). In 20a, YHWH's giving of "bread (*lechem*) of distress and water of affliction" likely pertains to punishment that YHWH brings upon his people in a siege through Assyria (e.g., 1:7; 3:1, 7; 5:13; 7:15, 22–25; 8:19–21; 36:16–17).[71] In 23a, a more positive gift of food emerges as a re-

67. Many date this passage to the Assyrian era, especially 701 B.C.E. See Blenkinsopp, *Isaiah 1–39*, 199; Sweeney, "Re-evaluating Isaiah 1–39," 109. Wildberger situates 3:1–11 within the time of Ahaz. *Isaiah 1–12*, 128. On blockades, see Bleibtreu, "Five Ways," 37–44.

68. If read in conjunction with Isa 1:19 where *twv* and *'kl* also occur, the idiom "they will eat the fruit of their works" (cf. Prov 1:31; 18:21; Jer 21:14) takes on a literal overtone as the prospect of eating will be a reward for the obedient in Zion in contrast to the starvation noted in 3:1, 7. See Williamson, *Isaiah 1–5*, 260.

69. For others interpreting Isa 4:2 as referring to agriculture, see Brueggemann, *Isaiah 1–39*, 44; Seitz, *Isaiah 1–39*, 42; Wildberger, *Isaiah 1–12*, 166; Williamson, *Isaiah 1–5*, 307–8; Gray, *Critical and Exegetical Commentary*, 1:78. For a messianic interpretation, see Baldwin, "Tsemach," 64–65. For an interpretation of this as a new community, see Blenkinsopp, *Isaiah 1–39*, 203; Goldingay, *Isaiah*, 50–51.

70. Watts, "Jerusalem," 213–14.

71. Blenkinsopp, *Isaiah 1–39*, 420; Oswalt, *Chapters 1–39*, 520; Smith, *Isaiah 1–39*, 518, 521; Sweeney, *Isaiah 1–39*, 392. See Beuken, however, who takes 20a positively as referring to the provision of food to the oppressed. *Isaiah 28–39*, 172.

sult of God's provision of rain resulting in blessing for humanity and their animals (23–24). Just as YHWH's call for the people to sow (*zara'*) in 37:30 asserts YHWH as the king who provides, not Sennacherib (36:16–17), so Isa 30:23 (*zara'*) makes it clear that they need not run to other empires for a reversal of this situation (30:2; 31:1)—YHWH will take charge of bringing restoration in the realm of food. In both food deprivation and promising agricultural abundance, this interpretation of imperial rhetoric takes on a covenantal tone.[72] In this way, Judah's experiences of food deprivation via the Assyrians gives rise to highlighting how YHWH uses such to punish the disobedient and provide for the faithful who are waiting for him in Zion.

While there are other passages from Isa 1–39 that could occupy our attention, these two examples provide some grounding for our suggestion that Isa 1 and 36–37 provide an imperial-covenantal orientation for interpreting other uses of food and drink in Isa 1–39. As with the frame, Isa 3–4 and 30 interpret Assyrian imperial tactics regarding food from a covenantal perspective in order to solicit allegiance to YHWH amidst his mission to establish Zion.

Conclusion

Eating plays a significant role in the empires of Isaiah's time as it does today. Focusing primarily on Isa 1 and 36–37 to gain perspective on the topic, it has been argued above that the primary function of food and drink in the rhetoric of Isa 1–39 is to highlight YHWH's supremacy amidst his quest for a new Zion in response to the politics of eating in the Assyrian empire.

72. See Sweeney, *Isaiah 1–39*, 396, for a lexical correspondence especially with Deuteronomic traditions. Laberge especially argues for a Deuteronomic influence on the food language in Isaiah 30. Laberge, "Is 30, 19–26," 35–54. Beuken helpfully points out however that such language is not limited to a Deuteronomic influence (*Isaiah 28–39*, 172–73).

3

Isaiah as Colonized Poet

His Rhetoric of Death in Conversation with African Postcolonial Writers

CHRISTOPHER B. HAYS

THE BOOK OF ISAIAH shows profound resonances with the ideologies, historical situations, and even literary methods of colonized authors in modern Africa. As Joseph Blenkinsopp has observed, "One of the most durable legacies of Israelite prophecy [is its] critique of imperial ideology,"[1] and indeed Isaiah repeatedly subverted the rhetoric of neighboring imperial nations such as Assyria and Egypt. When one reads Isaiah, one is reading some of the world's oldest surviving resistance literature. This is brought into focus by the way that much modern anti-imperial rhetoric by African postcolonial intellectuals has (apparently unknowingly) reflected Isaiah's emphasis on death as the outcome of submission to and cooperation with empire.

I. Isaiah As "Colonized Poet"

Frantz Fanon supplies particularly cogent models for thinking about Isaiah as a resistance writer, and so he is a touchstone for this essay. Fanon

I would like to thank Joel M. LeMon, Annie Vocature Bullock, Cameron Richardson Howard, and Seth L. Sanders for reading drafts of this essay, and Daniel Smith-Christopher for his friendly engagement with me on these topics, and his earlier work in conversation with Fanon, such as "Reading Jeremiah as Frantz Fanon"; "Ezekiel on Fanon's Couch"; "The Book of Daniel" and "The Additions to Daniel." I am also grateful to Andrew Giorgetti for his editorial assistance.

1. Blenkinsopp, *A History of Prophecy in Israel*, 105.

(1925–61) was born in Martinique, under French rule, and joined the French army during World War II.[2] After the war, he stayed in France and studied medicine and psychiatry, and in 1953 became head of the psychiatry department at the Blida-Joinville Hospital in Algeria, where he treated French colonists by day while also collaborating with the *Front de Libération Nationale* and treating Algerians by night. The next year, the Algerian War broke out; by 1956, Fanon, who was already highly critical of the colonial situation (as shown by 1952's *Black Skin, White Masks*), resigned his hospital post to devote himself to the Algerian resistance movement.

In his second major book, *The Wretched of the Earth* (1961), Fanon lays out a three-stage progression of the development of the "colonized poet." In the first stage, he says, "[T]he colonized intellectual proves he has assimilated the colonizer's culture"; in the second stage, the poet "has his convictions shaken" and begins to move toward the cause of his own people.[3] Although we know nothing of Isaiah's education and formation prior to his prophetic career, his knowledge of the cultures of Judah's imperial neighbors is reasonably well documented.[4] In any case, it is Fanon's third stage that is most relevant to the book as we know it; it is "a combat stage where the colonized writer . . . will rouse the people. Instead of letting the people's lethargy prevail, he turns into a galvanizer of the people. Combat literature, revolutionary literature, national literature emerges."[5]

Isaiah seems to have been part of just such a movement toward developing a national literature. In adopting and transposing the literary forms of the dominant neighboring empires, Isaiah (along with the authors of biblical covenants,[6] laws, prayers, and other genres) created some of the earliest Judean literature that we are able to reconstruct. Seth Sanders traces this process of the invention of Hebrew literature, noting that "History, law and prophecy are each old Near Eastern genres that circulated in the later Iron Age and appear transformed in the Bible."[7] Although Sanders does not

---

2. Among the biographies of Fanon is Macey, *Frantz Fanon*.

3. Fanon, *The Wretched of the Earth*, 158–59.

4. The literature on this topic is too large to cite with any thoroughness here. For a discussion of Isaiah's potential knowledge of Assyrian and Egyptian culture, see Hays, *Death in the Iron Age II*, 21–34, 60–66.

5. Fanon, *The Wretched of the Earth*, 159.

6. The idea that the authors of Deuteronomy adapted an Assyrian treaty-form to their use is well-known. As a specific example, William Morrow cogently argues that the expression *lškn šmw* in Deuteronomy "simultaneously acknowledges the reality of Neo-Assyrian hegemony while also subverting it." For the full argument, see "'To Set the Name.'"

7. Sanders, *The Invention of Hebrew*, 160.

explicitly employ postcolonial theory in his study, his understanding of the implications of this use of genres by the colonized would be very familiar to modern theorists: "If someone other than the ruler can speak in history, the genre begins to do something new"; it is able to "[found] something else."[8] The biblical authors took these literary genres out of the control of empires.

As luck would have it, theorists have adopted familiar religious language to describe the process of liberating the mind from the hegemony of empire. Pierre Bourdieu has dubbed as *doxa* the sum total of cultural notions that bound one's inquiry and interaction with the world.[9] Thus cultures have their own orthodoxies that inhibit questioning, and it is necessary for a resistance figure to "unthink the logic of empire," as Anathea Portier-Young has put it.[10] In this framework, one can perceive counter-cultural thinking as *heterodox*, and indeed *heretical*, with all the iconoclastic shock value that anti-religious speech once had (and has mostly lost). Thinking one's way out of imperial orthodoxy is a creative process, and it can be a difficult one; but like other biblical authors, Isaiah offers new visions on which a new world can be founded.

Fanon, too, sought to found something new, something other than what the empire intended. He wrote that "the first duty of the colonized poet is to clearly define the people, the subject of his creation."[11] And the name that he gives to that redefinition of the people is *decolonization*:

> Decolonization never goes unnoticed, for it focuses on and fundamentally alters being, and transforms the spectator crushed to a nonessential state into a privileged actor, captured in a virtually grandiose fashion by the spotlight of History. It infuses a new rhythm, specific to a new generation of men, with a new language and a new humanity. *Decolonization is truly the creation of new men.*[12]

This new energy is something that various strata of the book of Isaiah conceive of as *the revivification of a people who had previously been portrayed as dead*. In Isa 29:4, the prophet threatens that under the divine punishment of foreign siege the Jerusalemites will be like the dead:

8. Sanders, *The Invention of Hebrew*, 158.

9. Bourdieu, *Outline of a Theory of Practice*, 168.

10. Portier-Young, *Apocalypse Against Empire*, 44. (On *doxa*, see also p. 12.) Portier-Young's entire discussion of the theories of resistance is to be recommended.

11. Fanon, *The Wretched of the Earth*, 163.

12. Ibid., 2, emphasis added. Note that Fanon continues: "But such a creation cannot be attributed to a supernatural power: The 'thing' colonized becomes a man through the very process of liberation." I address Fanon's view of religion below.

You shall be brought low; from the ground you shall speak;
from low in the dust your speech shall come,
and your voice shall be like a ghost from the earth,
and your speech shall whisper from the dust.[13]

Furthermore, in 5:13–14, Isaiah mourns that his nation is going straight to hell:

[M]y people go into exile without knowledge,
its nobility dying[14] of hunger, and its crowd parched with thirst.
Therefore Sheol widens her throat
and opens her maw in a measureless gape—
down go her splendor and her crowd and her uproar,
and the one who exults in her.

Along with other, more subtle references, these texts exemplify a tendency of Isaiah to portray the people as dead when they forsake YHWH, the national god, in favor of necromancy, or other practices, which were the result of both foreign influences and indigenous traditions. Another example of this is his portrayal of the Jerusalem monarchy's strategic defensive pact with Egypt, sealed by a covenant ceremony at which the Egyptian national goddess Mut (in Egyptian: *Mwt*) was invoked as a "covenant with death" (Heb. *mwt*) in Isa 28:15, 18.[15]

In contrast to these negative images is the promise of life that Isaiah holds out to those who heed his Yahwistic (and nationalistic) message. In Hezekiah's Psalm (Isa 38:9–20), the king is portrayed (as the psalmists commonly were) as being at death's doorstep, only to be rescued by the Lord: YHWH Most High is the one who gives life to every heart, who gives life to the spirit![16] (38:16). This same powerful sort of life-giving imagery was elaborated by later tradents in Isa 25:8 ("[The LORD] will swallow up on this mountain/ the shroud that is wrapped around all the peoples,/ the covering that is spread over all the nations./ He will swallow up Death forever") and 26:19 ("Your dead shall live, their[17] corpses shall rise./ Those who dwell in the dust, awake and shout for joy!"). The combination of these last two images of removing the shame of the nations and thereby revivifying the

---

13. Translations of biblical texts are my own unless otherwise noted.

14. Reading *mētê* ("dying of") for *mĕtê* ("men of"), as the parallelism strongly suggests.

15. Hays, "The Covenant with Mut."

16. This translation of vv. 16–17a is based on the reconstruction of Barré, *The Lord Has Saved Me*, 153–68. For a summary of other significant suggestions, see also Wildberger, *Isaiah 28–39*, 441. See further discussion below.

17. Read (with the Peshitta) as "their corpses" (*nbltm*) rather than MT "my corpse" (*nblty*).

people of YHWH—which is very similar to Ezekiel 37's image of "national resurrection"—is particularly akin to Fanon's vision. Those who had been oppressed and practically dead under the shroud of foreign rule are miraculously restored to life when it is removed. Reflecting the cessation of Neo-Assyrian dominance in Palestine during the time of Josiah, this is truly an image of decolonization and the "creation of new men."

Isaiah's methods of decolonization are also akin to Fanon's, as we shall see in due course, but having sketched the outlines of the comparison, it is advisable to address briefly some theoretical issues that arise in the interplay of biblical texts and modern theory.

II. Judah and Africa: Theoretical Considerations

An initial task is to define terms. To the biblical scholar not immersed in postcolonial theory, the very term "*post*colonial" may seem problematic, since the Bible was written primarily by authors *under* imperial rule, not in its wake, as many modern postcolonial authors now do. One could further ask whether the rule of the Assyrians, Babylonians, and Persians is better defined as "imperialism" or "colonialism." Ronald J. Horvath defines colonialism as "that form of intergroup domination in which settlers in significant number migrate permanently to the colony from the colonizing power"[18] whereas imperialism is a form of intergroup domination in which few, if any, permanent settlers from the imperial homeland migrate to the peripheral colony.[19] The Assyrians in particular had a governing presence in Judah at such locations as the palace/fortress at Ramat Rachel. But whether this amounted to "a significant number of settlers" is not of crucial importance, since "postcolonial" has come to be defined broadly, as referring to "all the culture affected by the imperial process from the moment of colonization to the present day."[20] What makes certain writings distinctively postcolonial is that "they emerged . . . out of the experience of colonization and asserted themselves by foregrounding the tension with the imperial power, and by emphasizing their differences from the assumptions of the imperial centre."[21] This certainly describes Isaiah, and indeed much of the Bible.

---

18. Horvath, "A Definition of Colonialism," 50. Cited in Killebrew, *Biblical Peoples and Ethnicity*, 53.

19. Killebrew, *Biblical Peoples and Ethnicity*, 53.

20. Ashcroft, Griffiths, and Tiffin, *The Empire Writes Back*, 2.

21. Ibid.

Those wishing to use postcolonial theory in conversation with ancient data have been obligated to argue for the comparability of the ancient and modern contexts, since various scholars have cautioned against using terms like "imperialism" and "colonization" to describe ancient phenomena.[22] Postcolonialism began with analysis of modern empires, and often does not make reference to the ancient world at all; when its prominent theorists do so, they typically look back no farther than Rome or Greece.[23] For its part, the biblical studies guild has produced an increasing amount of scholarship on both the Old and New Testaments as resistance literature in recent years,[24] but the degree to which such studies engage with modern postcolonial thinkers varies widely.

Despite the objections, most existing definitions of "imperialism" and "colonialism" seem able to accommodate ancient empires. Paul Veyne has written that "imperialism, as distinct from an empire, does not exist unless one acquires a taste for unsought conquest"[25]—and no ancient empire was more frank about its imperial ambitions than the Assyrians. The move from classical antiquity to the ancient Near East is particularly straightforward; Garnsey and Whitaker described the structural roots of Roman imperialism as including "the ever-increasing need for warfare in the acquisition of personal riches, glory and clients . . . the militarism of the traditions . . . [and] the soothsayers' habit of predicting that a war that was imminent would advance the boundaries of the empire";[26] that could function reasonably well as a description of the Neo-Assyrians as well. In an exploratory manner, at the very least, the conversation needs to be stretched farther back than it usually is. The distinctions between ancient and modern may prove to be more a modern ideology than a reality.[27]

---

22. E.g., Purcell, "Colonization and Mediterranean History," 120, argues that what historians sometimes view as Greek colonization is actually only "aggressive opportunisms," and that ancient "colonialism" was more reciprocal than its modern counterparts.

23. See, e.g., Marshall, "Postcolonialism and the Practice of History," 98–99; Garnsey and Whitaker, eds., *Imperialism and the Ancient World*.

24. In addition to Portier-Young's *Apocalypse Against Empire*, one might mention Brett, *Decolonizing God*; Brueggemann, *Out of Babylon*; Horsley, ed., *In the Shadow of Empire*; Horsley, *Revolt of the Scribes*; Howard-Brook and Gwyther, *Unveiling Empire*; Moore, *Empire and Apocalypse*; and the various publications of Daniel Smith-Christopher and Warren Carter.

25. Veyne, "Y a-til eu un impérialisme romain?," 796.

26. Garnsey and Whitaker, "Introduction," in *Imperialism and the Ancient World*, 5.

27. In their programmatic introduction to a volume of essays on postcolonialism and medieval studies, Ingham and Warren make the telling point that by chronologically restricting the applicability of postcolonial insight to the modern period, postcolonial theorists treat "colonial 'modernity' as a fact of history rather than an ideology

The general similarities between the way experts describe modern and ancient empires are striking. Fanon wrote, "A blind domination on the model of slavery is not economically profitable for the metropolis. The monopolistic fraction of the metropolitan bourgeoisie will not support a government whose policy is based solely on the power of arms."[28] In the same way, the Assyrians preferred ruling through native puppet-kings, extracting wealth by tribute and taxation, and expanding their empire by treaties; these methods were less expensive than warfare and brought comparable economic benefits to the homeland.[29] Another common thread is "dislocation," which postcolonial theorists speak of as a common thread in various postcolonial literatures:

> A valid and active sense of self may have been eroded by dislocation, resulting from migration, the experience of enslavement, transportation, or "voluntary" removal for indentured labour. Or it may have been destroyed by cultural denigration, the conscious and unconscious oppression of the indigenous personality and culture by a supposedly superior racial or cultural model. The dialectic of place and displacement is always a feature of post-colonial societies whether these have been created by a process of settlement, intervention, or a mixture of the two.[30]

The Mesopotamian practice of exiling populations was precisely such an example of intentional dislocation. The northern kingdom of Israel suffered exile at the hands of the Assyrians in 721 B.C.E., and in Judah, there were incremental exiles carried out by the Babylonians in 597 and 586. The Mesopotamians' theological rhetoric, occasional despoiling of temples, and their practice of "godnapping"[31] were all examples of "cultural denigration" intended to assert the superiority of Assyrian culture and Assyrian gods.

When one turns to specifics, the ways in which ancient Judah and modern Africa have been compared are fairly numerous. Mary Douglas has advanced a type of postcolonial theory about the end of ancestor cults. She argued that the "colonial regime" imposed by the Neo-Assyrians

---

of colonialism." See Marshall, "Postcolonialism and the Practice of History," 99, citing Ingham and Warren, eds., *Postcolonial Moves*, 2.

28. Fanon, *The Wretched of the Earth*, 25–27.

29. Grayson, "Assyrian Rule of Conquered Territory," 961: "[T]he Assyrians came to prefer psychological warfare whenever it was feasible"; Parpola and Watanabe, *Neo-Assyrian Treaties and Loyalty Oaths*, xxiii: "No doubt the Assyrian kings preferred 'expansion by treaties' to expansion by aggression. Waging war was costly and time-consuming, and wasted resources."

30. Ashcroft, Griffiths, and Tiffin, *The Empire Writes Back*, 9.

31. Livingstone, "New Dimensions in the Study of Assyrian Religion," 165–77.

disenfranchised the Judean elders who were most likely to support an ancestor cult, and dishonored the young, who no longer had military outlet for their ambitions, making the time ripe for a religious revolution on the part of the young.[32] She especially emphasizes the role of the boy-king Josiah: "He is like the founder of a nativistic cult, mustering his young followers against the evil empire, going back to the pure origins of the old religion, rejecting accretions and impurities."[33] And indeed, the quest for "pure origins" in fact led to something quite new—in Judah's case, a religion purged of access to the dead. She summarizes: "[The rejection of the cults of the dead] has to be seen in a modernizing context of national rebuilding and reconciliation."[34]

Looking beyond biblical research that explicitly invokes categories such as "imperialism" or "colonialism" considerably expands the scope of comparisons between Judah and Africa. There is the seminal work of Robert Wilson[35] and Thomas Overholt[36] on prophets in Israel and divine intermediaries in traditional societies today, and scholars of ritual theory have also used African data to shed light on Israelite religion.[37] Regardless of the ongoing debate about the commensurability of ancient and modern, scholars continue to embrace such comparisons, and those comparisons continue to shed light.

Potentially more problematic than the ancient/modern divide is the overt contempt that Fanon generally showed for religion in his writings. Would Fanon himself not have objected to being compared to a biblical prophet? In keeping with his Marxist influences,[38] Fanon was extremely critical of religion as a distraction from what he saw as the real, practical concerns of decolonization. Certainly this critique falls most heavily on the "white man's Church," of which Fanon wrote, "The Church in the colonies is a white man's Church, a foreigners' Church. It does not call the colonized to the ways of God, but to the ways of the white man, to the ways of the master,

---

32. Douglas, "One God, No Ancestors," 191–92: "Enduring the frustration, bewilderment, and humiliations of a colonial dependency, the old men find their power is broken, but the young men, freed from their yoke, are relatively short of honour. This can make the country ripe for religious change instigated by the young."

33. Ibid., 193.

34. Ibid., 194.

35. E.g., Wilson, *Prophecy and Society*; *Sociological Approaches*.

36. Overholt, *Prophecy in Cross Cultural Perspective*; *Channels of Prophecy*; *Cultural Anthropology*.

37. In addition to the work of Douglas, note Kimuhu, *Leviticus*.

38. On Fanon's Marxism, see Martin, "Rescuing Fanon," 83–102.

the ways of the oppressor."[39] Fanon's critique also includes the church's leaders: "All [the colonized] has ever seen on his land is that he can be arrested, beaten, and starved with impunity; and no sermonizer on morals, no priest has ever stepped in to bear the blows in his place or share his bread."[40] Fanon was equally dismissive of other religions, including those traditional to Africa; he viewed them all as dead ends and distractions from the real work of decolonization:

> After years of unreality, after wallowing in the most extraordinary phantasms, the colonized subject, machine gun at the ready, finally confronts the only force which challenges his very being: colonialism. And the young colonized subject who grows up in an atmosphere of fire and brimstone has no scruples mocking zombie ancestors, two-headed horses, corpses woken from the dead, and djinns who, taking advantage of a yawn, slip inside the body.[41]

Although his language is indeterminate, Fanon seems to speak of (ostensibly political) decolonization in terms that are almost synonymous with religious deconversion.[42] Fanon's blanket suspicion of religion has found support among other prominent postcolonial theorists such as Gayatri Spivak.[43]

One can only be saddened that the abuses of Western religion (primarily Christianity) by modern imperial powers and the complicity of religions in unjust imperial structures caused Fanon and other resistance writers to overlook the fact that they have an ancient peer in Isaiah. There is no dismissing the anti-religious side of Fanon's thought, but one can note that other postcolonial authors have seen positives in religion that he did not.

---

39. Fanon, *The Wretched of the Earth*, 7.

40. Ibid., 9.

41. Ibid., 20–21.

42. "Once the colonists, who had relished their victory over these assimilated intellectuals, realize that these men they thought *saved* have begun to merge with the 'nigger scum,' the entire system loses its bearings. Every colonized intellectual won over, every colonized intellectual who *confesses*, once he decides to revert to his old ways, not only represents a setback for the colonial enterprise, but also symbolizes the pointlessness and superficiality of the work accomplished" (Fanon, *The Wretched of the Earth*, 158).

43. "It is my conviction that the internationality of ecological justice in that impossible undivided world of which one must dream, in view of the impossibility of which one must work, obsessively, cannot be reached by invoking any of the so-called great religions of the world because the history of their greatness is too deeply imbricated in the narrative of the ebb and flow of power. [. . .] I have no doubt we must learn from the original practical ecological philosophies of the world." Spivak, *Critique of Postcolonial Reason*, 383.

For example, Albert Memmi describes a type of "young intellectual who had broken with religions," but then returns (in this case, to Islam), and

> discovers that religion is not simply an attempt to communicate with the invisible, but also an extraordinary place of communion for the whole group. The colonized, his leaders and intellectuals, his traditionalists and liberals, all classes of society, can meet there, reinforce their bonds, verify and re-create their unity.[44]

Memmi concisely and adroitly captures this conflict within the postcolonial movement when he notes that at the Bandung Conference of African and Asian nations that opposed colonialism, "to the astonishment and embarrassment of the leftists all over the world, one of the two fundamental principles of the conference was religion."[45]

I take it as a given that religion generally—and the prophets specifically—have an inherent power that is available to be employed for the cause of liberation and justice. Theologians and postcolonialists are each free to decide for themselves whether they want anything to do with the other group, but I think it is worth facilitating a dialogue between the fields. Some have objected that Fanon's work has become something different to everyone who makes use of it (Henry Louis Gates Jr. called him "a Rorschach blot with legs"[46]), but what follows should demonstrate that the comparison with Isaiah is a most natural one, even if it is only one snapshot of him.

III. Isaiah and Fanon on Violence, Decolonization and Death

Isaiah and Fanon are most similar precisely where many interpreters are least comfortable with both of them: in their rhetorical employment of images of violence and death. Fanon puts violence in the forefront, at the outset of his work on decolonization: "National liberation, national reawakening, restoration of the nation to the people or Commonwealth, whatever the name used, whatever the latest expression, decolonization is always a violent event."[47] The book of Isaiah also begins with a threat of violence. The

---

44. Memmi, *The Colonizer and the Colonized*, 132–33. Memmi goes on to caution that "there is a considerable risk that the means become the end. Assigning attention to the old myths, giving them virility, he regenerates them dangerously. They find in this an unexpected power which makes them extend beyond the limited intentions of the colonized's leaders. We see a true return to religion."

45. Memmi, *The Colonizer and the Colonized*, 133.

46. Gates, "Critical Fanonism," 258.

47. Fanon, *The Wretched of the Earth*, 1.

nation has become like the (sinful, foreign) cities of Sodom and Gomorrah (Isa 1:9–10)—it is "desolate, as overthrown by foreigners" (1:7); it is
debased, watered down, and impure (1:22). Therefore, YHWH threatens:
"I will pour out my wrath on my enemies, and avenge myself on my foes,"
and thereby "restore your judges as at the first, and your counselors as at
the beginning. Afterward you shall be called the city of righteousness, the
faithful city" (1:24, 26). While this opening is perhaps not from the hand of
Isaiah ben Amoz, it functions as an effective overture to themes of violent
restoration that run throughout the book.

For Fanon, violence was a necessary means to an end. "For the colonized," he wrote, "to be a moralist quite plainly means silencing the arrogance of the colonist, breaking his spiral of violence, in a word ejecting him
outright from the picture."[48] This has a striking resonance with Isaiah's image of the dead "king of Babylon" in Isa 14. There, the Mesopotamian king
descends to Sheol and is greeted by the dead kings and chiefs of the land,
who mock him. I quote this passage at some length:

> How you are fallen from heaven, Hêlēl of the dawn!
> You are cut down to the ground,
> helpless on your back.[49]
> You said in your heart: "I will ascend the heavens,
> I will exalt my throne above the stars of El.
> I will be seated atop the mountain of the assembly,
> at the heights of Zaphon.
> I will ascend to the cloudy heights
> I will be like the Most High."
> But instead you are brought down to Sheol,
> to the depths of the pit.
> Those who see you stare at you,
> and they marvel:
> "Is this the man who made the earth tremble,
> the one who shook kingdoms,
> the one who made the world a wasteland,
> tore down its cities,
> and did not open the prison for his captives?"[50]
> The kings of the nations lie in glory,
> each in his "house."
> But you are cast out from your grave

48. Ibid., 9.

49. Here I read *'l-gwm* ("weak/helpless on [your] back") rather than MT *'l-gwym*.

50. Emending the MT to *bt hkl'*; this assumes that *kl'* was mistakenly grouped with
the following phrase in the process of transmission, resulting in the MT reading *kl-mlky
gwym* at the beginning of v. 18. Cf. Wildberger, *Isaiah 13–27*, 46.

> . . . clothed with the murdered,
> those pierced with the sword,
> those who go down to the stones of the pit
> like a trampled corpse.
> You shall not be joined with them in burial
> for you destroyed your land,
> you killed your people.
> The seed of evildoers will never again be named. (14:12–19)

Surely this is a song that Fanon would have been willing to sing about the colonizers, those who made the earth tremble, shook kingdoms, and despoiled the land. The boastful pride of the ruler—"I will exalt my throne above the stars of El. . . . I will be like the Most High"—is emphatically silenced as he goes down to the pit ("The dead do not praise the LORD, nor do any that go down into silence": Ps 115:17). He is also ejected from his eternal rest; indeed one may not even invoke the name of the dead ruler, which is a fate worse than death in the ancient Near East. This consignment of the enemy to hell was not merely implicit in Fanon's writings, but was explicitly enunciated: "I am no longer uneasy in [the colonist's] presence," he wrote. "In reality, to hell with him."[51]

The desecration of the king's corpse is another aspect of the Isaianic song's curse—"you are cast out from your grave . . . like a trampled corpse." Yet this wrath is not a negative in the world of singers; instead it is a precondition of happiness and flourishing. In verse 7, we read that with the end of the oppression, "all the earth is at rest, at peace—they burst out in song!" In a parodic inversion of mourning cries,[52] the whole earth, even the very trees, sings for joy at the sight of the royal corpse: "Since you were laid low, no one comes to cut us down" (14:8). The death of the ruler signifies life for others. Fanon viewed the corpse of the colonizer in a strikingly similar way:

> The arrival of the colonist signified syncretically the death of indigenous society, cultural lethargy, and petrifaction of the individual. For the colonized, life can only materialize from the

---

51. Fanon, *The Wretched of the Earth*, 10. For those who wish to see both Fanon's and Isaiah's "rhetoric of death" as something other than literal, there is an opening here. The colonized people are described as able to be reborn, so they were not really dead; in the same way, one could argue, the death of the colonist is not something that Fanon literally advocated, but rather his extirpation from the colonized's context. Tony Martin understood Fanon to intend that "if, once you have showed your determination for a fight, colonialism withdraws without a violent confrontation, then there is no necessity to pursue the retreating enemy and pick a fight simply for the sake of shedding blood" (Martin, "Rescuing Fanon From the Critics," 98).

52. Yee, "The Anatomy of Biblical Parody," 565–86.

rotting cadaver of the colonist. Such then is the term-for-term correspondence between the two arguments.[53]

To keep the metaphor organic, for Fanon, "the rotting cadaver of the colonist" serves as fertilizer for the soil from which the people grow, regenerated.

This passage also points to the Manichaean aspect of Fanon's thought; the colonizer and the colonized are in a life-and-death struggle which only one can win. For Fanon, the absolute opposition of the colonized and colonist reflects value judgments that each has made about the other. "On the logical plane, the Manichaeanism of the colonist produces a Manichaeanism of the colonized. The theory of the 'absolute evil of the colonist' is in response to the theory of the 'absolute evil of the native.'"[54] This sort of dualistic absolutism might seem to be absent from the early strata of Isaiah (it is more clear in later texts; e.g., 65:13–15), but a joyful reaction to death such as is demonstrated by Isa 14:7 (or 30:29) is only possible when the deceased is implicitly viewed in such terms. If one looks beyond Isaiah, one finds that his violence is not exceptional at all, but often partakes in an ancient tradition. Much as Isaiah rejoiced at the destruction of Judah's enemies, so in a seminal biblical passage such as the Song of Sea (Exod 15), the Israelites sing as Pharaoh's army drowns.

Fanon's interpreters have hastened to overwrite and recast his views of violence, describing him as "a man to whom violence was personally abhorrent."[55] That particular formulation seems difficult to substantiate, however. In arguing that Fanon abhorred violence, the best support Tony Martin could adduce from Fanon's writings is this: "It happens that one must accept the risk of death in order to bring freedom to birth, but it is not lightly that one witnesses so many massacres and so many acts of ignominy."[56] To say that one does not take massacres lightly is rather different from finding violence abhorrent.

Biblical categories might provide more adequate ways to frame and understand Fanon's violence. Marie Perinbam has termed Fanon's violence "Holy violence"[57]—a term never used by Fanon, but one that brings into focus the connection between him and his biblical forebears. Both shared

53. Fanon, *The Wretched of the Earth*, 50.

54. Ibid.

55. Hansen, "Frantz Fanon," 50.

56. Martin, "Rescuing Fanon From the Critics," 84. "Fanon abhors violence even while recognizing it as a necessary evil in some circumstances." Citing Fanon, *Toward the African Revolution*, 95.

57. Perinbam, *Holy Violence*. As my discussion shows, I do not share Perinbam's interpretation of Fanon's violence; she states that it should be interpreted as largely displaced from the political sphere.

an absolute certitude in the justice of their cause, like combatants in a holy war, which allowed them the rhetorical latitude to call for its achievement by any means necessary. They were not bogged down by the equivocation with which later theologians and postcolonial theorists have struggled. For example, Fanon made little mention of the problematic agency of the colonized in colonial systems, an omission that later theorists have tried to "rectify." (Ngugi referred to native enablers of colonialism as "comparador bourgeoisie," a group that might be fruitfully compared to the "scoffers who rule this people" in Isa 28:14, since Judah also seems to have had elite classes who benefited from Assyrian domination.) But Fanon is not troubled by fine distinctions in his most famous work; his appeal is that he sounds the trumpet clearly, without shame.

In all of the cases mentioned here, it is arguable that the cause of the oppressed is just; Algeria did not ask for French rule any more than Israel asked for Egyptian slavery or Judah asked for Assyrian hegemony. All these (allowing for the historicity of *some kind* of Semitic slavery in Late Bronze Age Egypt) were imposed with bloodshed; why should they not have been thrown off with bloodshed? Is it not an eye for an eye? Whether such logic is justified or not is a question for ethicists; but in any case, later postcolonial authors have seen Fanon's violence as a justifiable reaction to imperial violence. Aimé Césaire wrote:

> [I]t is true he instituted himself as a theorist of violence, the only arm of the colonized that can be used against colonialist barbarity. . . . But his violence, and this is not paradoxical, was that of the non-violent. By this I mean the violence of justice, of purity and intransigence. This must be understood about him: his revolt was ethical, and his endeavor generous.[58]

Another way of approaching the problem turns the focus onto the colonist, as Martin did: "[P]erhaps the most eloquent testimony to the depravity of French colonialism is provided by the fact that it could have driven a man as desirous of justice and a true humanism as Fanon was to the inescapable conclusion that violence was the only answer."[59]

Do these rationales apply to Isaiah as well? Was his violence just and pure? Was he a true humanist driven to violent rhetoric by the depravity of Assyrian imperialism? The horrific images of violence and torture that the Assyrians have left behind in their own reliefs and texts means that such arguments are easy to make, and the images of Assyria's punishment by fire in Isa 10:16–17 and 30:33 would then be acts of holy purification. From a

58. Aimé Césaire, quoted in Hansen, "Frantz Fanon," in *Rethinking Fanon*, 81.

59. Martin, "Rescuing Fanon from the Critics," 85.

standpoint that confesses the inspiration of Scripture, the conclusion that Isaiah was justified may be inevitable; but will these arguments convince readers without such theological commitments, and without a hermeneutical perspective that identifies "Israel" as "us" and "Assyria" as "them"? The same sort of question applies to the violence of the Algerian resistance. Is the perspective of history ever sufficient to answer such questions?

Christians and other thinkers who espouse nonviolent solutions to violent injustice may cite the examples of Jesus or Gandhi; but suffice it to say that absolute nonviolence has not, for many Christian thinkers, seemed an adequate philosophy. For me, the most significant recent example of this is Miroslav Volf's *Exclusion and Embrace*. Out of his wrenching experience of war and genocide in the Balkans, he writes that "it takes the quiet of a suburban home for the birth of the thesis that human nonviolence corresponds to God's refusal to judge. In a scorched land, soaked in the blood of the innocent, it will invariably die."[60] And so he concludes: "It may be that consistent nonretaliation and nonviolence will be impossible in the world of violence."[61]

IV. Isaiah and Ngugi:
The Culture Bomb and the Collective Death Wish

The resonances between the work of Fanon and Isaiah are probably not coincidental, but rather due to similarities between their (postcolonial) historical situations. A further example from the modern African context may support this thesis. The Kenyan author Ngugi wa Thiong'o is well known for having elaborated on the linguistic aspects of decolonization.[62] His book *Decolonising the Mind* (1986) was a farewell to the English language as he devoted himself to writing in his native Gikuyu. In a familiar passage, he writes:

---

60. Volf, *Exclusion and Embrace*, 304.

61. Very significantly, he goes on to add that "one should not seek legitimation [for violence] in the religion that worships the crucified Messiah." See Volf, *Exclusion and Embrace*, 306. In this essay, I choose not to make the distinction between divine and human violence, because I do not think that Isaiah's (or much of the OT's) "theologized violence" originally made such a distinction, even if it is present *in nuce*.

62. See also Ashcroft, Griffiths, and Tiffin, *The Empire Writes Back*, 10: "That imperialism results in a profound linguistic alienation is obviously the case in cultures in which a pre-colonial culture is suppressed by military conquest or enslavement. So, for example, an Indian writer like Raja Rao or a Nigerian writer such as Chinua Achebe have needed to transform the language, to use it in a different way in its new context and so, as Achebe says, quoting James Baldwin, make it 'bear the burden' of their experience."

> [T]he biggest weapon wielded and actually daily unleashed by imperialism against . . . collective defiance is the cultural bomb. The effect of a cultural bomb is to annihilate a people's belief in their names, in their languages, in their environment, in their heritage of struggle, in their unity, in their capacities and ultimately in themselves. It makes them see their past as one wasteland of non-achievement and it makes them want to distance themselves from that wasteland. It makes them want to identify with that which is furthest removed from themselves; for instance, with other people's languages rather than their own. It makes them identify with that which is decadent and reactionary, all those forces that would stop their own springs of life. It even plants serious doubts about the moral rightness of struggle. Possibilities of triumph or victory are seen as remote, ridiculous dreams. The intended results are despair, despondency and *a collective death-wish*.[63]

The resonances between this text and Isaiah's critique of the impact of empire on Judah are numerous. Let us widen the scope a bit to consider a text that is not one of Isaiah's prophecies, but that reflects his times: the exchange at the wall of Jerusalem in 701 between the Assyrian Rabshakeh and the Judean representatives.[64] (This account appears both in 2 Kgs 18–19 and in Isa 36–37.) The immediate goal of the Rabshakeh was to secure the military submission of Jerusalem (again, the Assyrians preferred to gain submission by force of rhetoric). In order to do this, he unleashed a cultural bomb. He sought to undermine the Jerusalemites' certainties. After impugning Judah's military and its reliance on Egypt, he goes on (in Isa 36:10) to challenge their theology, their trust in their own God. Quoting Sennacherib, he says: "Is it without the Lord that I have come up against this land to destroy it? The Lord said to me, Go up against this land, and destroy it." He plants doubts about the moral rightness of Judah's struggle by claiming that even their god was against them.

63. Ngugi, *Decolonizing the Mind*, 3 (emphasis added). Note the very similar language of Fanon, though without the reference to death: "colonialism is not content merely to impose its law on the colonized country's present and future. Colonialism is not satisfied with snaring the people in its net or of draining the colonized brain of any form or substance. With a kind of perverted logic, it turns its attention to the past of the colonized people and distorts it, disfigures it, and destroys it. This effort to demean history prior to colonization today takes on a dialectical significance." (*The Wretched of the Earth*, 149)

64. The text as we have it is almost certainly Deuteronomistic, and not Isaianic; but its portrait of imperial rhetoric has been shown to resonate with actual Assyrian practice. Machinist, "The Rab Šaqeh at the Wall of Jerusalem"; Cohen, "Neo-Assyrian Elements."

The tactic works. The officials respond: *Let's not speak our own language; let's speak the language of the empire.* "Please speak to your servants in Aramaic, for we understand it; do not speak to us in Judean within the hearing of the people who are on the wall" (36:11). They are frightened and shamed, and it is striking that their fear and shame manifest themselves in the request not to speak in the indigenous language, just as Ngugi observed about modern colonization. Whatever tactical motives this might reflect, the effect is to remove the conversation from the level of the common people. Furthermore, in the face of the Neo-Assyrian threat, the Judeans *did*, in Isaiah's view, fall back on the "decadent and reactionary," on the promises and cults of Egypt (Isa 20, 28, 30, etc.), as rulers in Palestine had done at least since the Amarna period, 500 years earlier. Many Judeans had no hope of triumph or victory on their own; they even gave up trusting in their own god.

In response to this loss of national identity, Isaiah, like Fanon's "colonized poet," created a "combat literature" to subvert both the imperial power and imperial sympathizers among his own people. Isaiah's vision was countercultural; he was unafraid to tell his audience that things were not what they seemed—the Lord was the true source of beauty and safety, and a covenant with Egypt was in fact a covenant with Death (Isa 28:15);[65] a collective death-wish.

Isaiah also condemned his opponents by describing them as advocates of necromancy, essentially worshipers of the dead (8:19–20). So did Ngugi, in his own way. In reference to the advice of a colonial school to learn Latin so as to understand English better, he raged: "Can you get a more telling example of hatred of what is national, and *a servile worship of what is foreign even though dead?*"[66] The non-native is repeatedly and purposefully associated by both prophets and postcolonialists with that which is dead or death-seeking.

It hardly needs to be pointed out that this is an intentional inversion of the colonist's own image of his culture; the colonist's positive self-image becomes negative when viewed through the postcolonial lens. As Fanon wrote, "All the Mediterranean values, the triumph of the individual, of enlightenment and Beauty turn into pale, lifeless trinkets. All those discourses enter into a discourse of *dead words.*"[67] But for Ngugi this inversion of the colonist's cultural values is in fact the restoration of order. For him, the fact that an African writer is asked why he writes in his own African language "is

---

65. On the covenant with Death as a covenant specifically with Egypt, see Hays, "The Covenant with Mut," and literature cited there.

66. Ngugi, *Decolonizing the Mind*, 19, emphasis added.

67. Fanon, *The Wretched of the Earth*, 11, emphasis added.

a measure of how far imperialism has distorted the view of African realities. *It has turned reality upside down*: the abnormal is viewed as normal and the normal is viewed as abnormal."[68] Again (and hopefully this is becoming less surprising) that description is a very close echo of Isaiah's charge against those who plot "in the dark," away from the influence and counsel of YHWH; he says to them: "you turn things upside down!" (29:15–16).

This effort at undoing the inversion suits a writer working under political domination, since "characteristic of dominated literatures is an inevitable tendency towards subversion," and that subversion typically entails "imaginative and creative responses . . . challenging the world-view" of the dominant power.[69]

V. Conclusion: "A Restructuring of the World"

Despite the significant body of scholarship that discusses the Bible in light of postcolonial theory and literature, the conversation is still in its infancy. It will have matured when it is no longer strange to many students and other readers to think of Isaiah (and nearly all of the biblical authors and tradents) as colonized intellectuals. For now, it is probably still uncomfortable for many people to accept that the rhetoric of the prophets was as angry as Fanon's, or that they were in as uncomfortable a position vis-à-vis a dominant imperial culture as was Ngugi. Lay readers of the Hebrew Bible are still conditioned to understand ancient Israel as the imperial power because of the descriptions of the Conquest of Canaan or the reigns of Solomon and David. Setting aside for the moment the question of the historicity of those accounts, there is no doubt that Israel and Judah were under imperial domination during the entire period that was most formative for the biblical texts that we read today—namely the eighth century B.C.E. onward. From the other side of the conversation, surely many postcolonial writers are unaccustomed to thinking of the biblical authors as their ancient intellectual forebears.

A postcolonial perspective, however, helps the reader to look squarely at the violence that the Bible often advocates. Though not comfortable, it becomes comprehensible as the reaction of a dominated people to their domination. As I noted in an earlier study of Ps 137, many would be more forgiving of extremism in resistance against more powerful oppressors—whether the oppressed are the Maccabees or Nat Turner.[70]

---

68. Ngugi, *Decolonizing the Mind*, 28, emphasis added.

69. Ashcroft, Griffiths, and Tiffin, *The Empire Writes Back*, 32.

70. Hays, "How Shall We Sing?"

Far more important than violence to both Fanon and Isaiah was its intended effect, which in both cases was "a restructuring of the world."[71] That formulation is Fanon's, but it reflects the goal of tearing up and washing away an unhealthy order and replacing it with a new one in which flourishing is possible. From the flood in Genesis to the new creation in Revelation, there is hardly a theme that is more widespread in the Bible than the hope (and threat!) of new creation. It is also the capstone of the book of Isaiah. Just before the final threat of violence in chapter 66 comes the promise that the threat is intended to reinforce: God will create new heavens and a new earth, and a new Jerusalem (65:17–18). Although this is (again) a later tradition, it is directly in line with the earlier threats and promises to cut down the mighty forests to make room for the shoot from Jesse's stump (10:33–11:1) and to overwhelm Jerusalem so that God himself can be its true foundation (28:15–18).

Many of Fanon's intellectual heirs realized that the "restructuring of the world" is not a return to a pure, pre-colonial past, because that is impossible. They focus instead "on the syncretic nature of post-colonial societies," recognizing that after colonization, even a literary work in a native dialect "is inevitably a cross-cultural hybrid," and that to fail to recognize that hybridity "is to confuse decolonization with the reconstitution of pre-colonial reality."[72] In Isaiah's case, too, the theological vision that he casts for his hearers, while it surely draws on older traditions, ends up being a new creation. One could point to any number of new ideas in Isaiah's theology, but the one that has drawn the most attention is the transition to monotheism. Although true monotheism is almost universally marked by scholars as an innovation of Deutero-Isaiah,[73] Baruch Levine has argued that monotheism has its roots in a reaction against the universalizing claims of the Neo-Assyrian empire.[74] Against the claims of the Assyrian emperor, who took titles such as "king of the universe," and "ruler of the four corners (of the earth)," Isaiah responds with the opposing claim, that YHWH was king of the universe. Thus already in eighth-century texts such as Isa 10:5–15 and 14:24–27, there is the assertion that YHWH controls the workings of the universe, which he deems "an explicit statement of Isaiah's monotheism."[75] Even if one prefers the older

71. Fanon, *Black Skin, White Masks*, 82.

72. Ashcroft, Griffiths, and Tiffin, *The Empire Writes Back*, 29.

73. Cf., e.g., Smith, *The Origins of Biblical Monotheism*.

74. Levine, "Assyrian Ideology." Levine builds on existing work by Peter Machinist showing that the biblical accounts of confrontations with the Assyrians reflect the Judeans' specific historical encounter with Sargonid rhetoric: See Machinist, "Assyria"; "The Rab Šāqēh at the Wall of Jerusalem." See also Aster, "The Image of Assyria in Isaiah 2:5–22."

75. Levine, "Assyrian Ideology," 423.

consensus that Deutero-Isaiah is the true, original locus of monotheism, it certainly echoes and transposes the rhetoric of empires. Thus monotheism, typically viewed as a great spiritual achievement of the Old Testament, is a product of postcolonial thinking.

Whether the thinking of modern postcolonial authors will render up a revolution at the level of ideas akin to that which Isaiah helped lead is no more clear now than Isaiah's intellectual impact was a half-century after his career. If it does, and if it is truly a manifestation of Fanon's philosophy, then it will be marked by a change in the way the world works. Fanon and Isaiah were both, in their own ways, intensely practical. Fanon was channeling the activist Karl Marx when he wrote:

> [W]hen one has taken cognizance of this situation, when one has understood it, one considers the job completed. How can one then be deaf to that voice rolling down the stage of history: "What matters is not to know the world but to change it"?[76]

For Fanon, understanding is not an end in itself; it must lead to change. In the same way, for the prophets, turning to God and away from sin is not merely an internal disposition, but is manifest in action: "do justice, love kindness, and walk humbly with your God" (cf. Mic 6:8).

In many ways, this essay settles for being suggestive, but I would consider it a success if it merely encouraged biblical scholars to incorporate insights from postcolonial studies and more postcolonial theorists to study the Bible—if only to correct my ideas! I do hope I have demonstrated that colonized intellectuals in ancient and modern times not only suffered from similar types of material and psychological oppression, but that they were even prone to express themselves in strikingly similar ways. Both types of "colonized poet" created combat literatures, sentencing the colonists to death so the colonized land could live; they rallied their own peoples to trust in their own languages and their own native resources; they veiled their words in images and wordplay from the understanding of the colonist; and they sought to restructure worlds they viewed as fatally flawed so that they could again sustain life for their peoples.

---

76. Fanon, *Black Skin, White Masks*, 17. Quoting Marx's comment, "The Philosophers have only interpreted the world is various ways. The point, however, is to change it." Cf. Martin, "Rescuing Fanon," 83

4

Living in the Empire

What Purposes Do Assertions of Divine Sovereignty Serve in Isaiah?

Tim Bulkeley

THE BOOK OF ISAIAH situates itself, and/or is situated by modern scholarship, in three quite distinct contexts. Each of these involves life on the periphery of a major regional empire, but each involved quite different political and cultural dynamics. Accordingly, the assertions of YHWH's sovereignty in the book of Isaiah are shaped within at least three different paradigms of theology, or at least, that is what this essay seeks to demonstrate.

Imperial Contexts

Judah as an Assyrian Vassal

The superscription in Isa 1:1, dating from the reign of Uzziah to that of Hezekiah, has been widely discussed. However long a "ministry" it might suggest for Isaiah as prophet, it neatly situates what follows during the period when the southern Levant was within the sphere of influence of the Assyrian empire and most states in the region were more or less Assyrian clients. Uzziah's reign marked the rise of Assyria and its growing control westwards. Hezekiah's reign was followed by Assyria's total domination of Judah, since the reigns of Manasseh and Amon can hardly be imagined a period of Judean independence as traditional maps of the growth of the Assyrian empire in fact make clear, showing Judah surrounded by imperial territory. Probably if we had national stories from many of the other cities in the region they too might claim local "kings" as the narratives in Kings and Chronicles do for Jerusalem. That is, I suggest our maps have been unduly influenced by the biblical narrative. Before Uzziah's reign Assyria's influence in the west was limited; after Hezekiah's it was, for a short period complete.[1] So, dating the texts that follow by naming these particular kings, links the speeches with this particular historical situation of Judah, as a small more or less independent vassal state of the dominant Assyrian empire. One marker of the change was Esarhaddon's campaigns in Egypt c. 671 B.C.E. perhaps intended to reduce the opportunity of smaller states to resist Assyrian pressure.[2]

So, the first part of the book of Isaiah is set in a period of Assyrian dominance in the region, and for most of the period Judah was a more or less faithful Assyrian client state. The main body of this first part of the book is bracketed by two prose accounts of threats to Jerusalem and its king. In chapters 7–8 Ahaz is threatened by Syria and Israel seeking to pressure him into joining their anti-Assyrian league; Ahaz' response most likely began the period of Judah's formal client status.[3] By contrast chapters 36–39 tell of the invasion by Sennacherib seeking to reimpose his authority after Hezekiah's more or less successful claim to independence.[4] As well as these two "bookends" there are other clues that this period of vassalage at the periphery of the Assyrian empire forms the backcloth for this section of the book.

Assyria is mentioned by name widely in chapters 7–38 of the book, 'ashshur (Assyria, Assyrian) is used forty-three times in chapters 7–38, but only once in the rest of the book. In 7:17–25 the king of Assyria is presented as the cause of suffering (brought by YHWH), the context suggests Assyrian raiding parties, or the foragers of an army passing near Judean territory, and here interestingly Assyria is mentioned in parallel with Egypt (7:18), the other regional power. While the second half of chapter 7 may or may not address the "Syro-Ephraimite crisis" it is clear that 8:1–8 does. There the king of Assyria is first presented as God's agent in humbling Damascus and Samaria, but then as threatening Judah also. The image of water that reaches the neck (8:8) vividly suggests the degree of Assyrian influence. Chapter 10 reinforces the idea that Assyrian power was permitted by YHWH for

1. See Ussishkin's paper in this volume for some discussion of Assyrian intentions and policy in invading Judah during Hezekiah's reign.

2. See, e.g., Grayson. "Assyria: Sennacherib and Esarhaddon," 103–41; Porter, *Images, Power, and Politics*, 161–62.

3. Cogan, "Into Exile;" though this is not without dissent. See Miller, "The Shadow or the Overlord," 146–47 esp. n4 and references there.

4. Seitz, *Isaiah 1–39*, 12.

the purpose of punishing idolatry, but that since this merely human power is overweening, it will in turn be destroyed (cf. 14:25; 30:31) and as 31:8 makes clear this eventual destruction will come at YHWH's hand rather than by any particular human power. Chapter 11 speaks of a future return from Assyria, reflecting Assyrian imperial policy of forced migration to weaken local opposition to imperial control (cf. 27:13). Chapter 19 invokes an even more ideal vision of the future when first Egypt and then Assyria will recognize YHWH's sovereignty and join with "Israel" to form a triple alliance. Chapter 20 returns to the world of *Realpolitik,* and suggests that since Egypt is destined (by YHWH) to fall under Assyrian control, there is no hope for Judah in an Egyptian alliance. In the context of a speech about the fall of Tyre and the Levantine Phoenician cities, reference is made to Assyrian dominance over "the Chaldeans" (23:13),[5] perhaps hinting at the power to which they will eventually fall.

Chapters 36–38 tell of the Assyrian invasion and capture of Judah, and their failure to capture Jerusalem (this telling is very close to that in 2 Kgs 18–20 and literary dependence is usually assumed, but its direction is debated)[6] illustrating powerfully the themes outlined above. Assyria is the dominant military power, but is subject to YHWH's control. The last reference to Assyria in the book (52:4) is part of a retrospective of Israel's past oppressors, namely Egypt and Assyria. This is the only mention of Assyria outside chapters 1–39.

Conquered by Babylon

Chapters 39–55 by contrast mention Babylon (39:1, 3, 6, 7; 43:14; 47:1; 48:14, 20),[7] the Chaldeans,[8] Babylonian gods (Bel and Nebo),[9] and the Persian ruler Cyrus (as a rising power).[10] These chapters speak frequently also of a return to Zion of her lost children and are therefore often perceived as addressing Judeans in Babylon around the fall of the Neo-Babylonian

5. The only other mention of Chaldeans in 1–39 is in 13:19 in a speech about the fall of Babylon.

6. For a brief summary of the issues see Childs, *Isaiah,* 259–66.

7. The strong presence of Babylon in chapter 39 is often seen as marking a transition of focus for the book; the city is however mentioned a few times in 1–38 (13:1, 19; 14:4, 22; 21:9).

8. Five times in chapters 40–55 (43:14; 47:1, 5; 48:14, 20), compared to no mentions in 56–66 and only two in 1–39 (see n5 above).

9. See Isa 46:1.

10. See Isa 44:28 and 45:1.

empire and the rise of Cyrus.[11] During this period, whether in Babylonia (as exiles) or in Judah it is likely that imperial policy favored the worship of Babylon's gods.[12] If we conclude that the text speaks to exiles in the imperial city then the number of passages in the second part of Isaiah would make particularly good sense given what we know about the uncertainty and anger towards the end of Nabonidus' reign occasioned particularly around his failure to play his ordained role in the Akitu festival in the month of Nisan.[13] However, given the significance of these events, it is likely that even inhabitants of the southern Levant would have some knowledge of the main features of the festival, and of Nabonidus' laxity in celebrating it. Thus if these chapters address (in whole or parts) a Judean context, these references might still make sense, and in either case they contribute to the overall focus of these chapters on Babylonian religion as well as on a promised return of Israelites to Jerusalem.

On the Periphery of Empire

The degree of unity, and therefore the imagined setting or settings of the third major section of the book are even more hotly contested, but it is widely accepted that this section addresses a period or periods during Achaemenid rule of Yehud during which various tensions in the community needed addressing.[14] There is for example a strong interest in ritual questions and the section opens with material presenting a wide understanding of the nature of the covenant community. I will not spend time here summarizing these issues as I did not discover such clear differences in the ways in which this section asserts the sovereignty of YHWH as for the other two major sections.

---

11 Tiemeyer argues powerfully in this volume that the composer(s) of these chapters should be envisaged as located in Judah rather than Babylon. In particular a Judean setting makes sense of the dietics of many of the mentions of return and of good news for Zion, which seem to speak from a Jerusalem perspective. However, I do not think that the points made in this paper are substantially different whichever decision one comes to on this issue. In each case the imperial setting is either late in the Neo-Babylonian or early in the Persian period. Judeans were then a scattered people and Judah weak and with no strong local identity, worship of Imperial gods was widespread and encouraged or required by the Empire.

12. See Beaulieu, *The Pantheon of Uruk*, 87, note the evidence from offering lists of the shift to the favored gods; cf. Cogan, *Imperialism and Religion*, 23 (cf. 119–21) on the vocabulary which expresses such policy.

13. Van der Toorn, "The Babylonian New Year Festival," 331–44.

14. See other contributions in this volume, particularly those of Brett and Goldingay.

Assertions of YHWH's Sovereignty

This paper argues that there is a strong and clear distinction between the forms in which YHWH's sovereignty is expressed in the three sections of the book (or at least in two since perhaps 56–66 uses the same forms as 40–55).[15] In chapters 1–39 the sovereignty of YHWH is often spoken of in contexts where YHWH is named with a string of epithets, usually containing the word *'adon*, lord (which only occurs once in 40–66)[16] or *'adonay* my lord.[17] On the other hand in chapters 40–55 often YHWH's sovereignty is affirmed by self-assertions (which are structurally and perhaps in terms of content similar to the aretalogies known widely in the ancient Near East)[18] which include the self designation *'ani YHWH*—a phrase which occurs twenty-two times (only once in 1–39 and only three times in 56–66). The form *'anoki YHWH* also occurs (43:11; 44:22). The paper will move on from this to argue that the purpose (as well as the form) of these assertions of sovereignty is different and that the differences correlate with the supposed differences of addressee in the sections of the book.[19]

The Lord of Israel and of Imperial Overlords (Isaiah 1–39)

The geopolitical and theological background of much of the material in chapters 1–39 envisages Judah on the periphery of a growing dominant Assyrian empire, which uses forced migration as an instrument of policy. However the claim that this empire is in turn being used unknowingly as a tool by YHWH also stands behind the texts which assert YHWH's sovereignty. How is this sovereignty cast, and how does it interact with this imperial context in the first part of the book?[20]

---

15. I am not claiming that these differences are absolute, evidently they are not, but the very markedly different frequencies of usage of the words and phrases alone (see below) do suggest that in some sense they are characteristic.

16. See Isa 51:22.

17. On rendering *'adonay* as "my lord" see Lust, "The Divine Title," 134–35. The form *'adonay* is found throughout the book, but outside 1–39 the longest string of titles it helps comprise is *'adonay YHWH*, so the sort of string of titles of YHWH discussed here seems typical of the first section of the book.

18. See below.

19. For a more detailed examination of these usages (comparing Isaiah with Ezekiel), see Lust, "The Divine Title."

20. Because expressions including the term "lord" are so sharply distinctive of this section of the book I will focus the discussion on these.

The opening chapter, which follows the superscription, is wholly concerned with Judah; it is framed as a plea by YHWH against his people (with the heavens and earth as witnesses). The chapter forms a whole and serves to introduce the book.[21] Judah (with the exception of Jerusalem) lies desolate and in the hands of "foreigners" (*zarim*), yet the focus is on Judah and Jerusalem rather than the imperial power. The nation fails to recognize God (1:2–4), and they have been punished without response (1:5–6). This means foreign occupation of most of the territory (1:7–9). The nation and its leaders are like Sodom and Gomorrah, and so their rituals are empty without justice (1:10–17). The piece then returns to the court case imagery and pronounces the final verdict (1:18–20).

The next section contains the first assertion of YHWH's sovereignty in the book. Isaiah 1:21–26 forms a quasi-chiasm, which begins and ends with talk of "the faithful city" first defiled then restored (1:21 and 26). The passage seems to center on the statement in v.24a that YHWH is making a declaration. Before this there is talk of false leaders and injustice using the imagery of impurities in wine and metalworking; after it YHWH declares that he will have vengeance purging the dross and impurities, and restoring leadership as at the beginning. The statement that God will speak is impressive in its agglomeration of titles: *ne'um ha'adon YHWH tseba'ot 'abir yisra'el*. This oracle or report of divine speech comes from one identified first as "the lord" (*ha'adon*) before being identified by name (YHWH), then qualified by the descriptor "of armies," who is then further identified as the "mighty one" who belongs to Israel.[22]

Such expanded oracle formulae are not uncommon in the prophetic books, and they usually include assertions of sovereignty using the word "lord,"[23] and often the ascription "of armies." What is less common is the self-identification of YHWH as belonging to Israel.[24] Here YHWH is Israel's "mighty one"; similar titles in Isaiah include: "mighty one of Jacob" in Isa 49:26; 60:6; "Rock of Israel" in 30:29;[25] "your holy one, the Creator of Israel"

21. Sweeney, *Isaiah 1–39*, 63–66.

22. The use of the definite *ha'adon* is found almost exclusively in Isaiah (the other uses are Mal 3:1 and the doublet verses Exod 23:17; 34:23 though there pointed without the *vav mater lectionis*).

23. Sometimes the form is as here *'adon* both in Isaiah and elsewhere the form *'adonay* is common. The distinction between the two terms is not clear.

24. In this passage though the people accused are Judean/Jerusalemite the divine self-description uses the wider "Israel" language. I take this to suggest that though the crimes are political/economic, and therefore local, YHWH is presented as beyond such regional interests. Paradoxically even though, at this stage, the interest is precisely in YHWH as *this* people's god.

25. This title only occurs here and in 2 Sam 23:3.

in 43:15; "King of Israel" in 44:6; "God of Israel" in 17:6; 21:10, 17; 24:15; 29:23; 37:16, 21; 41:17; 45:3, 15; 48:1, 2; 52:12;[26] and the most prominent "holy one of Israel" in 1:4 and 5:19 (on the lips of the addressees); 5:24; 10:17 ("light of Israel, their holy one"); 10:20; 12:6; 17:7; 29:19; 30:11, 12, 15; 31:1; 37:23; 41:14, 16, 20; 43:3, 14; 45:11; 47:4; 48:17; 49:7; 54:5; 55:5; 60:9, 14 (the only occurrences of such phrasing in chapters 56–66).[27]

So this assertion of YHWH's sovereignty is not concerned with his universal rule but most explicitly, as both the assertion itself and the surrounding text make clear, with his rule and relationship with "Israel." This claim to sovereignty is expressed in the context of an ongoing relationship, highlighted by the move from "once" (1:21) and "the days of old" (1:26) to the anticipated future. Despite and because of this relationship YHWH's sovereignty means that it is firstly "Israel's" leadership who are his enemies (1:24). The expanded divine name and title *ha'adon YHWH tseba'ot* functions similarly in 3:1, 15, again in a context concerned with leadership and sovereignty within the chosen community.[28]

Before the next usage of this title, however, chapter 6 provides a turning point in the book. This chapter may be a call narrative (cf. Exod 3; Judg 6; Jer 1) or tell of a prophetic commissioning (cf. 1 Kgs 22), perhaps forming part of a *Denkschrift* (Memoir) in chapters 6–10 or 11.[29] Whatever our conclusions on such issues, the account by its form looks back on a past event, and places this event in the literary context of the Syro-Ephraimite Crisis. With this in mind, the chronological setting "in the year that king Uzziah died" gains significance. According to the biblical accounts (alongside which the book of Isaiah is read) Uzziah's reign was long, prosperous and marked by divine approval, though it ended on a less clear note. Considering the year of Uzziah's death from a vantage point beyond the Syro-Ephraimite crisis (the time of the putative *Denkschrift*, or indeed beyond the fall of Jerusalem, exile and the struggles to rebuild, likely settings for the redaction of other parts of the book), this death marks a turning point in the story of Judah. Conrad notes that other significant points in the story of Judah's relationship with the Assyrian empire in the book of Isaiah are also marked by mention of the death of kings; the death of Ahaz in 14:28 is associated with the

26. Interestingly no such titles are constructed using Judah, Zion, or Jerusalem.

27. The phrase "holy one of Israel" is typical of Isaiah, occurring in each part of the book 19 times in total, and only once each in three other books (2 Kgs 19:22 [in a section concerning Isaiah]; Ps 71:22 and Jer 50:29).

28. We should not here follow Kaiser's suggestion that the word was a later addition in verse 15 (*Isaiah 1–12*, 75, n9.) or excise the phrase as BHS (following the LXX), see Lust, "The Divine Title," 136.

29. Proposed in its "classical" form by Budde, *Jesaja's erleben*, 42–44.

Assyrian invasion; talk of Hezekiah's mortality in 38:1 introduces thought of the Babylonian invasion, as in this vision Uzziah's death foreshadows the Syro-Ephraimite invasion and Ahaz's appeal to Assyria as protector.[30]

As well as these aspects of the chapter's situation, the wording of its opening, too, suggests that sovereignty is a significant motif: "seated/enthroned" (6:1). *yosheb* alone would suggest royalty, but specification is then made. First we are told that this *'adonay* is seated "upon a throne" (note that the "lord" is not named as YHWH in verse 1; only in verse 3 do the seraphs name him as "YHWH of armies," and then in verse 5 Isaiah echoes them adding that he is "king"). He is "high"; this verb has been used in chapter 2 of the arrogance and pride of human lords, although "lifted up" was also used in 2:2 for the raising of "the mountain of YHWH's temple" as well as of human pride and arrogance. Such cues, however, merely reinforce the image itself, a divine king enthroned, huge and exalted, with attendant seraphs.

Even without the *Denkschrift* hypothesis, in the process of redaction chapter six would be associated with those that follow. As we read the book, this chapter seems to mark a change, from the general accusations of failure in faithfulness to YHWH and in justice to each other which the first five chapters contain, to introducing the following section in which Isaiah seeks to persuade Ahaz to trust YHWH rather than Assyria, when his northern neighbors threaten his throne. In this context the vision sets the divine "lord" over all merely human lordships. For this lord, referred to as *hammelek YHWH tseba'ot* in 6:5, ought not even to be seen by a failing human.

It is striking therefore that in the next occurrence of the title "lord" in 10:16, 23–24, and 33 YHWH is explicitly exercising sovereignty not merely over the chosen community but over the imperial power. In 10:5–19 imperial power is heard vaunting its success (esp. 10:8–10), but already the true position had been explained; Assyria was YHWH's tool to discipline a particular apostate nation (10:5–6), but empire by its nature is overweening. Verse 11 expresses sharply the inherent irony of the message, for YHWH (the mighty one of Israel, etc.) sent his unknowing imperial vassal against Samaria and Jerusalem on account of their idols. So once "the lord" has finished his work, on the hill of Zion and in Jerusalem he will in his turn "visit" (for *pqd* carries here the sense of a visitation by an authority figure) the arrogant, boasting, proud king of Assyria (10:12). The term "lord" is used in verse twelve to speak of YHWH precisely to underline his sovereignty not only over "his people" but over the imperial power.[31]

---

30. Conrad, *Reading Isaiah*, 143–45.

31. For a summary of ways this passage echoes and subverts Assyrian royal ideology and literary tropes see Chan, "Rhetorical Reversal and Usurpation," 717–34.

Verses 13 and 14 with their claim by the imperial king to have achieved greatness by his own "hand" provide a nice foil for the imagery of the tools exalting themselves over the craftsmen who wield them. Verse 16 is once again prefaced by an assertion of sovereignty. The exact details of the invasion from the north at the end of the chapter can be debated, but the exercise of YHWH's power over this invader is clear.

In 19:4, it is explicit that the sovereignty claimed by/for YHWH is (at least) imperial, for Egypt will be handed over to harsh "lords" (*adonim*), while the same word (in the singular) is used to name YHWH as the one who orders this!

In chapter 22 the focus returns to the local, first to YHWH as Judah's lord, and then more local still to a concern with the doings of Shebna the Steward (22:15). But in 24:23 YHWH's sovereignty is over the "host of heaven" (*tseba' hammarom*) as well as the kings of the earth (24:21). Local sovereignty is a special case of YHWH's universal rule. In 25:8 YHWH's sovereignty is explicitly in the preceding verses *from* Zion, but *for* all peoples. The focus is also on Zion in 28:16, and again in verse 22 though here it is the strange act of this sovereign that is in view—the strange act of bringing enemies on his own subjects?[32]

Aretalogy of the Only God (Isaiah 40–55)

Isaiah 30:15 made clear that YHWH's sovereignty does not come from conventional military power, and that his vassals do not need such power. This is explained overtly in 40:10. There the lord YHWH comes in strength, and his arm rules for him—as some translations recognize these are military terms, and therefore the words for his payment at the close of the verse should be understood (as most translations do) as spoil or booty. In this chapter not only is YHWH's sovereignty over Israel and (implicitly) over the empire asserted, but his sovereignty over (or indeed incomparability with) all gods is again claimed too.

As we will see therefore, chapter 40 serves to link and transition between assertions of YHWH's sovereignty in 1–39 which primarily concern YHWH's rule over "Israel" and control over the Imperial overlords in which the divine power is contrasted to the frail power of human armed might, and chapters 40–55 where YHWH's sovereignty contrasts with the impotence or nullity of the idols. This is often expressed in self-assertions focused on the phrase *'ani YHWH* ("I am YHWH"). This phrase is repeated

---

32. Lust, "The Divine Title," 137–38, as befits a diachronic study, distinguishes the usage in 10:23–24 as later; such a historical account is not my interest here.

twenty-two times (Isa 27:3; 41:4, 13, 17; 42:6, 8; 43:3, 15; 45:3, 5–8, 18–19, 21; 48:17; 49:23, 26; 60:16, 22; 61:8) with the form *'anoki YHWH* used also in 43:11; 44:24. It is noticeable that only one of these comes from the first part of the book, and only three from the final part. Thus the phrase is typical of the second part, and as we will see is a repeated assertion of YHWH's sovereignty there.

The second half of the opening chapter of the second part of the book strongly stresses the incomparability of YHWH who is maker of all, though already both by implication (in possibly comparing YHWH's desert super-highway along which he will carry his people, to the gods of Babylon carried by their devotees in procession each New Year) and overtly (in the title "lord YHWH" in 40:10) this sovereignty was a theme of the first half of the chapter. In particular YHWH is the maker of the host of heaven, amongst whom were prominent members of the Babylonian pantheon. Nevertheless as at the start of the book, so here in chapter 40 (despite incomparability overt and implied with the imperial gods) the focus is on "Jacob/Israel" and the role of this sovereign for them.

By contrast chapter 41 opens with an appeal to the nations, and a series of rhetorical questions: ask who arouses the "righteous one from the East," commissioning him and handing over nations and kings to his authority. Verse 4 expands this asking: who has controlled history from the start? Then in 41:4b the answer is provided in the form of a self-praising aretalogy, very like those known from Egypt in both short and extended forms from texts of almost all periods.[33] It opens with the assertion "I am YHWH" and continues with a series of statements further defining what this means: "The first and the last, I am he" (41:4c). Despite their fear (41:5) the lands appealed to in the opening now seek refuge in useless idols (41:7).

So as in the first section of the book, here too an assertion of YHWH's sovereignty for Israel quickly turns to his universal sovereignty. However, while the first section was concerned to assert this over the imperial power, that sovereignty is assumed in the second part of the book, and a broader claim is foregrounded, that YHWH is creator and sovereign over all history, and so incomparable with the "gods" represented by idols.

In verse 13 the statement "I am YHWH," this time qualified as "Your God," is followed by a series of declarations (of present activity, intent, or continuing action expressed using participles). Notably this section uses the name "holy one of Israel" repeatedly, underlining that the thought is of YHWH's sovereignty for Israel, if not merely in or over Israel.

33. Lesko, *The Great Goddesses*, 195, who cites a coffin text (from c. 2000 B.C.E.), Spell 148, which read: "I am Isis, one more spirit-like and august than the gods" as a precursor of the aretalogies.

Although the overall structure and form of the list in 41:17–20 is similar, the morphology is different and here the verbs are *yiqtols* thus clearly expressing future intent. Here, the goal of this sovereign activity for Israel is expressed as:

> so that all may see and know,
> all may consider and understand,
> that the hand of the Lord has done this,
> the Holy One of Israel has created it.

In the next chapter, a presentation of YHWH as creator of all (42:5), is prefaced by a declaration that YHWH is *ha'el* ("the God"). This use of the article (*ha*) with *'el* is unusual (the form occurs less than twenty-five times in the Hebrew Bible). It can sometimes be used to point out one god from a pantheon, but often serves to distinguish God from gods, as it seems to here. The self-declaration which follows (42:6) introduces a commissioning speech, but it is introduced by the expression "the God" followed by a series of declarations by the speaker of who YHWH is; namely creator and sustainer (42:5). The focus then shifts from the widest possible frame to an individual one (for even if the Servant here is the nation of Israel, this servant is represented as an individual figure). The second self-assertion in verse 8 opens a polemic on the incomparability of YHWH who will not give his glory to another, or his praise to idols. In the following verse YHWH's control and announcement of history is presented as evidence that this is correct. The sovereign creator is not only Israel's God, but incomparable with the gods. The argument in the next chapter (with its two divine self-assertions) is very similar.

Chapter 45 has a huge concentration of these assertions. The chapter begins with the striking claim that Cyrus is YHWH's messiah, appointed by YHWH and for whom YHWH has prepared everything, even secret treasure, with a purpose *lema'an* ("so that" 45:4) Cyrus may know YHWH's self-assertion, and recognize that the God of Israel has done these things for him for their benefit. Once again the claim to sovereignty is both super-imperial and with a local focus. For readers aware of claims of the Cyrus Cylinder (which cast Marduk, Babylon's patron deity, in this role) this claim is an implicit assertion of YHWH's superiority to, or better reality over against the unreality of gods (cf. verses 5–7 with a string of such self-assertions).

The last section of the chapter begins in verse 18, also with a presentation of YHWH as creator. This verse ends with a divine self-assertion declaring the name and unique status of YHWH. The next two verses appeal to "the survivors of the nations" again affirming YHWH's incomparability to idols and uniqueness, and found these claims on his having declared "this" long ago. Verse 22 contains the much rarer self-assertion "I am God" (not found again in Isaiah, and elsewhere only a couple of times in Genesis and once in Job)—following it with the precision *we 'en 'od* ("there is no other"). Six of the nine biblical uses of this expression are in this chapter, so it is clearly thematic. Verse 23 gives the clearest and most complete statement of the divine imperium yet: "To me every knee shall bow, every tongue shall swear." But again the final verse of the chapter returns to YHWH's commitment that this sovereignty is for Israel's sake.

In 48:17 a conglomeration of titles and self-assertions link together the title common in 1–39 "lord" and the self-assertion (over against gods) common in chapters 40–55. The title "lord" returns in 49:22 when again it is a question of YHWH giving commands to the "nations." While the next verse uses the self-assertion formula, thus underlining their similar functions, the title "lord" is also strongly present in the servant poem of chapter 50, and is again in use (though this time qualified by the possessive "your" in 51:22 where again it is a question of YHWH's authority over Israel and their oppressors). Isa 52:4–6 is similar.

Israel's Lord (Isaiah 56–66)

The final part of this three part book opens by recalling themes of justice and righteousness from earlier in the book, while giving them a new twist linking them to Sabbath observance (56:2), then in verses 3–7 surprisingly (in view of this apparent "legalism") speaks of how eunuchs and foreigners will have a lasting name and a ministry in God's "house of prayer for all nations." Thus while the second part situated itself, and YHWH's sovereignty over against the gods, and seemed to address a people living in a pluralistic imperial city (usually assumed to be Babylon), this third part of the book situates itself in a more local context, where torah observance is a significant issue, and imperial powers seem distant.

In 56:8 a new speech is introduced by a formula in the name of "lord YHWH" who gathers Israel's outcasts claiming that he will now gather yet others to them. (Perhaps this is a reference to what has gone before?) The last four verses are a castigation of leaders who neglect their duty in favor of rest, their own ideas, or partying. Thus the turning point is introduced by explicit reference to YHWH's sovereignty, clearly marking the concern here that Israel should not assume that asserting YHWH's sovereignty over the universe and YHWH's special care for Israel somehow exempts them from that very sovereignty! The third section of the book contains fewer direct assertions of YHWH's sovereignty, but they are also more nuanced.

This sovereignty is again stressed in 60:16 in a context where (if it were not read in this book, and in the light of the careful distinction between God for/of Israel and a god whom Israel controls) the sense seems purely to be YHWH rules and exercises this rule on Israel's behalf:

> You shall suck the milk of nations,
> you shall suck the breasts of kings;
> and you shall know that I am YHWH, your Savior
> and your Redeemer, the Mighty One of Jacob.

Again at the close of the chapter the divine self-assertion serves to introduce the summary:

> I am YHWH, at the right time I will accomplish it quickly. (60:22)

So the commissioning poem in 61:1–9 (which Jesus read in the Nazareth synagogue) begins with such an overt use of the title "lord," and links this rule with the sort of events that marked new reigns in the ancient Near East.[34] Note, as well as the freedom for captives and prisoners, the phrase "the delightful year of YHWH." In verse 8 the self-assertion "I am YHWH" occurs, but in a context much less reminiscent of aretalogies, and more as a simple statement, "this is who I am . . ." The title "lord" recurs again in the last verse of the chapter, stressing that all this will be done in sight of all nations, thus again linking YHWH's sovereignty for or in Israel with clear indications that it is not limited to Israel.

Finally, towards the close of the section and the book, chapter 65 has been distinguishing between YHWH's faithful servants and those who are rebellious. The act of thus distinguishing is likened to a farmer who spares a cluster of grapes for the sake of the juice they may offer (65:8). This comes to a climax in the second half of the chapter, where the new speech is introduced, naming the speaker as "lord YHWH" (65:13), speaking of a series of paradoxical reversals his "servants" will suffer, culminating in the claim that they will bequeath their "name" as a curse, so that "lord YHWH . . . will call his servants by another name" (65:15). The chapter closes with a vision of total renewal, as befits such a total sovereign.

---

34. Weinfeld, *Social Justice*, 75–96, 152–78. To this accession tradition Bergsma adds interesting material concerning such liberation associated with cities dedicated to a god (*The Jubilee*, 27–30), which open interesting possibilities for reading this passage in context.

Conclusion

YHWH as sovereign, who rules over all, including empires, emperors, and their gods, is a key theme spread through the book of Isaiah and is especially prominent at its turning points in chapters 1, 6, 40, and 56. However, in the three parts of the book this divine sovereignty is asserted differently, and with different emphases. In the first part a major form is simply naming God as "lord YHWH," and commanding the imperial armies and the ultimate end of the empire is the primary focus of many of these assertions. In the second part the form of the assertions shifts to become more like the aretalogies known from other ancient near-eastern texts and the purpose also changes (affirming that YHWH is incomparable to the gods, who do not in fact rule history, indeed cannot act). Then at the close of the book the focus shifts and becomes more local, though in this as with other themes of the book the third part echoes the first two in many ways, claiming that YHWH's sovereignty is not only over "everything" but is most particularly over Israel and that his "servants" should serve as directed. Interestingly, at the very start, neat narrow understandings of who may appropriately claim this status of "servant" of the "lord YHWH" are overturned. Thus in this brief survey, assertions of YHWH's sovereignty serve different functions that are appropriate to the three broad brush imperial contexts often suggested for the parts. The overall effect is a trajectory that soars towards sublime heights in the second part of the book. YHWH is first presented as lord of the empire in the first part of the book, and then in the second part as incomparably more sovereign than the imperial gods. The third part returns to the everyday and shows what such sovereignty means in the nitty gritty of the here and now (or rather the there and then) of a community reconstructing Yahwistic life in Persian Yehud.

5

The Usefulness of a Daughter

Judith E. McKinlay

THIS PAPER IS DEDICATED to the late Rev Sonny Riini, remembering the injustices of colonialism borne by the Tuhoe people of Aotearoa New Zealand.

> Anyone who engages with texts knows that they are not innocent and that they reflect the cultural, religious, political, and ideological interests and contexts out of which they emerge. What postcolonialism does is to highlight and scrutinize the ideologies these texts embody and that are entrenched in them as they relate to the fact of colonialism.[1]

> Noho noa te tinana, ka nuka ki te haere
> He turehu naku i te ao, i te po
> Noho ana hoki au i Rua-toki ra,
> Te whenua i puritia, te whenua I tawhia . . .

> I sit here a captive, but my discontented spirit
> Yearns to be free
> I remain here in Ruatoki
> The land that was fought for, the land that was held . . .[2]

> Comfort, O comfort my people,
> Says your God. (Isa 40:1a)

---

1. Sugirtharajah, *Postcolonial Criticism*, 79.

2. A song (waiata) by Te Ahoaho, quoted in Binney, *The Encircled Lands*, 181, "depict(ing) the people's imprisonment at Ruatoki, in their own land."

The Puzzling Gap

I have long been intrigued and puzzled by the gap between chapters 39 and 40 in the Isaiah scroll, what Brueggemann describes as "the abyss" of "the brooding, doubting and suffering of Israel."[3] Sean McEvenue has described it as "like a movie where we are watching some people inside a car . . . and then suddenly we find ourselves walking among clouds and hearing persuasive voices. We know right away that an accident has happened and we are now in heaven."[4] But this "accident" is *the* key event of Israel's history; in this gap lies the disaster, the very tragedy of the Babylonian invasion with its subsequent forced removal of Israel's leaders, of the king, and seemingly of most of those who were part of Judah's political and economic administration. How could this have been passed over in a textual silence? How can one, in a scroll that has a concern for Zion throughout, move directly from chapter 39 to the comforting voice of chapter 40? Was the shame and humiliation too great, too overwhelming to be voiced?

The Postcolonial Question

Or has the poet writer of Deutero-Isaiah deftly included it "under erasure," recognizing the shame that must not be spoken and yet cannot be omitted? Did he recognize, to quote David Penchansky, that "[w]hen we live with this tension we will discover that it is the very thing that energizes our discourse"?[5] Certainly, there is an energy, a perhaps unexpected hopefulness in the opening call of Isa 40. Rather than anticipating the Derridean move of writing in and then crossing out any direct mention of this recent shameful event, has this Isaian poet turned quite intentionally to an intertextual strategy as a way of living with the tension? This would, of course, assume that his audience and readers would both recognize the allusions and know

3. Brueggemann, "Unity and Dynamic in the Isaiah Tradition," 96, 95.

4. McEvenue, "Who Was Second-Isaiah?," 216. This is not to deny any connection with the preceding chapters. Many agree with Conrad, "The Royal Narratives and the Structure of the Book of Isaiah," 78, that "Isa. 36–39 provides the narrative context for the message of hope in Isa.40ff. . . . Just as Yahweh brought to pass what he determined long ago concerning the Assyrians, so the audience of the book can assume that Yahweh will bring to pass what he determined long ago in Isaiah's pronouncements of judgment and salvation regarding the Babylonians." Others note "the former things" of 41:21 referring back to what has occurred before. See also Clements, "Beyond Tradition-History," 101, arguing that chapters 40–55 "were intended as a supplement and sequel to a collection of the earlier sayings of the eighth-century Isaiah of Jerusalem," with the caveat that not all of 40–55 fits this.

5. Penchansky, "Up for Grabs," 40.

exactly what they were signifying. Although many scholars have studied the intertextual aspects of the Deutero-Isaian texts,[6] this paper is choosing to look again at this literary strategy of the poet(s), this time through a postcolonial lens.

Whether the writer(s) of these chapters, 40–55, can be considered subjects of a postcolonial discussion might seem open to question, as Christopher Hays has noted.[7] The immediate issue is the relationship of the two terms, colonialism and empire. Although these are sometimes used almost interchangeably, many, such as Edward Said, see a sharp distinction: "'imperialism means the practice, the theory, and the attitudes of a dominating metropolitan center ruling a distant territory," whereas "'colonialism,' which is almost always a consequence of imperialism, is the implanting of settlements on distant territory."[8] If the whole middle section of the scroll is to be understood as having been written in Babylon, then this would not be a post-colonial writing at all, but a writing from within an imperial context. These would be texts written by a prophetic poet or poets living within "the dominating metropolitan center," in the very confines of empire. Although their anticipation of a return to their former homeland, now to be a settlement ruled over by a Persian empire, would at least hint of a colonialist situation. The distinction, however, is not necessarily a problem, for, as R. S. Sugirtharajah writes, postcolonialism is a "discipline in which everything is contested, everything is contestable, from the use of terms to the defining of chronological boundaries."[9] So here I would follow Fernando Segovia's call for "a more comprehensive" term, such as "imperial-colonial discourse," that sets a doubled focus on both "source and impact." While the imperial aspect "refers to whatever has to do with the originating and dominating center," the colonial "points to whatever has to do with the receiving and subordinate periphery."[10]

Matters of Dating and Historical Context

What is clear, is that Deutero-Isaiah is a political text. To quote Tod Linafelt, "[t]he poetry of Second Isaiah exists in the service of a particular sociohistorical context." For Linafelt, this is "preparation for the return of exile from

6. See, in particular, Tull Willey, *Remember the Former Things.*

7. See the essay in this volume by Hays.

8. Said, *Culture and Imperialism*, 9.

9. Sugirtharajah, *Postcolonial Criticism*, 12.

10. Segovia, "Mapping the Postcolonial Optic," 65–66.

Babylon to Judah."[11] Certainly, scholarly tradition has, for the most part, set these chapters, 40–55, in Babylon, yet, as Goldingay admits, "we do not even know for certain whether the material in Isaiah 40–55 is of Babylonian background, or perhaps of mixed origin."[12] Lena-Sofia Tiemeyer, in her detailed paper in this volume, argues that an apparent knowledge of Babylonian customs and Akkadian language "are not in themselves arguments" for a Babylonian provenance, and, indeed, in an earlier article, she has proposed a Judean origin, suggesting the writers were either a group of "newly returned exiles, who sought to convince the people of Judah that a return of their exilic brothers and sisters would be in their interests" or, following Ezra 6:21, a group of indigenous Judahites who were pro the exiles.[13] The matter of a "mixed origin" remains a possibility. While chapters 40–48 with their references to Cyrus would seem to imply a setting in the last years of the Neo-Babylonian Empire (ca. 550–539 B.C.E.), the possibility that the later chapters were written later, after the rise of Persia and the downfall of Babylon remains more open to debate.[14] Certainly there appears to be a change of focus in chapters 49–55.[15] While some have suggested that "the core of Isaiah 40–48 originated in Babylon addressing the *gola*, whereas Isaiah 49–55 was composed by a group in Judah to address the population of Jerusalem after 520 B.C.E.,"[16] Tod Linafelt is more cautious: "a geographical shift, from Babylon to Judah, has occurred between the two sections," but whether this is an imagined or physical shift, and whether that implies a different writer and a different audience, is more debatable.[17] Gottwald sees the difference in terms of time rather than location, with a "community debate" taking place over several years, asking such questions as "[w]hat are we Judahites to do about the deepening conflict between Babylon and

11. Linafelt, *Surviving Lamentations*, 63.

12. Goldingay, "Isaiah 40–55 in the 1990s," 240, adding "[t]he whole book of Isaiah may be of Jerusalem provenance."

13. Tiemeyer, "Geography and Textual Allusions."

14. Blenkinsopp notes in his review of John Goldingay and David Payne, *Isaiah 40–55*, 342, that while "the authors accept the majority opinion that those addressed . . . are the diaspora communities in Babylon ca. 540 B.C.E., . . . they urge the reader to bear in mind that the book in its final form was produced for the inhabitants of Jerusalem in the late Persian or early Hellenistic period and was intended to address their concerns." Gottwald, "Social Class and Ideology," 50, also recognizes the probability that it was "assembled" after the restoration.

15. Linafelt, *Surviving Lamentations*, 66: "The first section employs a rhetoric of release, while the second employs a rhetoric of reintegration."

16. Maier, *Daughter Zion, Mother Zion*, 162, with reference to van Oorschot, *Von Babel zum Zion*, and Berges, *Deutero-Jesaja*.

17. Linafelt, *Surviving Lamentations*, 67.

Persia?"[18] With these uncertainties, it might seem foolish to attempt to apply a template that would seem to require a particular political setting. What does, however, remain certain is that through reading this collection of texts we are hearing the voice of a people living with a very real and significant power imbalance, whether that is in Babylon or Jerusalem or later Yehud. As Mandolfo writes of "the anti-Babylon rhetoric" of chapter 47, it is not difficult to hear "the conflicted colonial status of this text."[19] My interest in this paper is to consider how this poetry both reflects such a political reality and strategizes its response.

Introducing Scott's Concepts of Hidden and Public Transcripts

Deutero-Isaiah opens with a strikingly up-beat hymn announcing the glad tidings not only of the exiles' return to Jerusalem, but of the imminent revelation of the glory of the exiles' God, a glory moreover that *all people shall see* (40:5), i.e., not only the returnees or those in Jerusalem.[20] Following the more general assumption of a Babylonian setting, my initial reaction is that for a poet or a community located and, indeed, confined within the centre of imperial power, to sing or circulate such a hymn would have been neither wise nor safe. Its promise would also have seemed utterly ridiculous, for the Babylonians had virtually destroyed the city, together with its temple. Just as, one might assume, in an attempt to account for the missing pieces between chapters 39 and 40, it would have been equally unwise to give public voice to the grief and anger caused by the destructive brutality of the Babylonian invasion. But was it possible to do this more surreptitiously, and is there evidence for this in Deutero-Isaiah?

To investigate this I am primarily drawing on the work of James Scott, in his study of public and hidden transcripts.[21] Although his work is highly nuanced, he primarily uses the binary categories of dominance and subordination, which might seem to permit the criticism that these dualistic categories are inherently reductionist, locking people into identities that reify both dominance and marginalization.[22] Yet it is, to quote Segovia, the "realization

---

18. Gottwald, "Social Class and Ideology," 46–47.

19. Mandolfo, *Daughter Zion Talks Back*, 107.

20. Translations, for the most part, follow the NRSV.

21. Scott, *Domination and the Arts of Resistance*.

22. See Carter, *John and Empire*, 78, "Such simplicity is deficient not only because imperial control is experienced in different ways by groups of differing societal status and interests . . . but also because imperial control is effected not only through force,

of the problematic of domination and subordination" that is the mark of "the postcolonial optic."[23] What is particularly helpful is Scott's discussion of the wide-ranging ways in which resistance and discontent are expressed.

For the Judeans, whether in exile or under foreign rule in Judah/ Yehud, it would surely have been expedient to pay due attention and conform, outwardly, to the ruling ideology undergirding the worldview projected by the imperial power. Any comment or reflection by the Israelite exilic community could therefore be expected to conform

> with how the dominant group would wish to have things appear[;]
> . . . it is in the interests of the subordinate to produce a more or less credible performance speaking the lines and making the gestures he knows is expected of him.[24]

This "performance" is what Scott terms "the public transcript," which, as he explains, will not only, "by its accommodationist tone, provide convincing evidence for the hegemony of dominant values, for the hegemony of dominant discourse" and, so, "naturalize the power of the dominant" but will also "conceal or euphemize the dirty linen of their rule."[25] The quite overt criticism of Babylon in Deutero-Isaiah might seem to be the very opposite of such a performance, but if the hymns of return either follow or anticipate the announcement of release by Cyrus, then this would be of little concern. As Jon Berquist notes of 44:24—45:8, with Cyrus named as the Messiah, God's anointed one, "the Persian imperializing ideology is unmistakable," the title not only affirming Persian power but giving it divine warrant.[26] It would seem a classic case of a public transcript. So, too, Deutero-Isaiah's railing against the Babylonian gods, for the Persian victory has shown them to be well and truly powerless. There is no danger at all in speaking against them. Gottwald, indeed, goes as far as seeing the author of Deutero-Isaiah as "a pronounced

---

intimidation, and spin, but also through complex and disguised means. . . . These strategies often benefited the subordinated in some ways, thereby mixing gift with obligation, benefits with dependency, accommodation with dissent."

23. Segovia, "Mapping the Postcolonial Optic," 65.

24. Scott, *Domination and the Arts of Resistance*, 4. The concept of the public transcript describes a way of responding to what the Kenyan author, Ngugi, refers to as the imperialists' "cultural bomb," which Hays discusses in his contribution to this volume.

25. Scott, *Domination and the Arts of Resistance*, 4, 18. See Newsom, "Response to Norman K. Gottwald," 75–78, and Goldingay, "Isaiah 40–55 in the 1990s," 238, regarding the language of children, sons and daughters rather than kings, princes, priests and prophets.

26. Goldingay, "Isaiah 40–55 in the 1990s," 232; Berquist, "Postcolonialism and Imperial Motives," 22.

Persian sympathizer."[27] Or is this a case of the public transcript convincing Gottwald?! There may, however, at the same time, be a Judean self-interest at play here: Mandolfo, for example, sees the attack on the gods as "part of the prophet's campaign to urge the exiles to support Persia and to ignite their passion to return and rebuild Judah."[28] Goldingay, too, sees this "overt" dismissal of the Babylonian gods as a "covert" word to Israelite exiles.[29]

My interest lies with that word "covert." Is there evidence within these chapters of a hidden transcript, that other "discourse that takes place 'off stage', beyond direct observation by powerholders"?[30] As Scott further describes it,

> the hidden transcript . . . is voiced in a sequestered social site where the control, surveillance, and repression of the dominant are least able to reach, and second, when the sequestered social milieu is composed entirely of close confidants who share similar experiences of domination.[31]

While it seems likely that the exiles were indeed a close and self-trusting community living in a "sequestered social milieu," this could also apply to the Judean survivors who remained in their now-dominated homeland. While much of their discourse would presumably have been voiced and circulated orally, I am assuming, heuristically, that despite the uncertainties of time and context noted above, portions, at least, of the work of the Deutero-Isaian poet(s) reflect such a community.

The Figure of Daughter Zion

It is one particular feature of the Deutero-Isaian text that I wish "to highlight and scrutinize," to use the words of Sugirtharajah quoted in the heading of this paper, to see if I can gain some sense of how the poet(s) may have used poetic prophecy as a response to their imperial-colonial reality. Gottwald has described these chapters as "a *bricolage* of fantasy."[32] The element of

27. Gottwald, "Social Class and Ideology," 48, "and the vocal supporter of an anti-Babylonian political orientation and strategy for his community." He sees the attacks on the Babylonian gods as directed at those exiles who had "embraced Babylonian religion and culture."

28. Mandolfo, *Daughter Zion Talks Back*, 106–7.

29. Goldingay, "Isaiah 40–55 in the 1990s," 232.

30. Scott, *Domination and the Arts of Resistance*, 4.

31. Ibid., 119–20. He adds, on page 135, that "[t]he social site at which they develop a hidden transcript is itself uniform, cohesive, and bound by powerful mutual sanctions that hold competing discourses at arm's length."

32. Gottwald, "Social Class and Ideology," 50.

fantasy is clearly seen in chapters 40–48, for, as Goldingay describes them, these chapters "portray an alternative world which the believing communities have wanted to be a real world whether it is so or not," adding that, with the persuasiveness of their rhetorical devices, "only a fool would dispute the matter under discussion."[33] The feature that interests me is the figure of Daughter Zion, Jerusalem explicitly personified as a daughter, which is but one use that the prophet-poet makes of the "multi-faceted" Zion symbol, more fully discussed by Joy Hooker in this volume. While the writer of Isa 62:11 also uses the term daughter, and, as is well recognized, concern for Zion "marks a thread" through the whole Isaiah scroll,[34] the focus of this paper is specifically the use that the Deutero-Isaian poet(s) makes of Daughter Zion, admittedly only one small feature in this richly imaged *bricolage*.

There is an initial technical and syntactical question as to whether *bat-siyyon* is to be read as a genitive of possession or location or as an appositional usage. As the options have been well rehearsed, I do not wish to repeat the pro- and anti-theses here, but will be following Christl Maier's proposal of a preferred "appositional genitive."[35] Possible ancient Near Eastern precedents that allowed the use of the daughter image have also been thoroughly discussed, although they must remain as hypotheses only, and will not be summarized again here.[36]

The other initial question is what personified Zion represents. Is it the spirit or spirituality of the temple mount, the earthly dwelling place of Israel's God, the city of the Davidic monarchy, or the inhabitants of Jerusalem? And how significant is the gendered aspect? Daughter Zion is a particular "metaphor, "that figure of speech whereby we speak about one thing in terms which are seen to be suggestive of another."[37] As G. B. Caird describes it, the two "are not grasped as two but as one. . . . Metaphor is a lens; it is as though the speaker were saying, 'Look through this and see what I have seen, something you would never have noticed without the lens!'"[38] But, equally, as one tilts the lens, different facets come into view, so that personified Zion may be seen sometimes as representing one particular aspect

---

33. Goldingay, "Isaiah 40–55 in the 1990s," 227. Such idealism, he suggests (229), "gives the impression that there will be achievement, closure, but there never is."

34. Maier, *Daughter Zion, Mother Zion*, 161. See Clements, "Zion as Symbol and Political Reality," 8, suggesting that the question pervading "the entire *traditio*" of Isaiah was "What future can there be for Zion, now that the temple has been destroyed?"

35. Maier, *Daughter Zion, Mother Zion*, 62.

36. See Biddle, "The Figure of Lady Jerusalem"; Dobbs-Allsopp, *Weep, O Daughter of Zion*; Maier, *Daughter Zion, Mother Zion*, 63–73.

37. Soskice, *Metaphor And Religious Language*, 15.

38. Caird, *The Language and Imagery of the Bible*, 152.

of Zion/Jerusalem, and at other times another. The metaphor of daughter does, however, view her specifically as gendered. To what effect is one of the issues to be explored.

In the Isaiah scroll Zion as Daughter had already made an appearance in 1:8, memorably and pathetically figured, *left like a booth in a vineyard, like a shelter in a cucumber field, like a besieged city,* before being charged as a prostitute (v. 21), although if one follows the view that a later hand composed chapter 1 to set at the start of the scroll as an introduction to the whole, then this verse can be seen as both Daughter Zion's Isaianic beginning and her closing. There are two references to *the mount (har) of Daughter Zion* at 10:32 and 16:1; while the dating of the latter is disputed, 10:32 would seem to reflect the Assyrian threat. Although Maier describes the daughter in 10:32 as "in need of protection" in contrast to "the mighty warrior,"[39] neither of these uses seem to highlight the personification.

Daughter Zion in Lamentations

Metaphorical and personified Zion had, however, been a significant figure in a collection of grief stricken and angry responses to the events of 587 B.C.E. These were the poems of Lamentations, most probably circulating sometime soon after 586 B.C.E., although, as Dobbs-Allsopp states, the book of Lamentations, like the collected poems of Deutero-Isaiah, "survives in a mostly decontextualized state," so that its dating and place of origin can only be deduced.[40] It would seem most likely, however, that initially these laments circulated among those Judeans who had survived the destruction, and apparently, perhaps soon after, were also known in Babylon. The interest for this paper is that in the outpouring of grief and anger, it is, as Maier observes, "[p]articularly in the voice of personified Zion" in the first two chapters that "the pain, anger, and desperation over the catastrophe finds a venue of expression."[41] Pictured and named in various ways within the poem(s), she is introduced by the narrator in 1:1, simply as "the city," perhaps, as has been suggested, carrying an echo of Isa 1:21, but a city that is now like a widow; though previously a princess she is now a vassal in forced labour, the poet adding female image to female image. While the title of daughter appears in verse 6, it is the ending of this introduction (vv. 1–9) that more immediately links with Deutero-Isaiah, in its bleak and poignant observation that there is *no-one to comfort her,* a line repeated as a refrain of

39. Maier, *Daughter Zion, Mother Zion,* 79.

40. Dobbs-Allsopp, *Lamentations,* 4.

41. Maier, *Daughter Zion, Mother Zion,* 143.

marked pathos (1:9, 16, 17, 21). Here, at its first utterance, it prompts Zion into voice herself, briefly in verse 9 but at greater length in verses 11c–16, 18–22. It is as if she has been standing by as the narrator has been describing her fate, including her own part in it, until she can stand it no longer, and so bursts out in a cry to God to notice her affliction, caused by the unnamed enemy. Those among whom the work circulated would, of course, have been in no doubt as to who this enemy was.

And yet, it is not Babylon that is seen as the ultimate cause; verses 12c–13 make it very clear that it is YHWH who has afflicted her, *on the day of his fierce anger*. The narrator reiterates this at length in chapter 2, but it is Babylon nonetheless that has acted as YHWH's agent (v. 13). Even if Zion does admit her own wrongdoing (vv. 18, 20), the punishment is clearly out of all proportion; it is roundly shown, detail after detail, as profoundly excessive. As Dobbs-Allsopp notes, the poems do not spell out or linger on the matter of Zion's sin; the intensity is in the images of suffering, so that "sin is effectively denied much of its purchase power."[42] So while it is accepted that YHWH is behind this disaster, and while the cries rise up to heaven, imploring YHWH to look and see the misery (1:9c, 11c, 20; 2:20), the fact remains that it is the Babylonian army that has caused the mayhem, acting with devastating brutality. There can surely be little doubt about the role of Lamentations: the survivors who remained in the land needed a vehicle to testify to the pain they had endured. This is the focus; unlike Deutero-Isaiah there is no overt concern for restoration, rebuilding or the return of the exiled. Rather, these poems are filled with the "horrifyingly dark and grizzly images of raw human pain and suffering,"[43] which both Zion and the narrator are protesting. As Maier notes, such imagery of Jerusalem's "wounded body . . . signifies resistance against the hopeless situation in its unwillingness to surrender. . . . The wailing body of Jerusalem signifies the protest of the survivors."[44] It would certainly not have been for Babylonian eyes or ears, and must therefore fall within the category of hidden transcript, which, as noted above, Scott describes as that "discourse that takes place 'off stage', beyond direct observation by powerholders."[45] The poetic intensity also fits well with Scott's observation that where "the domination is particularly severe, it is likely to produce a

---

42. Dobbs-Allsopp, *Lamentations*, 32.

43. Ibid., 2. Note his discussion on page 11 of some opposing views re restoration possibilities.

44. Maier, *Daughter Zion, Mother Zion*, 152.

45. Scott, *Domination and the Arts of Resistance*, 4.

hidden transcript of corresponding richness."[46] And a significant feature of this richness is the female image of Daughter Zion, which the Deutero-Isaiah poet carries through and adopts for another purpose.[47]

The Matter of Isaiah Chapter 40

That the opening of chapter 40 appears to be a conscious and quite deliberate response to the Lamentations refrain of there being no comforter for Daughter Zion is well recognized.[48] Is this, then, Deutero-Isaiah's strategy for dealing with the gap, after chapter 39? And, if so, further questions follow. Who were the intended readers or audience, and how would they have understood the connection with Lamentations? Once again, as with Deutero-Isaiah as a whole, we are faced with uncertainties of both dating and context. As Goldingay notes, there is a real possibility that this chapter, or at least verses 1–11, were a later addition, placed here as an introduction to what follows.[49] And again that question: was it, then, written and circulated in Babylon or in Jerusalem? As Goldingay writes of Deutero-Isaiah as a whole, "[e]ven if their original covert audience was exclusively one or the other, both are possible audiences for them."[50] Both have deep concern for Jerusalem. While I would suggest that in either case such a poem would have circulated as a hidden transcript, kept away from the eyes of imperial overlords, what I further wish to suggest is that by bringing the words of the Jerusalem survivors into this opening chapter, albeit indirectly, the poem acts as a doubly "hidden transcript."[51] For, while it would seem, in hymning

---

46. Scott, *Domination and the Arts of Resistance*, 27.

47. It is notable that the Isaiah poet goes a step further and also uses female imagery of God as well as Zion (42:14; 45:10; 49:15). Gruber, "The Motherhood of God in Second Isaiah," 358, noting that "Deutero-Isaiah polemicized against idolatry more than any other prophet . . . in the Bible," suggests that women were particularly attracted to "idolatrous" cults, having been turned away from their own by the polemical gendered language of the marriage metaphor used by Jeremiah and Ezekiel, where maleness identified with YHWH was a positive and femaleness associated with a wayward Israel a negative. There is, however, also the possibility that the idolatry passages are from another hand, as noted by Clements, "Beyond Tradition-History," 111.

48. See among others, Korpel, "Second Isaiah's Coping with the Religious Crisis"; Brueggemann, "Unity and Dynamic in the Isaiah Tradition."

49. See Goldingay, "Isaiah 40–55 in the 1990s," 242, with reference to the work of Merendino, *Der Erste und der Letzte*, who sets it in a post-exilic Jerusalem; Tiemeyer, "Geography and Textual Allusions."

50. Goldingay, "Isaiah 40–55 in the 1990s," 242.

51. See Newsom, "Response to Norman K. Gottwald," who uses the work of Bakhtin to highlight the force of Judahite speech in Deutero-Isaiah.

a God-given return with no mention of Cyrus' decree of release, to be a hidden transcript itself, it also, with its strong opening call for comfort, immediately reminds its audience of that earlier hidden transcript lamenting the suffering experienced by their own friends and relatives.[52] Whether or not it was penned in Babylon, this indirect reminder of Daughter Zion's pain and humiliation, written "under erasure," would seem to be a strategy devised as a way of expressing that which is not to be expressed, a ploy of the hidden transcript. For, as Scott notes, in

> any established system of domination, it is not just a question of masking one's feelings and producing the correct speech acts and gestures in their place. Rather it is often a question of controlling what would be a natural impulse to rage, insult, anger, and the violence that such feelings prompt.[53]

He further notes that such feelings are all the more intense when some are forced "to look on helplessly" while others closely related to them are abused or degraded. If the writer(s) of these chapters were drafted to Babylon either in 597 B.C.E. or immediately before the worst of the destruction in 587 B.C.E. they would have known and heard of the brutality and violence meted out in Jerusalem, but would indeed have been powerless to help in any way. The challenge of controlling their natural impulse to rage at the violence Babylon had perpetrated against their people and their homeland would have been very real. This does not override the possibility that a later Judean poet also under imperial rule would have felt the same constraint. In either case, introducing a response to a key refrain of Lamentations, a set of poems in which the Judean survivors had given voice to their own grief and anger, would have allowed some expression, albeit vicariously, of their emotive responses in turn.

If, as many assume, these verses, and verse 11 in particular, assume a return, a God-gifted homecoming from Babylon, then there would seem to be a silence, or, at least, no overt reference to a Judean community still living in the land. If this is so, then a similar strategy of overt silence would seem to be in play. It was not only expedient but a matter of their own survival to seem to assume the impossibility of a surviving Judean

---

52. Tull Willey, "The Servant of YHWH and Daughter Zion," 302, states "there is no marker in the text for the inhabitants of Judah who have not been exiled. They are either subsumed into Zion or they do not exist at all." On the contrary, as Newsom, "Response to Norman K. Gottwald," 74, points out, "their utterances inhabit the text" through these intertextual or dialogic echoes.

53. Scott, *Domination and the Arts of Resistance*, 37.

community maintaining a strong sense of national identity.[54] The covert message conveyed through the Lamentations allusions was, of course, significantly different. It also follows another of Scott's observations, that for any expression of outrage or resistance to be owned or adopted by a group, it needs to "carry effective meaning for them and reflect the (group's) cultural meanings."[55] Lamentations fits this well. Of course, if this Deutero-Isaian hymn were to fall into imperial hands, without knowledge of Lamentations this coded aspect of the poem would have been indecipherable. This would fit once again with Scott's observation that "[t]he meaning of the text . . . is rarely straightforward; it is often meant to communicate one thing to those in the know and another to outsiders and authorities."[56]

Yet the Lamentations' echo is not only a reminder of present and past miseries and shame. Nor is it the only scriptural work that the Deutero-Isaiah poet(s) drew upon, as Patricia Tull Willey, in particular, has demonstrated in considerable detail. All of these allusions and re-workings function, as she argues, to help "a people reevaluating their national self-understanding in the wake of the destruction of their capital city, monarchy, and temple."[57] The Lamentations' echo is part of this, and here at the beginning of chapter 40 it sets a foundation for the new message: there is to be a homecoming, the exiles are to return. The Babylonian disaster is not the end of Jerusalem nor the exiles' place within it. Gottwald suggests the Deutero-Isaian chapters, as a whole, are "a creative act to make the deliverance and restoration so palpable to the community's imagination that, believing it actual, the audience will join the author to make it happen insofar as the deliverance depends on them."[58] If Lamentations is survival literature,[59] then these chapters are utopian. Once again, Scott sets such utopian writing in the context of

---

54. Goldingay, "Isaiah 40–55 in the 1990s," 239, acknowledges that there are varying ways of interpreting "the silence about the Jerusalem community." This paper however is suggesting that the use of Lamentations keeps that community well within view, when understood as a hidden transcript.

55. Scott, *Domination and the Arts of Resistance*, 118.

56. Ibid., 184.

57. Tull Willey, *Remember the Former Things*, 1. The use of trauma and disaster studies by O'Connor, "Reclaiming Jeremiah's Violence," could be equally applied to Deutero-Isaiah, in that he, too, 41, "names and reframes [his audience's world] by imaginatively re-inventing traditions that they share."

58. Gottwald, "Social Class and Ideology," 50. See, too, Newsom, "Response to Norman K. Gottwald," 75–76.

59. Maier, *Daughter Zion, Mother Zion*, 142. See Dobbs-Allsopp, *Lamentations*, 2: "Lamentations may well be the most remarkable and compelling testament to the human spirit's will to live in all of the Old Testament."

subordinated communities, as a way of imaginatively negating or reversing "an existing pattern of . . . status degradation."[60]

It may be even more than that. As Goldingay suggests, by "taking up" and responding to the speech of Lamentations, Deutero-Isaiah may be implying that both communities, the survivors in Jerusalem and the exiles, are one people. If written in Babylon, it may be allowing the exilic group to "see itself as one in destiny with the Judean community rather than set over against it."[61] For the exiles the immediate destiny, to be heralded from a high mountain, is a future of happy and even glorious return. Goldingay further suggests that by assuming "the right to declare God's response" to the prayers of Lamentations, the exilic prophet is, in fact, staking the exiles' "claim to power in the future Jerusalem community."[62] Under Persian rule, any hint of a power claim at all would be risky, for the reality for any future for Zion was only to be considered in terms of a small and rather unimportant part of the now mighty Persian empire, a future of relatively insignificant vassalage, useful only as a buffer, no other to be considered, or even hinted at. There is certainly a whiff of fantasy here, a redescription of the world of Judah, and an implied critique of the prevailing dominant ideology.[63] Carol Newsom, in her response to Gottwald's observation that "nothing explicit is said about the constitution of the new community,"[64] also senses some underlying political manoeuvres, seeing the use of the Judahite language of Lamentations as "an oblique acknowledgement that there are some social and ideological problems attached to going home again."[65] Persia would surely have taken a dim view of any political jockeying among underlings, which again, if these scholars are right, would argue for the writer recognizing the need for a hidden transcript. The power issue can also, however, be understood in the context of a further observation of Scott, that "[t]he power relations generated among subordinate groups are often the only countervailing power to the determination of behavior from above."[66]

---

60. Scott, *Domination and the Arts of Resistance*, 81. He comments, on page 91, that this way of coping is "so common . . . that it is plausible to consider it part and parcel of the religiopolitical equipment of historically disadvantaged groups."

61. Goldingay, "Isaiah 40–55 in the 1990s," 238.

62. Ibid., 244.

63. See Brueggemann, "Unity and Dynamic in the Isaiah Tradition," 93.

64. Gottwald, "Social Class and Ideology," 51.

65. Newsom, "Response to Norman K. Gottwald," 75. She also suggests that, by using a common language and shared imagery, the poem is also "an implicit appeal to the Judahite community" to welcome the exiles back, and highlights, 77–78, the affective appeal of the "children, sons and daughters" terms applied to the exiles.

66. Scott, *Domination and the Arts of Resistance*, 27.

While the specific term *bat siyyon* has not been used in this opening chapter, the Lamentations echo has clearly brought her into this idyllic or utopian picture of return. It is she, Daughter Zion, the city who has been sitting lonely (Lam 1:1), with no-one to comfort her (v. 9 *et al.*), who has been trodden and brought down to the ground by YHWH (1:15, 2:2), who is now to be comforted. It is she, Daughter Zion, who is now summoned to *get up to a high mountain and lift up* her voice.[67] It is she, Daughter Zion, who is to be shown tenderness—by a God who is tenderness itself (v. 11).

The Speaking Daughter of Chapter 49 Who Becomes a Mother

Yet, curiously, no more is heard of Daughter Zion until chapter 49.[68] Once again, there are the uncertainties of placing this chapter in time and place. If written in Babylon the imagined scenario is one where, "the exiles have been freed and have departed from an utterly powerless and humiliated Babylon."[69] As already mentioned, it is possible that chapters 49–55 were composed later in Yehud, sometime after 520 B.C.E.[70] If verse 21 is from the same pen and belongs to the same poem this would seem to assume an exilic setting, although it could all be simply poetic fantasy. In any case, there is a change of key: the scenario has changed. Poetically, at least, YHWH's people have now been comforted by YHWH, the god who shows compassion upon the suffering (v. 13). In an imperial Babylonian setting this would clearly have only been possible as a hidden transcript, but even if it were written either on the cusp of release under Cyrus, or later in Yehud, to imagine return as due to YHWH rescuing *prey from the mighty* and *captives of a tyrant* would hardly have warmed the hearts of Persian overlords. And

---

67. Taking *mebasseret* in apposition to *siyyon*.

68. Where Zion or Jerusalem are named between chapters 40 and 49 there is no indication of personification nor are they directly addressed.

69. Linafelt, *Surviving Lamentations*, 68.

70. Although many still hold to the view that Deutero-Isaiah, as a whole, is Babylonian based. The alternating and complementary pattern of Zion and servant passages is a significant feature throughout these chapters, as has been well recognized. See, for example, Sawyer, "Daughter of Zion and Servant of the Lord in Isaiah"; Tull Willey, "The Servant of YHWH and Daughter Zion"; Tull Willey, *Remember the Former Things*, 221–26. See, too, Linafelt, *Surviving Lamentations*, 71, "If one takes the servant to be a personification of Israel, then the alternation between Zion and the servant is a concrete manifestation of the rhetoric of reintegration." My interest, however, for this paper, is solely in the use of the Daughter Zion personification.

attributing release and return as solely determined and carried through by the exiles' god!

Dramatically, Zion now speaks, at last! Elsewhere in these Deutero-Isaiah poems, to quote Mandolfo, "she is spoken about, spoken to, and alluded to, but not allowed a voice of her own."[71] Just this once! Moreover, she not only speaks, she interrupts, and not only does she interrupt verse 13 with its repeated call for joyful singing,[72] but, as Tull Willey points out, her challenge comes "after eight chapters of nearly continuous divine speech. Heaven, earth, and mountains have been invited to rejoice at the news of YHWH's redemptions."[73] It is no less than a full "cosmic celebration" that she interrupts, protesting that the words of a comforting and compassionate YHWH simply do not ring true. Finally, the echo of Lamentations in verse 13 that now insists that YHWH has comforted his people, is too strong, and so she replies, with further echoes of Lamentations, using words of the Jerusalem survivors from the very last verses (Lam 5:20), words taken from their hidden transcript. This, she now protests, is a YHWH who forgets and abandons. The divine response, so remarkably lacking in Lamentations, is immediate. With a rhetorical question that seemingly demands that the audience respond, "of course, not!"[74] But, as Tull Willey comments, Lam 2:20 "has borne witness to the ravages that war may visit even on maternal care." Once again the echoes of Lamentations, provoked by words from both Zion and YHWH, are functioning as statements under erasure: they are to be heard, for they are real, and underline the misery of the past but they are not allowed to negate the new message. For there is now an updated transcript, still hidden, but looking to a future of hope, of comfort indeed, where Zion still has a role to play. For, to quote David Penchansky, "as a mediatrix between Yahweh and his people" she is "the link to the home for which the exiles longed and the God that they worshiped."[75] By verses 19–21 the usefulness of the daughter imagery seems, however, to have been exhausted. In verse 18, in a poetic conceit, Zion is promised that she will wear all those

---

71. Mandolfo, *Daughter Zion Talks Back*, 114.

72. Although its verbs of (not) comforting and afflicting carry the echo of Lam 1:9. Note, too, there is some question as to where verse 13 fits. BHS has it concluding the section from verse 8, whereas the NRSV has it attached to what follows. It is, as Blenkinsopp, *Isaiah 40–55*, 307, notes, a brief hymnic stanza, although he sees it following "the stylistic pattern of chs. 40–48." Linafelt, *Surviving Lamentations*, 74–75, sees a point of transition here, between concern for YHWH's people in exile in verse 13, and the move to Zion, understood as Jerusalem in verse 14.

73. Tull Willey, "The Servant of YHWH and Daughter Zion," 281.

74. Tull Willey, *Remember the Former Things,"* 191.

75. Penchansky, *Twilight of the Gods*, 73.

returning *as an ornament,* binding them *on like a bride.* She is now on the way to motherhood—for the rest of this chapter.

What has been the effect of the daughter metaphor? Michael Williams some years ago urged caution in discussing gendered imagery, setting the question: "when a gendered image is used, is it used primarily *for the sake of its gendered character,* or is it for some other reason . . . when are feminine images actually images *of the feminine?*"[76] I am suggesting that the quite particular feminine image of daughter has been significant and carefully chosen. I would agree with Julia O'Brien that its effect is both "to evoke pathos," and "provoke sympathy." While she is writing of its use in Lamentations her comments hold just as true for Deutero-Isaiah: just as daughters in Israel were wholly dependent on their fathers, so here, by making "explicit the daughter's total dependence on the power of others . . . [t]he subordinate status of the daughter and her helpless state do not lurk in the background of the prophetic description of Jerusalem as a daughter: they take centre stage." But, as she points out, it is even more that: there is the view that daughters are "sexually vulnerable, able to be penetrated against their will."[77] It is this that allows the metaphor of rape to be heard in the lament that *goyim* have entered Zion's *holy place* (Lam 1:10), and lies behind the call to Zion to rise from the dust in Deutero-Isaiah (52:2).[78] Ben Sira, admittedly some centuries later, shows real anxiety about daughters, his most developed section on daughters (42:9–12) being part of a longer section directly concerned with shame (41:14—42:8). Claudia Camp sums it up nicely: for an Israelite father "daughters . . . are a wild card."[79] What, then, are fathers to do? Protect them and guard them very carefully, although this does not necessarily mean that there is no affection. It is the powerlessness that is the *raison d'être* of a hidden transcript. Lamenting a daughter's degradation and abuse also fits well with the purpose of what Sugirtharajah terms as "dissident" texts, which is to highlight "the awful things that colonization had done or was capable

76. Williams, "Variety in Gnostic Perspectives on Gender," 4 (Williams' italics).

77. O'Brien, *Challenging Prophetic Metaphor,* 139–40, 147. She makes this comment regarding its use in Lamentations.

78. Which, as Maier, *Daughter Zion, Mother Zion,* 168, notes, follows the line that gentiles will not *enter* her again.

79. Camp, "Understanding a Patriarchy," 36–37. She refers here also to Philo, *Spec. Leg.* 3. 81, for while "an adulterous wife can be divorced . . . a sexually deviant daughter has no place to go but home. She is an everlasting blot on her father's name, which is all, in the sage's view, a man has to live for." Note, too, how Boaz uses the term "daughter" in a context of protection in Ruth 2:8.

of doing."[80] In this respect the metaphorical daughter would seem to be a highly useful postcolonial tool.

Now, however, the Deutero-Isaiah poet wishes to emphasize the return, picturing a great crowd of people all on their way back to Jerusalem. The daughter in need of fatherly protection no longer fits this happy homecoming scenario. Yet, although the focus is now to be on the returnees, the poet wishes to keep a female Zion—and in her female finery (52:1). The solution: the bride has to become a mother—with all her maternal care for her children, now so many that there is hardly room for them all (49:20). Once again the poet follows Lamentations, where a similar need of mother/child imagery to express the pain of loss was felt and answered, most shockingly in 2:20; here, however it is used with different purpose and effect. A further striking reversal is that YHWH, whose silence virtually reverberated throughout Lamentations, has now become, in Linafelt's words, "positively loquacious," in contrast to Zion, who challenged YHWH so directly in Lamentations, but is now rarely to be heard.[81] But in a further echo of Lamentations, the once *bereaved and barren* mother Zion, is now heard, albeit indirectly, *saying in her heart* that this return of the children is virtually beyond belief (49:21). As Newsom comments,

> [b]y representing the Babylonian community not as Zion in exile but as Zion's children, Second Isaiah emphasizes the most affectively charged image relating the exiles' relationship to Jerusalem . . . representing them as . . . children of Zion, provides the symbolic model for their reincorporation.[82]

Daughter Zion in the Later Chapters of Deutero-Isaiah

Yet Daughter Zion is not entirely forgotten; she may not be addressed with this title, but in 51:3 the echo of the Lamentations' refrain leaves it in no doubt that it is she whom YHWH will comfort. In a welter of positive images, she will be like a second garden of Eden, joyously singing hymns, presumably to YHWH. It is she to whom the ransomed will come with singing (v. 11), contrasting with the mourning roads and desolate gates of Lam 1:4. It is she whom YHWH addresses directly, assuring her that it is YHWH alone who is the comforter (v. 12). The focus, however, is no longer on Zion but on YHWH, whose speech addressing her is a mixture both of reproach and reassurance,

80. Sugirtharajah, *Postcolonial Criticism,* 44.

81. Linafelt, *Surviving Lamentations,* 79.

82. Newsom, "Response to Norman K. Gottwald," 76–77.

ending in verse 16 with the ancient covenant formula addressed directly to her, and leading to another stanza of maternal imagery. For the extreme pathos of the children's fate in Lam 4, heard here beneath the text in verses 17–20, calls again for maternal, not daughter imagery. But it is YHWH who is the speaker; as O'Connor wryly notes of verse 20, YHWH, "the missing voice of Lamentations, quotes that book (Lam 2:11; 4:1), as if he had been listening to her all along."[83] Verse 19 had already returned to the *devastation and destruction, famine and sword* of Lamentations, and if 1QIsaᵃ is followed the cry is heard once more, *who will comfort you?* Reassurance is given in verse 22, but with an uncomfortable echo of Lam 4:11 and 21 that leads in turn to an equally uncomfortable promise of vengeance on *the tormentors,* who are now, themselves, to receive the *bowl of wrath* which she herself has drained (v. 17)—yet another indication that we are still reading a hidden transcript.

There is one last turn to Zion addressed as Daughter in 52:2, in terms that once again recall the shameful degradations of Lamentations, although the image of a daughter sitting *in the dust* had already been used of Babylon in 47:1.[84] Always the echoes, always those reminders of the miseries of the past and the fate now to be left behind, hidden behind or under the words on the page. Here it follows the calls in verse 1 where Zion and Jerusalem are paralleled, and Jerusalem addressed as *the holy city,* the concept of holiness so crucial for this scroll. The Zion, who is to put on *your beautiful garments* and is finally addressed as daughter, now appears about to rise as a queen, if the command is to be interpreted as "ascend your throne."[85] In a reversal of 40:9, and echoing Nah 2:1, verse 7 announces she is to receive good news from a messenger.[86] It is another utopian hymn; the poet repeats the comforting declaration of 49:13 (v. 9), adding that YHWH has redeemed Jerusalem, before using words from Ps 98:3 to declare *all the ends of the earth shall see the salvation of our God* (v. 10).

The one called to sing out in chapter 54 is not Zion the daughter but Zion the once abandoned wife, although, in fact, the chapter never addresses

---

83. O'Connor, "'Speak Tenderly to Jerusalem,'" 290.

84. Blenkinsopp, *Isaiah 40–55,* 340, sees a deliberate contrast here. See also Tull Willey, *Remember the Former Things,* 168–71.

85. Following Blenkinsopp, *Isaiah 40–55,* 338–39, who reads the MT form "as an imperative fem. *>ysb,* 'sit,' as in 1QIsaᵃ *vsby*" and equivalents in LXX, the Vulgate and Targum. The implied reference to a throne would also carry the reference to Babylon's dethronement in 47:1.

86. Tull Willey, *Remember the Former Things,* 120, explains the use of Nahum, also a feature in verse 1, "by invoking a similar articulation of Nineveh's defeat, Second Isaiah confers historical significance on new events."

Zion by name.[87] In the final section, verses 11–17, she is once again the afflicted and uncomforted one, but only for a brief moment, for the promise comes that she will be a city of extravagant richness, before verse 13 returns to the children, who will, in turn, be prosperous, in a striking reversal of Lam 4:1–2. YHWH, the warrior god, who previously attacked Zion will deal, brutally, with any oppressor. The address is all directed at Zion before turning in the final verse to draw together the two main Deutero-Isaian figures, Zion and the servant of YHWH, in a final reassurance to the servants of YHWH. If these are, indeed, as Linafelt reads them "the returning exiles," then indeed, as he continues, "[t]he goal of the poet in Second Isaiah has been met. A way to imagine the homecoming has been found."[88] Chapter 54 is not, however, the last of this collection, as it is traditionally ordered. What follows is a resounding call to those who thirst, to *come to the waters, . . . come, buy and eat, . . . come to me; listen, so that you may live* (55:1–3b). The puzzling question: who is the caller? There are echoes here bringing to mind the call of that other personified feminine figure, Wisdom, who notably calls out, offering an invitation to a feast that brings life in Proverbs 9:4–6.[89] Moreover, if, as Baltzer and Paganini argue, the 3s suffix on the final word of verse 5 is a rare form of the feminine, and the verse addressed to Zion as the parallel in 60:9 would suggest, this strengthens the case that it is Zion who is speaking once again.[90] And if, as Paganini also suggests,[91] this call is read as a fulfillment of YHWH's promise to Zion in 49:18, then perhaps this is Daughter Zion's last appearance in Deutero-Isaiah, now, finally and actively, calling the people to come (back?) to her, and offering the feast and words of life.

---

87. See Tull Willey, *Remember the Former Things*, 234. "Lamentations' question of forgetting had been answered in 49:15, but the second accusation (i.e., of abandoning in 5:20) was left unaddressed. In chapter 54 it is finally answered." She further notes that the terms *reject* (*m's*) and *be angry* (*qtsf*) in Lam 5:22 "appear together nowhere else in the Bible except in Isa 54:6–8, where they appear along with *'zb* (abandon)."

88. Linafelt, *Surviving Lamentations*, 72.

89. Similarly Ben Sira 24:19–21. So Begrich, *Studien zu Deuterojesaja*, 59–61. Clifford, "Isaiah 55: Invitation to a Feast," 28–29, finds an Ugaritic precedent in Anat's invitation to Aqhat, as well as Proverbs and Sira.

90. Baltzer, *Deutero-Isaiah*, 468; Paganini, "Who Speaks in Isaiah 55.1?," 86–88. I am grateful to Lena-Sofia Tiemeyer for alerting me to this possibility at the colloquium.

91 Paganini, "Who Speaks in Isaiah 55.1?" 90.

Conclusion

Admittedly, the imagery of Zion as mother and wife has played a major role in this imaginative construal, allowing for some of the most emotionally charged texts, but her beginnings as daughter have allowed me a glimpse of the Deutero-Isaiah prophet-poet(s) at work, subtly drawing upon one resistant collection of poems, in order to create another. Mandolfo has described Deutero-Isaiah as "a document trapped between two urgent but potentially mutually exclusive needs—the survival of an authentic indigenous identity and survival, period."[92] My suggestion, applying Scott's template, is that at least the first of these was met as the poems circulated as hidden transcripts. Did they lead to more than a sense of survival? As Gottwald carefully states, "the extent to which" these led to political resistance "is uncertain," although he implies this would have been likely.[93]

Has it been an anachronism to apply a term such as "postcolonial" to these ancient texts? I find myself in agreement with Colleen Conway when she writes "postcolonial studies may well be concerned with what happened in the past, but typically only insofar as a view of the past informs a particular reading of the text in the present."[94] I will therefore conclude with two further quotes:

> to read this alien text from the past is to share in a vision of the future. As a text that calls into question the fleeting security of regimes that do not look beyond themselves in pursuit of security and peace in their own days, the book of Isaiah ceases to be remote. . . . Like readers of other canonized literary works, we can find in the Book of Isaiah shared insights as we face our own future.[95]

> To what extent can those who have suffered innocently at the hands of modern empires find their experience addressed in this tradition? There is no single answer to this question. But the *ideal* of a justice that can restore life . . . is a biblical principle that no postcolonial society can do without.[96]

92. Mandolfo, *Daughter Zion Talks Back*, 107.

93. Gottwald, "Social Class and Ideology," 49, referring to "the overriding authorial ideology . . . sharply focused on the prospect of a Judahite restoration by the Persians." Scott, *Domination and the Arts of Resistance*, 191, makes the point that the hidden transcript is more "a condition of practical resistance rather than a substitute for it."

94. Conway, "There and Back Again," 86.

95. Conrad, *Reading Isaiah*, 161–62.

96. Brett, *Decolonizing God*, 111, referring to the prophetic tradition as a whole (emphasis original).

Postcolonial theory has deep Marxist roots. As the Marxist scholar Frederic Jameson writes, it is "the simultaneous recognition of the ideological and utopian functions of the artistic text" that moves us to praxis.[97] Deutero-Isaiah, with its doubled hidden transcripts, both honors the memory of those who suffer the inhumanity of imperial powers, and uses that same memory, in a poetic force of reversals, to reassure all who read this work that these powers do not have the last word. Utopian it may be, but the "ideal" of a divine power that honors and restores life is indeed what "no postcolonial society can do without." The challenging question is: does it lead us to praxis?

I have framed this paper with a lament from the Tuhoe people, whose treatment at the hand of the colonizing powers in my country of Aotearoa New Zealand was deeply shameful, with long lasting consequences yet to be resolved. This is the lens for a paper considering how a collection of ancient Isaianic poems may have responded to the powers of domination. If, as Sugirtharajah describes it, postcolonialism is "an undertaking of social and political commitment,"[98] then it is to be undertaken with one eye firmly on the ways in which our own postcolonial countries presently order society, and account for their histories. To read these ancient biblical texts, is to be reminded that these histories, these strategies reach over time and continents, urging us to remember and work towards the *tikkun 'olam* in our own land and context.

> Noho noa te tinana, ka nuka ki te haere
> He turehu naku i te ao, i te po
> Noho ana hoki au i Rua-toki ra,
> Te whenua i puritia, te whenua i tawhia . . .

97. Jameson, *The Political Unconscious*, 299.
98. Sugirtharajah, *Postcolonial Criticism*, 14.

6

Zion as Theological Symbol in Isaiah

Implications for Judah, for the Nations, and for Empire

Joy Hooker

WHILE THE NAME ZION occurs throughout the book of Isaiah,[1] it is utilized in a number of different and interesting ways. It can refer to a geographical place or a people, and is used as a theological symbol.[2] Goldingay says,

> Jerusalem-Zion (like "servant") is a tensive symbol, capable of having more than one referent. It can denote a location, a physical city, the people who live in the city, the corporate personality of the city, even that corporate personality as a metaphysical entity that in some sense exists independently of its population,

---

1. This essay supports the view of Isaiah as a composite unity spanning several hundred years. It is generally agreed, however, that a threefold division of the material exists where some sections are clearly pre-exilic, exilic, or post-exilic. While these divisions may not be clearly defined, for ease of reference this essay will assume Isa 1–39 and 40–66 as having separate contexts, with some division between 40–55 and 56–66 also being noted. While I refer to the book and author by the name "Isaiah" throughout, this does not prejudge the question of authorship.

2. For a list of theological themes incorporated within Zion see Ryken, Wilhoit, and Longman, *Dictionary of Biblical Imagery*, 980–81. Dekker discusses Isaiah's references to Zion as "Mt Zion" which he says has theological connotations, "Daughter Zion" which is a personification of the city of Jerusalem and its inhabitants, and independent use of "Zion" which can either stand for Jerusalem (with or without its inhabitants), or for the place of God's presence and/or salvation. *Zion's Rock-Solid Foundations*, 265–75. Berges interestingly notes Isaiah's four uses of the term "Daughter Zion" at strategic points in the book. "Personifications and Prophetic Voices," 57.

and perhaps even the city's people living elsewhere but identified with it.[3]

This essay explores how the book of Isaiah utilizes Zion as a powerful
symbolic tool. The Isaianic author wields this tool with consummate skill,
bringing practical application in various ways, as he confronts not only the
leaders of Judah, but also engages nations and empire with the implications
of God's righteous order and ultimate sovereignty. We begin with a brief
overview of Zion's historical and symbolic development. This will be followed by an exploration of how Isaiah uses Zion symbolism to confront accepted norms and initiate change. We will find that Isaiah boldly proclaims
an alternative view of reality to that of empire.

Zion's History and Symbolism

Zion's place in Israel's history begins with King David and the city of Jerusalem. Having been made king over all Israel and Judah (2 Sam 5:1–5), David turned his attention to Jerusalem and the stronghold of Zion, which he
conquered (2 Sam 5:6–10; 1 Chr 11:4–9) and renamed as the City of David
(2 Sam 5:7; 1 Chr 11:7).[4] By transferring the Ark to Jerusalem, Zion became
both the religious and political capital of the nation as David established the
cult alongside his throne (2 Sam 6; 1 Chr 15:1—16:6).[5] This unity was not only
a ploy that called the attention of the people to Zion as the legitimate religious
center, but also "advertise[d] the state as the patron and protector of the sacral
institutions of the past."[6] Having a king on Zion became an important aspect
of the Jerusalem cult, and "in association with Zion the fundamental role of
the king is that of executor of Yahweh's rule."[7]

The core of the Zion tradition revolves around the belief that God had
chosen Zion as his dwelling place where he rules as king, with his cosmic
order as supreme. It may have been the golden age of David and Solomon

---

3. Goldingay, "The Theology of Isaiah," 176.

4. The terms Zion and Jerusalem are used largely interchangeably throughout Isaiah. Amos 1:12 and Isa 8:18 record the use of the name Zion for Jerusalem. Davies
discusses Jerusalem and the temple as almost inseparable realities. *The Gospel and the
Land*, 150–54.

5. This connection between religion and politics was common in the ANE. Roberts,
"The Davidic Origin," 341.

6. Bright, *A History of Israel*, 201.

7. Ollenburger, *Zion, the City of the Great King*, 59, cf. 59–66 for further discussion
of Zion and David.

that inspired and produced the Zion tradition as Roberts suggests,[8] where "Israel's political and religious center is symbolically transformed into the mountain and city of God."[9] While incorporating many of the central aspects of the Zion tradition, Isaiah's treatment of the subject is not confined to the tradition.[10] The book's portrayal of Zion is far broader than the tradition allows with an orientation toward the future rather than the past.[11]

Even though kingship and cult were linked together at Zion, Isaiah shows that God's purposes were not dependent on having an actual king ruling from geographic Zion. In this regard it is interesting to note that the prophetic vision of peace of Isaiah 65 is likely without any reference to a king, though some may find an allusion to a king in 65:25 (cf. 11:9). Here, Isaiah maintains that restoration and peace no longer encompass the city, or even the nation, but the whole world is made new (v. 17). It is God's sovereign rulership over all things that is the primary focal point for Isaiah's Zion. This focal point affects how Isaiah views Zion's present state and its future. It also underlies Isaiah's confrontation with Judah's kings, the nations and empire.

Zion was therefore far more than simply a geographic location or historical place. Jerusalem and Zion are symbolic of another order that goes beyond the realm of history.[12] While Isaiah's final visions "do not abandon hopes for the Jerusalem of history and geography; nevertheless, the language in the texts opens the concept of Zion to deeper interpretations released from such restrictions."[13]

Isaiah begins by presenting two distinct views of Zion. Firstly, the book graphically portrays Zion's present state and future glory, and secondly Zion is viewed as a theological symbol of God's sovereignty and order. Each of these aspects will be looked at in turn, before examining how Isaiah draws them together in order to confront the rulers of Judah, the nations, and empire.

---

8. Roberts, "The Davidic Origin," 344.

9 Cohn, "The Mountains and Mount Zion," 115. Further examination of kingship is beyond the scope of this essay.

10. For Isaiah's use of Zion tradition motifs, see Levenson, *Sinai and Zion*, 89–184; Roberts, "The Davidic Origin," 329–40; Dekker, *Zion's Rock-Solid Foundations*, 283–318; Ollenburger, *Zion, the City of the Great King*, 15–19. See also Hayes, "The Tradition of Zion's Inviolability," 419–26, who proposes that Isaiah modified the Zion tradition by (a) adding faith as a precondition to salvation and protection (Isa 7:9; 31:4–9), and (b) placing the attack and purging of Jerusalem within God's activity and work (Isa 10:5; 29:1–8).

11. Dekker, *Zion's Rock-Solid Foundations*, 349–53.

12. Levenson, *Sinai and Zion*, 101.

13 McConville, "Pilgrimage and 'Place,'" 23.

Isaiah's Depiction of Zion—
Present Reality and Future Hope

Isaiah 1–39 describes Zion's present state as rebellious and degenerate. Isaiah graphically portrays Zion as wounded and filthy (1:6), desolate (1:7) and destitute (3:26) and has experienced devastating judgment at the hand of invading empires. This is because the people are sinful (1:4), unfaithful (1:21) and rebellious (30:9). They have spoken and acted in defiance against God, and this has caused their downfall (2:6; 3:8; 29:13).[14] Yet alongside this, Isaiah maintains that Zion is chosen by God (14:32) as his dwelling place (8:18; 12:6) and is the place where he reigns (24:23). Zion will therefore be redeemed (1:27), will be holy (4:3) and will be cleansed (4:4). Chapter 1 of Isaiah clearly spells out God's judgment on the nation in the form of a lawsuit.[15] Yet in chapter 2:1–4, there is a promise of future restoration and hope. While Isa 1–39 seems largely to be a catalogue of the nation's sin and God's judgment (3:13), windows of restoration and hope, such as 2:1–4, are also present throughout.[16]

Isaiah maintains that as Zion has been chosen by God as his dwelling place, he will bring justice and righteousness to Zion (1:27). Israel's sin has brought them out of God's order, but God will restore them and bring them back into order. As the book unfolds, we find that this does not just concern Israel, but will affect all the nations of the earth, including empire.[17]

From chapter 40, Isaiah's focus shifts away from Judah's sinfulness onto God's promises for the future[18]—coming to Zion (40:9–11; 51:11–16; 52:3–12), his creative power (40:12–31), promises of election (41:8–10) and help (41:14–20; 49:8–13), sovereignty (42:5–9), promise of protection (43:1–13), blessing (44:1–8; 51:1–6), redemption (44:21–28; 54:1–17), choice of instruments (45:1–17; 49:1–7; 50:4–11), salvation (46:8–13), judg-

---

14. From the beginning of the book, Isaiah continually speaks not just of Zion's desolated state, but also of the people's relationship to God. They are God's rebellious children (1:2, 4) and a wife that has been unfaithful (1:21). "Here we encounter the West-Semitic idea of the high god of the pantheon as husband of the city." Berges, "Personifications and Prophetic Voices," 57.

15. The witnesses are the same as are found in Deut 32. Watts, *Isaiah 1–33*, 15.

16. E.g., Isa 4:2–6; 11:10–16; 12; 14:1–2; 27:6; 32:16–20; 35.

17. E.g., Philistia (14:28–32); Moab (15:1—16:14); Damascus (17:1–14); Ethiopia (18:1–7); Egypt (19:1–17); Tyre (23:1–18); the earth (24:1–23); all the nations (34:1–4); Edom (34:5–17; 63:1–6); Babylon (13; 14:3–22; 47:1–15); Assyria (14:24–27).

18. First person verbs with God as subject occur sixty-nine times in Isa 40–66, thirty-seven of which are in Isa 56–66, all with positive reference to bringing hope and restoration. By contrast, the bulk of these verbs in chapters 1–39 are in reference to God bringing judgment.

ment on Babylon (47:1–15), powerful word (48:1–8), purposes (48:9–22) and lordship over the nations (49:22–26).

The contrast between Zion's current state and Isaiah's depiction of Zion's future is even more explicit in Isa 40–55 than in chapters 1–39. Zion's wretched state is again graphically described. Yet alongside each of these descriptions is God's promise of restoration:

Zion's current state	God's promise
Forsaken (49:14)	"I will not forget you" (49:15)
Ruined (51:3)	God will have compassion (51:3)
A wasteland (51:3)	God make her like Eden (51:3)
Sorrowful and sighing (51:11)	God will ransom (51:11)
Fearful (51:12–13)	God brings comfort (51:12)
Sold (52:3)	Redeemed (52:3)

While Zion herself maintains: "The Lord has forsaken me, my Lord has forgotten me" (49:14), Isaiah insists that Zion stand up (51:17), awake and put on beautiful garments (52:1), and to shake off their dust and loose their bonds (52:2).[19] They have a part to play and need to begin to see themselves from God's viewpoint. It is God's promises and God's return to Zion that needs to have their attention (52:7–10).

It is interesting to note that, in contrast to Isa 1–39, there is little mention of sin and judgment from chapters 40–55. The only times Zion's sin is mentioned is in reference to it being pardoned (40:1–2; 43:25; 44:22). As Seitz says, "God is concerned to register that Zion's condition of bereavement and desolation has come to an end, and that it is now to be comforted."[20] The change in context (from pre-exile to exile) may help in explaining this. It seems that Isaiah does not negate the reality of Zion's condition, but sees beyond this reality to another reality—not just God's promises of comfort and hope, but Zion's total transformation to bring it into alignment with God's desired order. How Isaiah demands the engagement of Judah, the nations and empire, will be explored below.

Isaiah 56–66 is a chiasm that coordinates around Zion's glory in 60–62.[21] Alongside the glorious promises of chapters 60–62 are instructions to maintain justice (56:1; 59:1–21) and worship God correctly (58; 66:1–4). The future vision of chapters 60–62 therefore has implications for how they are to act in their current situation. This is similar to Isaiah's call to "walk in

19. For discussion on the personification of Zion see Berges, "Personifications and Prophetic Voices," 54–82.

20. Seitz, *Zion's Final Destiny*, 203.

21. Westermann, *Isaiah 40–66*; Oswalt, *Chapters 40–66*, 461–65.

the light of the Lord" (2:5) which is in response to the vision of 2:1–4 and covers similar themes. Isaiah 60–62 also contains promises of deliverance (63:1–6; 65:1–16), the vindication of Zion (66:5–13), and new heavens and new earth (65:17–25; 66:14–23). It is important to note that Zion's glory does not come from within Zion. It is YHWH's glory that will shine over Zion (60:2). While Zion becomes the centre of the universe, YHWH becomes the focal point of attention (e.g., 60:19–22).

From the beginning of the book, Isaiah describes Zion's current condition in terms of desolation and ruin. As the book progresses, these sobering descriptions are countered with God's glorious promises of comfort and restoration.

Isaiah's Depiction of Zion—As Theological Symbol

Alongside the book's graphic descriptions of the desolation of Zion and God's promises of restoration, Isaiah also uses Zion as a multi-faceted theological symbol of God's sovereignty and order.[22] Symbol is used here of a reality "that stands for and gives insight into some other reality because of the analogy between the two."[23] Symbolism does not usually point to a one-on-one relationship, but can be multivalent and point to many things.[24] This is how Zion symbolism is utilised throughout the book of Isaiah.[25]

Symbolism and myth often work together in the Old Testament. In the ancient Near East (ANE), myth defined the foundations of reality. While there are many ways of understanding myth,[26] here the term will refer to traditions about the past (origins) which are expressed in such a way that

22. As Ollenburger maintains, "Like any other central symbol Zion was capable of being placed in designs of more than one configuration, and was capable of evoking more than one response." *Zion, the City of the Great King*, 18. While Ollenburger's study examines Zion as a central symbol within the Jerusalem cult, this essay focuses on Isaiah's use of Zion as a symbol of God's sovereignty and order.

23. Macky, *The Centrality of Metaphors*, 56. Koester defines a symbol as "an image, an action, or a person that is understood to have transcendent significance." *Symbolism in the Fourth Gospel*, 4 n29.

24. Knudsen, "Symbol," 669, says that a "characteristic of a symbol . . . is that it draws together facets of that which it symbolises, concentrating or compressing them in a pregnant fashion." See also Macky, *The Centrality of Metaphors*, 49–56.

25. For further discussion of Zion as central symbol in Isaiah, see Ollenburger, *Zion, the City of the Great King*, 19–22.

26. For a range of perspectives, see Childs, *Myth and Reality*; Bultmann, "New Testament and Mythology"; Gunkel, *The Legends of Genesis*; Rogerson, *Myth in Old Testament Interpretation*; Jeppesen, "Myth in the Prophetic Literature"; Otzen, "The Concept of Myth"; Marshall, "Myth"; Oswalt, *The Bible among the Myths*.

they bring understanding to the present and future. In particular, we will be mindful of how Zion corresponds with mythic patterns from creation to temple and kingship.

As Zion and Jerusalem are important focal points in Israelite history, they would therefore be expected to show up in some form in the creation accounts of Gen 1–11.[27] Explicit reference to Zion or Jerusalem is, however, absent from these Genesis passages.[28] Robert Gordon says, "Early Genesis denies Jerusalem/Zion a mythological presence in its account of beginnings."[29] The concepts of sanctuary and holy place do exist, however, in the Genesis account of primeval history, with both the creation and Eden narratives echoing temple traditions.[30] These same concepts are also resident within Zion symbolism. Zion therefore "extends the significance of both the city and temple right back to the creation of the world."[31]

Genesis 1:1—2:4 narrates God's creation of the cosmos. In six days, God created everything, and according to John Walton, this did not just entail material creation, but that God put everything in order and gave it a function.[32] On the seventh day, God rested as sovereign ruler, in his temple. Michael Fishbane explores the significance of the links between creation and tabernacle/temple saying, "[T]he opening biblical passage seeks to enforce the theological value of a primal order and harmony created by God."[33] These links are also seen in other ANE writings such as the Mesopotamian epic of *Enuma Elish* and also in Canaanite mythology.[34] When a tabernacle or temple is built on earth, divine rulership by deity is no longer restricted to pre-history, but becomes an event on earth, yet one that has cosmic significance. When King David brought the Ark of the Covenant to Jerusalem, he united the temple tradition and the presence of God with the place of kingship and order. Zion then became more than a geographical site; it was the place where God dwelt and the place from where he ruled.

Many ANE writings view creation as emanating from a central point—where heaven and earth meet.[35] Brevard Childs helpfully explores

27. Other cities such as Babylon/Babel which are present in Gen 1–11.

28. Gordon, *Holy Land Holy City*, 5–26, explores this.

29. Ibid., 26.

30. Levenson, *Sinai and Zion*, 142–45; Sparks, "*Enuma Elish* and Priestly Mimesis," 625–48; Halpern, *From Gods to God*, 427–78. See also Isa 11:1–9; 65:23–25.

31. Gordon, *Holy Land Holy City*, 7; Ollenburger, *Zion, the City of the Great King*, 54–58.

32. Walton, *The Lost World of Genesis One*.

33. Fishbane, *Text and Texture*, 15.

34. Ibid., 13. Sparks, "*Enuma Elish* and Priestly Mimesis," 625–48.

35. Childs, *Myth and Reality*, 111.

the mythical concept of space in his book *Myth and Reality in the Old Testament,* identifying Eden and Zion as having the same mythical space. He says, "When two spaces possess the same content, then distance is transcended. These are not two different spaces, but one."[36] Isaiah also identifies Zion with Eden. Isaiah 11:6–9 depicts Zion as having the harmony of Eden.[37] While the context of these verses is the Davidic king (vv. 1 and 10), it is YHWH's work that is being highlighted over Davidic kingship. Zion is the site of YHWH's sovereign rule, and it is the knowledge of YHWH that brings peace to all of God's creation (vv. 2, 9).

Reference to Eden also occurs in Isa 51:3. The context here is 51:1— 52:12, where Zion is explicitly mentioned seven times, with Jerusalem named a further five times. These verses utilise past stories of Abraham and Sarah (51:2), Eden (52:3), the defeat of Rahab (51:9) and creation (51:13, 16) to portray what YHWH will do for Zion. Isaiah 51:3 maintains Zion will become like the garden of Eden. Zion is pictured as having a quality that sets it apart from ordinary or "common" space. Yet, as Childs points out, "While Zion is pictured as a manifestation of Eden, there is never a simple identification between the two as in the myth."[38] Zion is not projected back to the beginning, but is shown to be *like* Eden. God's continuing revelation in history is added into the original understanding, in order to develop something beyond that of the primeval era. Verses 13 and 16 state that YHWH is the creator of the cosmos.[39] Yet YHWH's action as Creator is not restricted to past action, but continues in the present. As Zion's Maker (v. 13), YHWH is the one who will bring comfort (v. 12) and restoration (v. 3).

Verse 16 directly links YHWH's creative sovereignty over the cosmos with Zion.[40] Goldingay suggests therefore that "in creating heaven and earth, Yhwh was on the way to designating Israel."[41] Rather than the usual "stretched out the heavens" (v. 13),[42] in verse 16 YHWH states that he is "planting the heavens." This "planting" suggests a remaking of the heavens and the earth according to the Creator's design (cf. 65:17) and a remaking or transforming of Zion as God's people (cf. 65:18–19).[43] Interestingly, the

---

36. Childs, *Myth and Reality,* 86.

37. See Isa 35 and 65:17–25.

38. Childs, *Myth and Reality,* 90.

39. See also Isa 40:22.

40. Cf. Isa 43:1, 15.

41. Goldingay, *The Message of Isaiah 40–55,* 439. See also Isa 44:23.

42. Cf. Isa 42:5, 15; 45:12; Ps 104:2; Jer 10:12.

43. Oswalt, *Chapters 40–66,* 348–49.

theme of God as Creator comes to the fore from chapter 40 on.[44] This is the same point where promises of restoration and total transformation of Zion begin to come to the fore.

This transformed reality is described in terms of *quality* of space rather than geographical location. Both Eden and Zion are spaces that belong to God and reflect his rule. It also looks to the future, rather than the past. As Childs says, "The Old Testament's understanding of space was eschatological, not mythical. . . . However, it chose a mythical category to express the tensions within this new spatial reality."[45] Establishing Zion as part of Israel's history therefore demythologizes its mythical substance transforming it into a symbol of a new reality.

Mythic patterns from creation are also seen in Isa 24–27, the so-called "Apocalypse of Isaiah." These chapters incorporate mythic and eschatological themes centred in the reign of YHWH on Zion.[46] Chapter 24 begins with YHWH's impending judgment on the earth and the heavens (vv. 1–23a), finishing with a declaration of YHWH's reign on Zion (v. 23b). A psalm of rejoicing (25:1–5) precedes the announcement of a banquet on Zion ("this mountain," vv. 6–10a).

Sharing a meal in the context of divine war is a well-known mythic metaphor. Smith says, "When the battle has been won, the gods assemble and celebrate the victory with a great banquet."[47] This is depicted in *Enuma Elish* where a banquet follows the victory and subsequent kingship of Marduk.[48] Chapter 25 ends with a declaration of victory over Moab (vv. 10b–12), and chapter 26 encompasses a song of victory (vv. 1–19) and a warning of further judgment (vv. 20–21).

Chapter 27 begins with YHWH's defeat of Leviathan and the dragon (v. 1). These are mythic creatures found elsewhere in Scripture (e.g., Isa 51:10; Ps 74:13–14; Job 26:13) and also in Ugaritic myths.[49] While the myths

---

44. Isa 40:26, 28; 41:20; 42:5; 43:1, 7, 15; 45:7, 8, 12, 18; 48:7; 54:16; 57:19; 65:17, 18. The only reference to God as Creator in Isa 1–39 is in 4:5 which links Zion with the Exodus.

45. Childs, *Myth and Reality*, 93.

46. For discussion of mythic themes in Isaiah 24–27, see Day, *God's Conflict with the Dragon and the Sea*, 142–51; Johnson, *From Chaos to Restoration*. For discussion of the function of Isa 24–27 within the book of Isaiah, see Sweeney, "Textual Citations in Isa 24–27," 39–52; Skjoldal, "The Function of Isaiah 24–27," 163–72. Watts includes chapter 23 in his story of these chapters, proposing a chiastic structure, the center of which is the divine banquet of YHWH on Mount Zion (25:6). Watts, *Isaiah 1–33*, 354–56.

47. Smith, "Messianic Banquet," 4:789; cf. Blenkinsopp, *Isaiah 1–39*, 358.

48. *Ancient Near Eastern Texts*, 69.

49. Day, "God and Leviathan in Isaiah 27:1," 423–36; Oswalt, *Isaiah 1–39*, 490; Blenkinsopp, *Isaiah 1–39*, 372.

locate the battle at the beginning of history, Isaiah projects it to a future time when YHWH defeats these creatures. "On that day" (vv. 1, 2, 12, 13), Israel will be restored (vv. 2–12), culminating in worship of YHWH on Zion (v. 13).

Together, these chapters maintain that YHWH is in complete control over nations and empires. All enemies, including death (25:8), will be overcome, and Zion will be transformed to become the centre of worship for all peoples.

Zion therefore becomes a symbol that draws together both mythical and historical concepts. As Knudson says, "characteristic of a symbol . . . is that it draws together facets of that which it symbolizes, concentrating or compressing them in a pregnant fashion."[50] Creation, Eden, temple and kingship are some of the facets that have been incorporated into Zion symbolism, as have been outlined above. Isaiah maintains Zion will be transformed to reflect God's glory and his sovereignty, finally being embodied in a new heavens and a new earth.

Isaiah's Use of Zion Symbolism

Having briefly examined Zion's roots, Isaiah's portrayal of Zion's current wretched state alongside God's promises of future restoration, and Zion as a theological symbol, it now remains to consider how Isaiah draws these threads together in a prophetic message to those with claims of supremacy. The practical application of Zion symbolism can be seen throughout the book. It is not only the leaders of Judah that are challenged, but the breadth of Isaiah's message also impacts the nations, empire, and indeed all of creation, with the absoluteness of God's sovereignty and order.

Isaiah maintains that God has chosen Zion as his dwelling place (Isa 8:18). As such, Isa 1–39 specifically critiques the political leadership whose rule is centered in Jerusalem, for disobeying God (e.g., 1:21–26). In these chapters, one of the ways Isaiah utilizes Zion symbolism is to set God's righteous order as the only valid order. The prophetic message then demands Judah's active engagement with this order. Both King Ahaz and King Hezekiah are faced with the challenge aligning themselves with God's order and trusting him with the city's future, or turning to other nations for help when Jerusalem comes under siege.

---

50. Knudsen, "Symbol," 669. Brett says, "The prophetic utopias are more like a collage than a coherent set of images." *Decolonizing God*, 109.

Ahaz (Isaiah 7–8)

During the Syro-Ephraimite war, Isaiah presents King Ahaz with a major decision. With the city under siege, Ahaz has three main choices—to surrender, to turn to the superpower of Assyria for aid, or to stand firm and trust in God's deliverance. Isaiah maintains that God reigns on Zion and has established his everlasting covenant with David (2 Sam 7; Ps 89:3–4). God is to be the only source of security and refuge and the only object of faith and trust (Ps 2). Isaiah therefore stands against alliances with other nations and dependence on armies. Isaiah tells Ahaz to be quiet and stand firm before his enemies as they would not stand (Isa 7:3–9). Ahaz, however, chooses political action, turning to Assyria for help (2 Kgs 16; 2 Chr 28).

The book of Isaiah does not seem concerned with giving an accurate historical account of the event. Isaiah stresses that it is God's purposes, Ahaz's alignment with those purposes, and faith in God's word that will decide the outcome. The narrative presents Isaiah's confrontation with Ahaz as taking place "at the end of the conduit of the upper pool on the highway to the Fuller's Field" (Isa 7:3). This formed part of the water supply for the city.[51] To Ahaz, the water system was vital to the survival of the city. To Isaiah, "[T]he conduit recalls everything enveloped in the myth of the paradise at the cosmic center—the presence of God, an abundance of grace, the childlike simplicity of existence in the Garden of Eden."[52] The geographical setting at the conduit and the Zion symbolism therefore connect together in Isaiah's presentation of God's sovereignty and order to King Ahaz. When Ahaz rejects God's word, Isaiah uses what is possibly a second analogy of Eden and the temple to portray the consequences of Ahaz's action. Instead of the gentle waters of Shiloah (identified with the sacred stream of the temple in Pss 46:4–5; 36:8–9), the violent waters of the Euphrates will engulf them (Isa 8:5–8).[53] Assyria will wipe over them like a devastating flood and only a remnant will remain.

Hezekiah (Isaiah 36–37)

A second crisis happened during King Hezekiah's reign that is also set "by the conduit of the upper pool on the highway to the Fuller's Field" (36:2).[54] This

---

51. Watts, *Isaiah 1–33*, 92.

52. Levenson, *Sinai and Zion*, 161.

53. For more on this this, see Levenson, *Sinai and Zion*, 159.

54. For further discussion of the Assyrian crisis, see Clements, *Isaiah and the Deliverance of Jerusalem*; Childs, *Isaiah and the Assyrian Crisis*; Seitz, *Zion's Final Destiny*.

echoes the similar event of Ahaz's time outlined above. Hezekiah's reaction to the threat of the Assyrian crisis of 701 B.C.E. was to go into the temple (37:1) and to call for the prophet. The Assyrians had called into question the king's reliance on Egypt (v. 6) and on God (v. 7). Like Ahaz, Hezekiah's faith in God is put to the test. The central question asked of Hezekiah is, "On whom do you now rely?" (36:5). While Ahaz looked for a political solution, Hezekiah turned to God.[55] The Hezekiah narrative demonstrates that God is creator and sovereign ruler. He is the only source of security and refuge and is to be the only object of faith and trust. As Watts says, "The events and oracles of 701 B.C. showed that Yahweh was still in control, that he valued Zion as his city, and that he would not be bullied by the emperor" (37:33–35).[56]

The Nations (Isaiah 40–55)

Isaiah not only demands Judah's engagement with God's righteous order on Zion, but widens it to include all the nations, their rulers and their gods. In the ANE, rulership was associated with deity. Defeat of a nation was viewed as the defeat of the ruling deity. When Judah was defeated by the Babylonians, it appeared that Marduk was victorious over YHWH. Isaiah, however, boldly continues to proclaim that YHWH is supreme and that his sovereignty extends beyond the nations and their gods to encompass the cosmos. Deutero-Isaiah describes the nations as "nothing," "less than nothing" and "emptiness" (40:17, 23) in comparison with YHWH's supremacy. Similar terms are used to describe idols (41:24, 29; 44:9–11; 46:1–2), prompting Watts to state that "nations, like idols, have no ultimate substance in God's eyes."[57] It is not the myths of the gods that determine history, but YHWH, the sovereign Lord of all creation who is supreme. In other words, "[T]he particular history of Israel and its relation to other nations of the Near East can be viewed as Yahweh's action in accordance with the world-order he established."[58] Isaiah maintains that YHWH has chosen Zion as his dwelling place. His order is the only valid order. All nations are called to acknowledge this and are therefore summoned to Zion and worship YHWH there (45:14; 49:7, 22–23).[59]

---

55. It is interesting to note that Isaiah does not record Hezekiah's previous unfaithfulness (2 Kgs 18:13–16). This may possibly be in order to contrast Hezekiah's faith with Ahaz's lack of faith.

56. Watts, *Isaiah 34–66*, 48.

57. Ibid., 91.

58. Ollenburger, *Zion, the City of the Great King*, 157.

59. MacDonald says this is "a universal recognition of the glory of Israel's God,

Empire

The book of Isaiah falls under the shadow of the Assyrian, Babylonian, and Persian empires. Isaiah's overarching perspective, however, is that the empires of this world are subject to a greater world order and are instruments in God's hand and for his cosmic purpose. The empires are called to do God's "work on Mount Zion and on Jerusalem" (10:12), as he continues to fulfil his purpose for Jerusalem and Zion (44:28). Isaiah tells us God will "signal" and "whistle" for a nation far away to invade Judah and carry them off as prey (5:26–30). It is God who summons Assyria to destroy (10:5, 6) and Cyrus to rebuild (44:28). Empire has no choice but to obey God's command.

Isaiah also appears to be aware of a deeper understanding of empire's claim to rulership. Empire in the ANE primarily ruled through exercising domination and exploitation. This expression of order within the ANE was derived from the kind of power that a society's god was viewed as exercising in creation. Cosmic creation was believed to come about as a result of divine conflict. According to myth, conflict was an essential part of the creative process. Imperial society was a reflection of this creative process involving conflict, whereby justice was generally enforced by military might and domination. As Janzen says, it is "the discernment and exercise of this power [that] constitute[s] ruling wisdom" within an imperial society.[60]

Isaiah, however, proclaims that YHWH operates with a totally different kind of power which is in complete contrast to the kind of rulership endorsed by empire. This contrast begins with a different story of creation and therefore how the founding order of the cosmos is to be understood. Rather than any mention of conflict, Gen 1 and 2 are devoid of struggle or conflict as being characteristic of creation. The Babylonian and Israelite creation stories are fundamentally different in their conception of reality. These stories "represent not merely two different divine claimants for world rule, Yahweh and Marduk, but, by their differing accounts of the way the divine creator has brought the cosmos into existence, represent two different conceptions of life-giving and community-building power."[61] Indeed, Deutero-Isaiah's assertions of YHWH as creator would have been seen as counter-imperial.[62]

One of the ways Isaiah uses Zion symbolism is to present a concept of God's sovereignty and order that challenges the ANE concept of empire as the primary understanding of reality for the ordering of society. Janzen

---

rather than all nations partaking on equal terms in the worship of YHWH." "Monotheism and Isaiah," 54.

60. Janzen, "On the Moral Nature of God's Power," 461.

61. Ibid., 464.

62. Berquist, "Resistance and Accommodation," 56.

argues that the Judean community to whom Deutero-Isaiah is speaking, still does not understand the true nature of God's sovereignty and justice. He suggests that while Isaiah rejects the dominant ANE model of cosmic origins, the voice of the people reflects a mindset of myth and empire. Isaiah 51:9–11 records the community calling on God to take action on behalf of his people, yet using the motif of mythical conflict.[63] YHWH acts in a different manner than is expressed in verses 9–10. It is his presence that YHWH promises (v. 12), rather than any kind of mythic power.

> Salvation comes from the Creator who continues the creative process and from the Lord of History whose plan opens the door to rebuilding Zion's Temple and restoring Israel's freedom to worship there. It grows in the potential for spiritual communion with Yahweh and from knowledge gained from his law, not from a flashy repetition of exciting myths.[64]

Isaiah looks to a new era of God's rulership that will begin with a new world order centered on Zion. Isaiah 55–66 reveals that participation is through relationship with YHWH and ethical (rather than ethnic) righteousness.[65] It was an obedient response to God that would bring about a new reality.[66] Childs says, "God's redemptive purpose in the world was seen only in the tangible shape of Israel who did justice, loved kindness, and walked humbly with her God."[67] Oswalt argues that ethics are a matter of cosmic concern and are derived from a society's understanding of reality based on their creation story. He contrasts ethics in the non-biblical ANE with ethics in the Bible, showing that while there are similarities in practice, expression and

---

63. Janzen, "On the Moral Nature of God's Power." Levenson takes a slightly different view of this passage. He says, "The verses on each side of the mythic allusion underscore by juxtaposition the jarring incongruity of the community's experience with the great victory that the 'arm of the Lord' won in primordial times." Rather than conflict and victory over chaos, he underscores the fact "that YHWH will triumph is predestined and inevitable." *Creation and the Persistence of Evil*, 20. Even in Jesus' time, his disciples did not seem to truly understand the nature of God's kingdom. In the account of two of his disciples wanting to sit at his right and left hand, Jesus himself insists on a difference between earthly rulership and the kingdom of God (Mark 10:35–45).

64. Watts, *Isaiah 34–66*, 211–12. See also Oswalt, *Chapters 40–66*, 339–43.

65. Lind argues "that the unity of the cosmos and history under the oneness of Yahweh includes a distinctive moral quality." He examines the evidence in Isaiah found in Yahweh's trial speeches against the gods, the Cyrus poems, and the Servant poems. "Monotheism, Power and Justice," 432–46.

66. "The Old Testament conceived of the experiences of Israel as the process by which God brought into being a new form of existence." Childs, *Myth and Reality*, 97.

67. Ibid., 97.

thought process, the Israelite way of thinking was to be completely different from other ANE cultures.[68]

One of the seeming paradoxes of Isaiah's claims of God's sovereignty and rulership of creation is that Zion, the geographic center of God's presence and rulership, remains under the shadow of empire. Zion itself, however, is not subject to empire, and as has been previously discussed, it is of a whole different nature and quality of space.

Isaiah ultimately envisages a time when "the earth will be full of the knowledge of the Lord as the waters cover the sea" (11:9). All the nations of the earth and every empire will count as nothing as God's glory is revealed in Zion (52:7–10). The goal is that all nations will see the glory of God (66:18) as indeed Isaiah had seen in Isaiah 6, and that all people will worship God (66:23). YHWH, the sovereign ruler who created all things, will create a new heavens and new earth (65:17–25). In Isaiah's eyes, however, Zion and Jerusalem remain as the focal point for worship of YHWH (Isa 60; 66:22–23). For Isaiah, this is not just a vision, but a statement of the way things really are. As Ollenburger maintains, "It is not offered as a wish for the way things could be, or a hope for what they will become, but as a positive affirmation of what is 'really real.'"[69]

Conclusion

In exploring the "other-worldliness" of Zion symbolism and God's sovereignty and order, Isaiah reminds us that God's work is also firmly anchored in the historical experience of God's people. Isaiah uses Zion as a symbolic tool to call Judah's kings to account, the nations to come and worship, and boldly sets forth an alternative to empire's view of reality. Zion is the place where God has chosen to dwell. Zion also reaches back into primordial creation to proclaim that YHWH alone is sovereign ruler of everything that exists. For Isaiah, Zion is the center point for the fulfilment of all God has promised, not just for Judah, but for the whole of creation. In direct contrast to the rulership of empire, Isaiah looks to a new era of God's rulership that will begin with a new world order centered on Zion. Any claims that empire has laid, pale in comparison to the glorious vision Isaiah portrays of God's ultimate plan and purpose for Zion.

---

68. Oswalt, *The Bible among the Myths*, 85–107.
69. *Zion, the City of the Great King*, 157.

7

Imperial Influence on the Language and Content of Isaiah 40–55

LENA-SOFIA TIEMEYER

Introduction

IT IS COMMON TO regard Isa 40–55, as a whole or in part, as the product of the Babylonian exile. This view is only very loosely based on the biblical text itself, however. The present article challenges one of the key claims of the proponents for a Babylonian-based author of Isa 40–55, namely that the language and content of Isa 40–55 is influenced by (1) close similarities between the language of Isa 40–55 and Akkadian, (2) by explicit references to Babylon, and (3) by familiarity with its religion and culture.[1] I shall examine these three claims and determine to what degree they really support a Babylonian origin of Isa 40–55. As we shall discover, most, if not all, of these claims do not *support* a Babylonian setting of Isa 40–55 but rather *presuppose* it.

I shall first discuss the methods involved in comparative studies of the Bible and the ancient Near East, showing what one can and cannot prove. Secondly, I shall argue that the Neo-Babylonian and the preceding Neo-Assyrian Empires exercised considerable influence over their neighboring nations throughout the eighth to the sixth centuries B.C.E. Superficial knowledge of Babylonian customs in a text stemming from that time period can therefore not be an argument for a Babylonian-based author of Isa 40–55. Thirdly, I shall examine the alleged Akkadian influence on the language and literary style of Isa 40–55 and conclude that nothing in Isa 40–55 necessitates a Babylonian-based author. Fourthly, I shall look briefly

1. This article is an abbreviated version of chapter 3 of my monograph *For the Comfort of Zion*, 77–130.

at select texts in Isa 40–55 that scholars often cite as evidence of a Babylonian provenance of Isa 40–55 and show that, on the contrary, these texts are better understood as composed in Judah. I shall conclude that none of the aforementioned arguments proves that Isa 40–55 was composed in Babylon. Nothing in the text lends itself as an argument for seeing Isa 40–55 as a Babylonian-based composition. Indeed, they do not disprove it either, and they also do not prove that Isa 40–55 was composed elsewhere (such as in Judah). Yet they serve as a caution for exegetes not to take a Babylonian provenance of Isa 40–55 for granted and not to build a house of interpretation on sand.

Methods in Comparative Studies

Before we can begin to investigate whether or not Isa 40–55 betrays Babylonian influence, it is important to establish the method that can be used for undertaking such an investigation. In the ensuing discussion, I depend in particular on three of Talmon's guidelines for comparative studies of the Bible and the ancient Near East: (1) the interpretation of biblical features— whether socio-political, cultic, general-cultural, or literary in nature— should give priority to inner-biblical parallels and only thereafter look to extra-biblical parallels; (2) if comparisons with extra-biblical material are made, priority should be given to parallels from societies contemporary with the biblical text; (3) likewise, when studying social phenomena, the study of a particular phenomenon within Israel must be given priority before looking for extra-biblical parallels.[2] I maintain that, when we investigate a societal function or a cultural and/or religious custom referred to in Isa 40–55, we should begin by asking whether this phenomenon can be explained satisfactorily by other biblical texts before looking to Mesopotamian material.

It is furthermore important to pay heed to Barr's cautionary remarks pertaining to philological influence in a biblical text. Barr highlights the tendency among scholars to detect loanwords and philological influence from languages that are their own speciality. In other cases, scholars are affected by the simple matter of availability of certain data. Yet again, scholars often display a preference for one cognate language over another, although it is often impossible to detect any decisive reason for this preference. Barr therefore suggests three principles. First, comparisons with sources near to the Hebrew Bible *in time* are to be given priority. Secondly, sources closer to Israel and Judah *geographically* are likely to be more reliable. Thirdly, closer

2. Talmon, "The 'Comparative Method' in Biblical Interpretation," see summary 356.

linguistic affinity within the classification of the Semitic family will in general yield the most convincing results.[3]

In view of these words of warning, we shall proceed to consider the comparisons that scholars have made between the text of Isa 40–55 and the world of the Neo-Babylonian Empire.

Neo-Babylonian Imperialism

There is no doubt that the Neo-Assyrian Empire and the subsequent Neo-Babylonian Empire exerted major cultural and religious dominance over the areas under their control. Imperial ideas and institutions were exported to the countries under their control, and both resistance to and familiarity with these ideas naturally developed among the conquered peoples.[4] We should therefore expect to find a relatively large degree of Mesopotamian influence in the intellectual life of Israel and Judah, both in terms of language and in terms of societal, cultural, and religious phenomena. For instance, we can detect such imperial influence over pre-exilic Judah in the cuneiform texts that have been found in the territories of Israel and Judah. In the present context, the seventeen texts that belong to the Neo-Assyrian period, as well as the few isolated texts from the late Neo-Babylonian and Persian periods, are of special interest.[5] These texts reflect a situation in which several Assyrian administrators lived and worked in Judah and Israel.

In view of the cultural and religious dominance of the Neo-Assyrian and the subsequent Neo-Babylonian Empires, it should come as no surprise to find ample references to Babylonian practices in the biblical texts stemming from the eighth to the sixth centuries B.C.E. In fact, we should expect to see evidence of influence in terms of literary and religious concepts. It is, for example, widely accepted that there is significant Neo-Assyrian influence on the book of Deuteronomy. As van der Toorn states, there is little doubt that the pre-exilic Judahite scribe responsible for what van der Toorn deems to be the first edition of the book of Deuteronomy, was "a professional with a thorough knowledge of the legal tradition and the conventions of international treaties."[6] This in turn suggests that at least the scribes, and possibly also the rest of the people of Judah, had at least a rudimentary understanding of Mesopotamian religious ideas. Likewise, Machinist argues that the

3. Barr, *Comparative Philology*, 111–13.

4. See, e.g., the discussion in Vanderhooft, *The Neo-Babylonian Empire*, 111–16.

5. W. Horowitz and T. Oshima, with S. Sanders, *Cuneiform in Canaan*, 4–6.

6. Van der Toorn, *Scribal Culture*, 152–55. See also Parpola, "Assyria's Expansion in the 8th and 7th Centuries," 105.

significant Neo-Assyrian influence in the language of Isa 1–39*, including several cognate expressions, is the direct result of Assyrian propaganda in Judah.[7] Although the prophet may have known some of these expressions and idioms from his own native tradition, it is more feasible that his selection and formulations of them resulted from the direct impact of the Neo-Assyrian idioms, familiar from Assyrian literature known in Judah at this time, or from Assyrian propaganda on public monuments and the like.[8] Along similar lines, Smith maintains that although the degree of knowledge of the Akkadian language and its literature in Judah is uncertain, and although some of this cultural familiarity may have been filtered through Aramaic, there is little doubt that the basic structure of Neo-Assyrian views on divinity were known in Judah.[9]

To sum up, the Neo-Assyrian and the Neo-Babylonian Empires were major centres of power whose influence spread beyond their borders, and they had direct impact upon life in Judah in the seventh and the sixth century B.C.E. We can therefore assume that the people in Judah during the ascent of the Neo-Babylonian power were roughly familiar with Mesopotamian religious customs and beliefs. This, in turn, means that the mention of Assyria/Babylon, or indeed a display of knowledge about Babylonian customs, or even the occurrence of Akkadian idioms in a biblical text, are not in themselves arguments for the Assyrian or the Babylonian provenance of the same text. Likewise, polemic against Babylon and its religious practices does not on its own suggest that its author lived in Babylon.

Akkadian Influence in Isaiah 40–55:
Loanwords and Literary Style

One key reason for regarding Isa 40–55 as a Babylonian composition has been the Akkadian influence on its vocabulary and expressions and/or the literary influence of Mesopotamian texts on its ideas and ways of writing. Barstad has already discussed this issue.[10] The present discussion therefore builds upon his research, as well as incorporating the scholarly findings subsequent to his publications. My conclusion will, however, differ from Barstad's in one important aspect. While Barstad concludes that "we have not a single word in Isa 40–55 which may indicate any Akkadian influence on the writer of this text," I shall argue that it is indeed possible to detect Akkadian influence in Isa 40–55.

---

7. Machinist, "Assyria," 719–28.

8. Ibid., 732–33.

9. Smith, *God in Translation*, 149–57.

10. Barstad, "Akkadian 'Loanwords' in Isaiah 40–55," 36–48.

This influence, however, does not constitute an argument for a Babylonian domicile of the authors responsible for Isa 40–55. As we shall see, the question that needs to be asked is not whether there are Akkadian loanwords in Isa 40–55—we can take that for granted, given the dominance of Mesopotamian culture over Judah and Israel from the eighth century and onwards—but rather whether there are *significantly more* Akkadian loanwords in Isa 40–55 than in other texts from the same time period. Furthermore, if this indeed were the case, we would have to explain why Isa 40–55 contains *Akkadian* rather than *Aramaic* loanwords, given that by the sixth century B.C.E. the spoken language of the Neo-Babylonian Empire was no longer Akkadian but Aramaic. Finally, we would also have to demonstrate that the authors of Isa 40–55 had access to and the ability to read texts written in Akkadian. Only then would we be able to argue that this alleged high number of Akkadian loanwords in Isa 40–55 is best explained by a scenario where its authors resided in Babylon.

Akkadian Influence over the Language of Isaiah 40–55

The scholarly claim that Isa 40–55 is influenced by Akkadian goes back to the end of the nineteenth century. In 1898, Kittel laid the foundation for much of the subsequent research on the Akkadian influence on Isa 40–55. He detected similarities between Isa 45:1–5 and the so-called Cyrus Cylinder, and, in order to explain these similarities, Kittel postulated that both texts drew upon a common tradition, namely the style of the Babylonian court.[11]

Following in Kittel's footstep, Stummer provides a detailed discussion of the similarities between expressions in Isa 40–55 and in cuneiform literature. He discusses specific expressions,[12] or literary motifs in Isa 40–55,[13] and he lists parallels between Babylonian texts and Isa 62:3. These parallels are found in a multitude of texts, ranging from hymns to Marduk, oracles to Esarhaddon, the covenant between Shuppiluliuma and Mattiuaza, to more epic texts of Marduk's return from Elam and *Enuma Elish*.[14] Many of these examples demonstrate similarities in vocabulary. These similarities are, however, better explained as cognate Semitic expressions rather than evidence of explicit influence. One cannot help but suspect that had the author done a similar search of, for example, the book of Hosea, he would have detected a comparable amount of lexical parallels. Stummer's suggested par-

11. Kittel, "Cyrus und Deuterojesaja," esp. 159–61.

12. Isa 40:3–5 (*kbd yhwh, pnw drk*); 40:12–16 (*tkn, my mdd bsh'lw mym, shlysh*); 41:9–10 (*'l-tyr' m'styk*).

13. Isa 41:13//42:6//51:18; 41:22–24; 42:7; 43:10; 43:11; 43:13; 44:24; 52:7; 53:7.

14. Stummer, "Einige keilschriftliche Parallelen zu Jes. 40–55," 171–89.

allels between Isa 62:3 and Babylonian literature rather proves the point as very few scholars today stipulate a Babylonian setting for Isa 60–62.

Building upon the research of Kittel and Stummer, Behr's 1937 monograph discusses the general cultural influence on the writing of Isa 40–55. Behr claims that, although Isa 40–55 contains no references to a Babylonian locale, its author speaks of cultural and religious aspects of Babylonian life as an eye witness.[15] However, Behr gives virtually no specific indications to support this claim beyond the fact that Cyrus is mentioned by name in Isa 44:28; 45:1 and that the doom of Babylon is described as pending (Isa 46:1; 47:1–3; 48:14). Along similar lines, having adopted many of Behr's arguments, Paul aims to demonstrate that much of the language in Isa 40–55 reflects knowledge of cuneiform royal inscriptions.[16]

A closer look at Behr's and Paul's suggested similarities leads to a different conclusion, as many, if not most, of these similarities are better explained through inner-biblical parallels (cf. Talmon above). In some cases, Isa 40–55 may be the earliest time a certain expression is attested. Even so, its appearance elsewhere in the biblical corpus is a strong indication that it is integral to the Hebrew language.[17]

For example, Behr claims that the expression *qr' bshm* (Isa 43:1) corresponds to the Akkadian expression *nabu nibitta*, found in the royal inscriptions of Nebuchadnezzar and Nabonidus where it denotes how Marduk called these monarchs by name. These two expressions are only semantic parallels and not linguistic cognates, however. "To call by name" is a general expression that can appear in two languages independent of each other.

Behr also argues that the expression *hzkyr shm* (Isa 49:1) corresponds to the Akkadian expression *šuma zakāru*.[18] The two expressions are clearly cognates, yet it is unlikely that this is a case of direct influence from Akkadian upon Hebrew. The Hebrew expression is integral to Hebrew (see, e.g., Exod 31:2; 35:30).[19] Therefore, following Talmon's guidelines (above), it is preferable to see it as an example of inner-biblical influence.

Behr further claims that the expressions *hchzyq bymyn* (Isa 41:12; 42:6; 45:1) corresponds to the expression *qātu tamāḫu* in the Cyrus Cylinder

---

15. Behr, *The Writings of Deutero-Isaiah and the Neo-Babylonian Royal Inscriptions*, 15–16.

16. Paul, "Deutero-Isaiah," 180–86.

17. For a discussion of all the alleged instances of Akkadian influence, see *For the Comfort of Zion*, 88–91.

18. See also Kittel, "Cyrus und Deuterojesaja," 160, and Paul, "Deutero-Isaiah," 181.

19. Maynard, "The Home of Deutero-Isaiah," 233. See also Barstad, "Lebte Deuterojesaja," 77–87, esp. 83.

and in the inscriptions of Nabunidus.[20] Again, the expression *hchzyq byd* is attested in Gen 19:16; 21:18; Judg 16:26; and Jer 31:31.[21] Thus, as Barstad points out, Isa 40–55 contains a well-known idiomatic Hebrew expression, and its Akkadian equivalent is equally commonly attested. This is not a matter of influence but rather of two texts expressing the same general idea using similar, though not cognate, idioms.[22]

Looking at the issue from the wider scope of the Hebrew Bible, the issue of Akkadian influence in Isa 40–55 must be put in its right perspective. First, I would claim that *most texts* in the Hebrew Bible betray Akkadian influence. A brief glance through Paul's commentary to Amos reveals that Paul detects a high number of Akkadian loanwords in the book,[23] yet he nowhere makes the claim that the authors of Amos resided in Babylon. This example demonstrates how relatively easy it is to find verbal and conceptual parallels between a Hebrew text and an Akkadian text of roughly the same age. The occurrence of such cognates in the book of Amos further shows that the Hebrew language throughout the eighth to the sixth century B.C.E. incorporated a number of words from Akkadian, the politically dominant language of the time, either directly or *via* Aramaic. Aramaic was spoken not only in the areas in Babylon where the Jewish exiles lived in the sixth century B.C.E. but it was also becoming the new *lingua franca* of the Levant and Mesopotamia, thus having significant impact on the local languages. Therefore, a loanword that has entered Hebrew via Aramaic cannot by any stretch of imagination be an acceptable argument for a Babylonian setting of Isa 40–55.

Secondly, there is evidence to suggest that the relative amount of actual loan-words in Isa 40–55 is neither more nor less than what is attested in the rest of the Hebrew Bible. Mankowski, having looked at the distribution of Akkadian loanwords in the Hebrew Bible, shows that the major prophetic books Isaiah (seventeen loanwords), Jeremiah (fifteen loanwords), and Ezekiel (eleven loanwords) contain the largest number of Akkadian loanwords. All three books are long and many of the texts within these books were composed, although probably not in their final form, during the height of Neo-Assyrian and Neo-Babylonian imperial power. Taking the varying length of these books into account, it is true that the book of Isaiah contains the

20. See also Kittel, "Cyrus und Deuterojesaja," 160.

21. Maynard, "The Home of Deutero-Isaiah," 233.

22. Barstad, "On the So-Called Babylonian Influence," 99–100.

23. Paul, *Amos*, finds Akkadian cognates to most expressions in the book of Amos. See, for example, p. 22 (*hlk 'chry // arki alaku*—characteristic of the Dtr writings, found in Amos 2:4), p. 97 (Amos 2:15; *tps qsht // tameh qashti*), p. 98 (Amos 2:16—the motif of "fleeing naked" is also found in the Prism of Esarhaddon), to name but a few.

highest ratio of loanwords.[24] Even so, a closer look reveals that Mankowski recognizes but three Akkadian loanwords in Isa 40–55, namely Isa 41:18 and 42:15 (*'gm* = "pond"); 41:25 (*tyt* = "mud"); and 49:2 (*'shph* = "quiver").[25]

Thirdly, turning the issue around, there are words in Isa 40–55 that have cognates in Ugaritic. For example, the *Paal* verb *tsht'* ("to be dismayed") in Isa 41:10 is probably an example of shared Ugaritic-Hebrew vocabulary. Likewise, the word *qb't* in Isa 51:22 is a cognate of the Ugaritic word for "chalice."[26] Even so, few scholars since Duhm[27] have seriously contemplated placing the authors of Isa 40–55 in Syria although, it must be admitted, Dahood uses this very argument for claiming that the author of at least Isa 52:13—53:12 lived in Phoenicia.[28]

There is also a question as to what extent a person living in Babylon in the Neo-Babylonian period actually *spoke* Akkadian. Most assyriologists today agree that by the time of the Neo-Babylonian Empire, Akkadian was no longer the vernacular in Babylon, having been replaced by Aramaic. Akkadian was preserved as the language of rituals, culture, and administration.[29] This can be deduced primarily by the clear Aramaic influence over the royal inscriptions,[30] from the iconographic evidence from Assyrian sculpture where scribes of tablets and scribes of scrolls are depicted as standing side by side, and from a few clay tablets with Aramaic writing.[31] This means that unless we assume that the authors of Isa 40–55 were involved in the administration of the Empire or present at court, there would have been no need for the Jewish exiles in Babylon to learn Akkadian.[32] As neither biblical nor extra-biblical texts suggest any larger involvement of the Jewish

24. Isaiah (1,292 verses), Jeremiah (1,364 verses) and Ezekiel (1,273 verses). Source: www.deafmissions.com. I am indebted to Dr David Reimer for drawing my attention to these statistics.

25. Mankowski, *Akkadian Loanwords*, 44–45, 58, 173–74.

26. See the discussion and accompanied footnotes in Cohen, *Biblical Hapax Legonema*, 44–46.

27. Duhm, *Das Buch Jesaia*, xviii.

28. Dahood, "Phoenician Elements," 63–73.

29. Van de Mieroop, *A History of the Ancient Near East*, 265. For more details, see George, "Babylonian and Assyrian," 58, who states that "at the Assyrian and Babylonian courts and in the market place, the more vital language of literary expression and oral literary tradition was undoubtedly Aramaic". This transition from Akkadian to Aramaic as the vernacular began already in the Neo-Assyrian period. In the same volume, see further Millard, "Early Aramaic," 92, for a more tentative opinion. See also Tadmor, "The Aramaization of Assyria," 449–70.

30. Schaudig, *Die Inschriften Nabonids*, esp. 315.

31. Fales, *Aramaic Epigraphs*.

32. S. Dalley, The Oriental Institute, Oxford, email communication.

community in Babylon with the imperial administration, and as I find it difficult to imagine the clearly Yahwistic authors of Isa 40–55 having had any deeper involvement in the Babylonian cult, I fail to see how *Akkadian* parallels would support a Babylonian domicile of the authors of Isa 40–55.

To sum up, the occurrence of expressions in Isa 40–55 with Akkadian cognates, as well as the occurrence of idiomatic expressions or literary motifs in Isa 40–55 with parallels in Mesopotamian texts, is not evidence of a Babylonian provenance. Rather, the cognate expressions testify to the fact that Hebrew and Akkadian, as two Semitic languages, use related expressions to express related ideas. Likewise, the similar idioms and cultural outlook are better explained as either the shared cultural heritage of the ancient Near East and/or as a matter of imperial influence of the dominant culture of Assyria and Babylon upon its vassal states.

Akkadian Influence over the Style of Isaiah 40–55

A few scholars also suggest that the so-called "self-predication" formula, attested throughout Isa 41–45, 48, 49 and 51, is influenced by Akkadian, and argue that this influence supports a Babylonian origin of Isa 40–55. This "self-predication formula" contains two parts: (1) God presents himself ("I am YHWH"), and (2) a short hymnic statement that assigns an attribute to God (e.g., "the first and the last one" [Isa 41:4]; "the one who strengthens your right hand" [Isa 41:13]).[33] Gressmann, the prime advocate of this view, maintains that although the comparable "self-presentation formula" is attested throughout the biblical corpus (Gen 15:7; 17:1; 26:24, 28:13; 35:11; 46:3; Exod 6:2), the self-predication formula in Isa 40–55 is derived from Babylonian sources.[34] From a different perspective, Dion detects similarities between the writings of Isa 40–55 and a Sumerian hymn form where the deity praises him/herself (*hymne à soi-meme*), and, on the basis of this similarity, concludes that the author of Isa 40–55 learned about this type of literature in Babylon.[35]

33. For a complete list and a detailed discussion of all the occurrences in Isa 40–55, see Diesel, *Ich bin Jahwe*, 284–342.

34. See further the extended discussion in Diesel, *Ich bin Jahwe*, 95–118, 187–367. She focuses her discussion on the self–identification formula "I am YHWH" in Exod 6:2–8 which she regards as a post-exilic key expression for monotheism, but she also discusses the occurrences throughout Lev 18–26 and in the prophetic literature where it is primarily attested in Ezekiel and Isa 40–55 but also found in Hos 12:10; 13:4 and Jer 32:27.

35. Dion, "Le genre littéraire sumérien de l'hymne à soi-même,'" 215–34. For a translation of the relevant text (Enki and the World Order), see Kramer, *The Sumerians*, 171–83.

These claims are untenable for multiple reasons. Following Talmon's guidelines, it is methodologically preferable to give precedence to the inner-biblical evidence. While not doubting that the "self-predication" formula existed in Sumerian and Akkadian literature, it is overall more plausible that the authors of Isa 40–55 drew from their own, already existing, tradition of the "self-predication" rather than borrowing it from Babylonian texts. This remains true regardless of whether the authors lived in Judah or in Babylon. Although it may be true that the "self-predication formula" in Isa 40–55 ultimately stems from Sumerian culture, we have to distinguish direct literary influence from shared cultural heritage.[36]

The original *Sitz im Leben* of the "self-predication" formula can probably be located in prophetic circles.[37] Weippert highlights the similarity between the formula 'ny/'nky yhwh in Isa 40–55 and the Akkadian self-predication formula *anāku Ištar ša Arbail* in the Neo-Assyrian prophetic texts.[38] These attestations of the formula "I am + divine name" in the Neo-Assyrian prophetic texts suggest that any influence must have occurred already in pre-exilic times.[39] How, then, do we explain the similarities between Isa 40–55 and the Neo-Assyrian prophecies? Weippert rules out the possibility that the authors of Isa 40–55, whom he presumes to be living in Babylon, could have been directly familiar with the Neo-Assyrian prophesies. The latter were composed seventy-five years earlier in Nineveh and nothing suggests that the traditions surrounding these prophecies relating to Neo-Assyrian monarchs were brought to Babylon.

The situation is the same with regard to other cases of affinity between Isa 40–55 and Neo-Assyrian prophecies. In their discussion of the similarities in terms of theology between Isa 40–55 and a letter of Ashshurhaatu'a to Ashshurbanipal (State Archives of Assyria 13, 139), Nissinen and Parpola reject any notion of direct influence as "the Assyrian documents we have at our disposal were already buried with the city of Nineveh." In their view, the evident influence is the result of cultural and ideological interaction between

---

36. Barstad, "On the So-Called Babylonian Influence," 107–9.

37. Zimmerli, "Ich bin Jahwe," 186–92. Zimmerli is aware of the use of the formula in prophetic texts from Neo-Assyria and Mari (195–96), but nevertheless argues that this formula does not have its *Sitz im Leben* in the prophetic literature bur rather in the cult. Its occurrences in the book of Ezekiel are due to the priestly theology of this book (p. 202).

38. Weippert, "'Ich bin Jahwe,'" 42–58. In contrast, Diesel, *Ich bin Jahwe*, 184, notes the relatively high frequency of this formula in both the Ishtar oracles from the time of Esarhaddon and the royal inscriptions from the same time period, and she sees both as suggesting that at this time this formula became characteristic of powerful speech.

39. Nissinen, "Die Relevanz der neuassyrischen Prophetie," 235. Nissinen is open to the possibility of additional influence in Babylon during the time of the exile.

the people of Marduk and the people of YHWH.[40] More broadly, de Jong argues that Neo-Assyrian prophecy and ancient Israelite prophecy were part of the same phenomenon. More specifically, de Jong detects a number of similarities between Neo-Assyrian prophecies and those attributed to Isaiah ben Amoz, dated to roughly the same time period in the eighth century B.C.E.[41] Taking this reasoning one step further, as Isa 40–55 clearly stands in the same tradition as the preceding Isaianic material,[42] we should almost expect it to display affinity with its Mesopotamian counterpart.

To sum up, the fact that the self-predication formula exists in both Isa 40–55 and in Neo-Assyrian prophetic texts is best explained as an expression of two distinct attestations that form part of the shared prophetic heritage. In addition, given the political ties between the Neo-Assyrian Empire and both Israel and Judah, direct influence cannot be ruled out. The authors of Isa 40–55, staying close to the traditions of their prophetic antecedents, adopted and further developed this formula in order to address the needs of their audience following the destruction of Judah in 586 B.C.E.

Akkadian Influence—Conclusion

As we have seen, there is a resilient tendency among scholars to assume that Isa 40–55 was composed in Babylon, and then, based on this assumption, to detect similarities between this text and various Mesopotamian texts. This whole process is methodologically questionable, however, as the Babylonian background of Isa 40–55 is not beyond doubt. There are similarities between Isa 40–55 and several Mesopotamian texts which justify concluding that the authors of Isa 40–55, alongside many other prophetic authors in the Hebrew Bible, were familiar with Babylonian ideas, either through direct influence or through shared cultural heritage. Likewise, biblical Hebrew and Akkadian share many cognate linguistic parallels. These similarities, however, should come as no surprise. By the sixth century B.C.E., the imperial powers of the Neo-Assyrians and the Neo-Babylonians had dominated the culture of Mesopotamia and the Levant for nearly 200 years and Akkadian had served as the *lingua franca* of the ancient Near East for an even longer time. It would actually be peculiar if the material in Isa 40–55, alongside other Hebrew texts from the same time period, did not share linguistic and stylistic elements with

---

40. Nissinen, and Parpola, "Marduk's Return and Reconciliation," 199–219 (esp. 218).

41. De Jong, *Isaiah among the Ancient Near Eastern Prophets*, esp. 283–85.

42. See especially Williamson, *The Book Called Isaiah*.

Akkadian compositions. A conclusion that we cannot draw, however, is that the authors of Isa 40–55 must have been residents of Babylon.

Specific Texts in Isaiah 40–55

Apart from the general claims that Isa 40–55 displays Akkadian/Babylonian influence, several scholars have also detected examples of direct knowledge of Babylon in specific passages and used these examples as part of their argument for a Babylonian origin of Isa 40–55. These texts fall into two general groups. First, we have texts that refer to *religious practices* that can be associated with Babylon. This category contains the so-called idol fabrication passages (Isa 40:18–20; 41:6–7; 44:9–20) as well as Isa 46:1–7 and 47:12–13. Secondly, we have texts that contain *explicit references* to Babylon and/or to Babylonian deities (Isa 43:14; 44:24–25; 46:1–4; 47; 48:14, 20).

Idol Fabrication Passages

Beginning with the idol fabrication passages, the critique of idol worship is, in itself, as likely to be levelled against the people in Judah as against the exilic community in Babylon. On the one hand, a person living in a land full of images of deities (such as Babylon), which are understood as symbolizing the essence of the deities that they represent, could easily be influenced by this type of thinking. On the other hand, the tendency to worship idols is nothing novel to the situation after the fall of Jerusalem. Both the DtrH and the pre-exilic prophetic texts habitually accuse the people of Israel and Judah of worshipping other gods and their images. These accusations are born out by the archaeological remains from Judah which testify to the worship of a variety of idols.[43] It is thus possible that the people who remained in Judah either continued (depending on our evaluation of the accusation of DtrH and the prophets) or resumed worshipping idols following the catastrophe in 586 B.C.E. After all, from their perspective, worship of YHWH had not prevented the disaster. In view of this, the idol fabrication passages in Isa 40–55 *per se* do not hint at the whereabouts of their original target audience.

---

43. See, e.g., the overviews with cited bibliography in Vriezen, "Archaeological Traces of Cult," 45–80, and in Hess, *Israelite Religions*, 297–332. Note that parts of the material discussed in these surveys are significantly older than the sixth century B.C.E.

Babylon in Isaiah 40–55

The references to Babylon (Isa 43:14; 46:1–2; 47; 48:14, 20) and to Babylonian practices (Isa 44:24–25; 47:12–15) have also often been treated as evidence of the Babylonian origin of Isa 40–55.

Isaiah 44:24–25 and 47:12–15 mention (stereo)-typical Babylonian divination practices. Based on these references, several scholars maintain that these verses testify to their Babylonian setting,[44] yet a closer look does not support this conclusion. Although the interpretation of some of the technical terminology is debated, and although some of the terms used have Akkadian cognate forms, these two passages do not contain any Akkadian loan-words and all the terms for the various religious experts are attested in the Hebrew Bible outside of Isa 40–55.[45] There is thus no reason, on the basis of the language itself, to postulate direct Akkadian influence on Isa 44:24–25 and 47:12–15. As to the content, Babylon was widely known for its knowledge of the stars. In fact, astrology, divination, and magic are exactly the kind of things that the peoples throughout the ancient world would have associated with Babylon. These passages therefore do not contain any details that should cause us to assume that its author had any deeper knowledge of Babylonian customs beyond that which was generally known.[46]

It is also commonly held that the imagery of Isa 46:1–4 reflects an insider's knowledge of Babylon.[47] As we shall see, a closer look at Isa 46:1–4 does not support this claim. The oracle in Isa 46:1–4 mentions Bel (Marduk) and Nebo (Nabu), the chief deities of the Neo-Babylonian Empire. The oracle contains polemic speech against these deities in which YHWH declares that he is mightier and more dependable than they are, and therefore best suited to take care of Jacob-Israel.

The imagery of verses 1–2 has been interpreted in three main ways: (1) the *akitu* festival, (2) the Babylonians bringing their idols to safety, or (3) the Babylonian idols being carried into captivity. The third interpretation is the most likely. It comports well with the general message of Isa 46:1–2: the idols themselves are unable to deliver a burden (v. 2ab) so instead they have to be carried (as a burden) (v. 2b). It also sets the scene for the contrasting

---

44. E.g., Behr, *The Writings of Deutero-Isaiah and the Neo-Babylonian Royal Inscriptions*, 16; Muilenburg, "The Book of Isaiah Chapters 40–66," 397.

45. For a detailed discussion of the Hebrew terminology, see Vanderhooft, *The Neo-Babylonian Empire*, 182–84, with cited bibliography.

46. Kapelrud, *Et folk på hjemferd*, 28. See also Duhm, *Das Buch Jesaia*, 312, and Maynard, "The Home of Deutero-Isaiah," 216.

47. E.g., Kittel, "Cyrus und Deuterojesaja," 161.

imagery in the following verse 3 where God carries his people Israel.[48] The image is that of humiliating defeat, either mirroring the reality of post-539 B.C.E. or the prophet's vision in which the Babylonians are defeated and their idols are being loaded onto pack animals. The fact that Cyrus is not reported as having dethroned the statues of Babylon but having supported and sought to reinstate the cult of Marduk in Babylon renders the latter interpretation likely. It is a future prediction rather than a report of an event that has already taken place.[49]

Nothing in this interpretation demands an author who resides in Babylon. In the words of Blenkinsopp: "No local features and no individuals are mentioned, and there is nothing that calls for more than an active imagination nourished with a minimum of general cultural information."[50] A prophet in both Babylon and Judah would be able to envision the fall of Babylon along the lines of the well-known Near Eastern ideology of the deportation of its statues. In fact, there are factors that actually point in the opposite direction. As Maynard, Kapelrud and more recently Hägglund emphasize, Isa 46:1–2 reveals a conception of the Babylonian gods that does not fit the situation in Babylon during the last years of the Neo-Babylonian Empire. Presumably a prophet living in Babylon would have been familiar with Nabonidus' attempt to replace the worship of the traditional Babylonian chief deities Marduk and Nabu with that of the moon god Sin. This lack of familiarity with the cultic issues of Nabonidus' reign invites the conclusion that the author of Isa 46:1–2 lived at some distance from Babylon.[51]

Conclusion

There is little in terms of specific knowledge of Babylon in Isa 40–55. Furthermore, the linguistic evidence in Isa 40–55 does not warrant the claim that Isa 40–55 was written in Babylon.[52] What there is in terms of familiarity of Babylonian customs and deities is broad in character and best explained as shared cultic heritage. Judah had lived in the immediate military and

48. Cf. Franke, "The Function of the Satiric Lament," 415; Koole *Isaiah*, 497.

49. See the Cyrus Cylinder. Cf. Schaudig, "'Bēl Bows, Nabu Stoops!'" 570–71; contra Berges, *Deutero-Jesaja*, 446–49, who argues, on the same grounds, for a later dating to the reign of Cyrus around 522–21 B.C.E.

50. See Blenkinsopp, *Isaiah 40–55*, 268.

51. Maynard, "The Home of Deutero-Isaiah," 215; Kapelrud, *Et folk på hjemferd*, 28, 31–32; Hägglund, *Isaiah 53*, 153.

52. For in-depth discussions of the archaeological and exegetical evidence often listed in support of a Babylonian provenance of Isa 40–55, see further my monograph *For the Comfort of Zion*, esp. 53–203.

cultural shadow of Assyria and Babylon for nearly a century before the fall of Jerusalem. We can therefore safely assume that the people of Judah, long before the catastrophe in 586 B.C.E., were well aware of the customs and religious beliefs of these dominant superpowers in the east. In addition, a conquered people learn the customs of the conqueror quickly, regardless of whether they are deported or not.

8

Transforming Word and Empire

Isaiah 55:10-11 Considered[1]

TIM MEADOWCROFT

Attendance at worship was falling. The young people in particular were conspicuous by their absence. When the elders gathered, they grumbled about accommodation, looked back on better days, and wondered whether God was yet working (or even present) in their midst. Each day brought reports of someone from the flock who was "selling out," turning toward the values of an increasingly alien world, chasing after other gods—a better spot in the market, the trust and respect of those in power, a secure and stable life for them and their family. Other congregations were growing and growing rapidly, but the gods they worshiped did not seem to be the God of the ancestors, the Lord who had always brought them victory in the past. Where was this God, they wondered, now?[2]

RICHARD BOYCE'S IMAGINATIVE DEPICTION of the gathered life of Jewish exiles under the Babylonian empire could describe church life in the West at the beginning of the twenty-first century. The church seems to have less and less to say to society, or even to its own adherents. Religious enthusiasm, when it is expressed, is often clumsy and out of touch with the questions of the age. The promotion of the marketer as the new high priest in society results in an

1. Much of the material in this chapter is also covered in Meadowcroft, *The Message of the Word of God*, 46–60. I acknowledge the permission of IVP to use it here. I am grateful also for comments from participants in the original colloquium on which this volume is based.

2. Boyce, "Isaiah 55:6–13," 56.

obsession with appearance over substance at almost every level of public life, from fashion to politics, and even to matters of faith. The materialistic apathy that surrounds the faithful is profoundly debilitating in its effects. And the difficulty in achieving a moral consensus in society leaves believers uncertain how to respond with both grace and truth. In a post-Christian world, Christians find themselves increasingly on the edge, at odds with the empire.

From what we know of life in the Babylonian exile, the Hebrew people were free—indeed, commanded by God—to make a living in Babylon (Jer 29:4–7), to go about their daily lives more or less undisturbed, to form their own religious communities and even to "seek the welfare of the city" (Jer 29:7).[3] Yet still they ached for something more as they tried to make sense of life in an exilic context and to come to terms with being surrounded by a Babylonian cosmology (Ps 137). In short, they struggled in the terms laid out by Boyce. Into that context, the words of the Isaiah scroll in chapter 55 spoke of new hope and possibility, a possibility formed around a renewed covenant brought into being by the ever-reliable word of God.[4] The very word or speech of God acts to bring new possibility into being.[5]

It does so against the imperial background to the Isaiah scroll. In saying that, I am making certain assumptions about the formation of that scroll. First, I take it that Deutero-Isaiah was formed in the context of the Babylonian and perhaps Persian exile experience, but in conscious response to and interaction with the work of the earlier Isaiah of Jerusalem, work which is reflected in Isa 1–39.[6] At the same time, I assume that the final formation of the scroll, as evidenced from Trito-Isaiah, is a conscious incorporation of the earlier material into the later Palestinian Second Temple context.[7] As

---

3. All English quotations of Scripture are from the NRSV unless otherwise stated.

4. Westermann, *Isaiah 40–66*, 289: "For our prophet the word is not primarily something with a content, but the instrument by means of which something is effected. . . . This view of the word dominates the whole of prophecy."

5. In that God's word is sent forth with a task to do, *speech* and *act* come together. It is no accident then that Speech-Act Theory within the discipline of linguistics has come to prominence in the study of biblical interpretation, as interpreters search for greater understanding of the process whereby the voice of God in Scripture may be said to be effective. Speech-act focuses on the category of *locution* and thinks about the intended effect of a piece of communication and its outcome, as well as the act of communication itself. Speech-act understandings of locution and of its applicability to reading a sacred text are presumed in this treatment of the notion that God's word goes forth. See for example the contributions from Vanhoozer, Stiver, Wolterstorff, and others in Bartholomew, Greene, and Möller, eds., *After Pentecost*.

6. See the argument of Seitz, *Zion's Final Destiny*, esp. 32–35.

7. Although I accept that the discussion as to which material in Trito-Isaiah reflects redactional activity as against original composition from a later period continues, the point I make about the incorporation of material into a Palestinian context does not

a result, the words of Isa 55:10–11 are spoken into a time when much has been lost, and assumptions of power may no longer be made by the hearers of the prophetic message.[8] At the same time, it is read from a perspective of having returned to the land of promise but in markedly different imperial circumstances from those that obtained before the collapse in 586 B.C.E.[9] A certain amount of self-determination has been regained, but such sovereignty as there may be remains at the pleasure of a foreign imperial power.[10]

As Walter Brueggemann has argued, the Isaianic sense of being on the margins of an alien world is to some extent analogous to the struggle of the church to maintain a fingerhold in a Western society that has largely rejected a Christian account of life.[11] Like the exilic community that formed Isaiah 55 and like the Palestinian community that read it, the church is in regular need of being re-invigorated by Christian hope and possibility. In that respect, Isaiah's account of God at work through the agency of God's word speaks as much to the Western church today as it did to the people of Israel all those generations ago.

And like the communities that formed and first incorporated the Isaiah scroll, the church in the West occupies a liminal space with respect to the imperial powers of the day. The church has lost its place as privileged companion of the empire, but still exists to some extent in collusion with the empire. Whether the imperial context is hostile or characterized by self-interested complicity, transformation for the marginalized party is a requirement and a possibility. The purpose of this paper is to consider the dynamics of transformation with respect to the "word of God" in such a context by means of a close reading of Isa 55:10–11, which is then set into the literary context of ch. 55 as a whole.[12]

---

require the debate to be settled. For further see Williamson, *Variations on a Theme*, 167–72; Stromberg, *An Introduction to the Study of Isaiah*, 48–53.

8. Westermann, *Isaiah 40–66*, 291, comments that this utterance "forms in actual fact a bridge between the exile and the new Jerusalem."

9. Contra Barstad, *The Myth of the Empty Land*, 30–39, my use of the word "collapse" takes its lead from the evidence for a weak Jerusalem and a depopulated Judah during the exilic period adduced by Kessler, "Reconstructing Haggai's Jerusalem," 144–51.

10. For one analysis of the situation on the ground, see Smith-Christopher, *A Biblical Theology of Exile*, 38–45.

11. Brueggemann, *Hopeful Imagination*, 6.

12. I leave an explicitly postcolonial analysis to other essays in this volume. But I note in passing that Deutero-Isaiah is potentially a postcolonial text, both in that it represents a coming to terms with a lost status as colonizer and in that it speaks from a context of remaining to some extent colonized by the Persian empire.

Structural Matters

While the focus of this paper is the transforming word of God as described in verses 10–11, it is important to understand that word in the wider context both of Isa 55 and of the second half of the book of Isaiah as a whole. I am convinced by the argument that the entire chapter 55 may be read as a coherent literary unit.[13] I am also convinced by the logical flow of the chapter as described by Walter Brueggemann:[14] verses 1–5 describe the invitation into a renewed covenant that God offers to his people on the basis of the ancient covenant with the house of David; verses 6–9 then switch to the imperative mood as God appeals to the people to accept the invitation, assuring them of forgiveness as he does so; verses 10–11 concern the word of YHWH which both looks back to the earlier promises and also brings to fulfillment the renewed promises of God; the concluding verses 12–13 are then a vivid picture of the transformation that comes through accepting YHWH's invitation and obeying his commands. As Brueggeman puts it in summary, "The transformation occurs because life is now given (vv. 1–5). Israel turns to life (vv. 6–9) and Yahweh guarantees it (vv. 10–11)."[15] Additionally, I would want to say that YHWH does more than guarantee it; he brings it about by the act of his speech.

Some have also linked the message of Isa 55 with what immediately precedes it, namely the reference to the "heritage of the servants of the Lord" (54:17b).[16] If the thirsty and penniless people of God think they are bankrupt, then think again. They have an inheritance, which the prophet now reveals as a renewed covenant brought into being by the word of God. Indeed, the link goes back further because the comfort promised in chapter 40 is on the basis of the fact that "the mouth of the Lord has spoken" (40:5).[17] This promised comfort culminates in the reflection of chapter 55 on the effective word of YHWH in formulating a new covenant with God's people.[18] In fact, the words of chapter 55 reach further back than just chap-

---

13. Korpel, "Metaphors in Isaiah LV," 48. Contra those who read verses 1–5 and 6–13 as units distinct from each other.

14. Brueggemann, "Isaiah 55," 193–94.

15. Ibid., 194.

16. See Goldingay, *The Message of Isaiah 40–55*, 543.

17. Childs, *Isaiah*, 437–38, argues that chapter 55 concludes the train of thought commenced in chapter 40.

18. One of the assumptions of a speech-act approach to language is that language implies relationship. Vanhoozer, "From Speech Acts to Scripture Acts," 1–49, demonstrates that it is therefore no surprise that the act of God's word is closely connected to the formation of covenant.

ter 40. They can also be read as the culmination of the response of God to the situation set up by the puzzling material of 6:9–13.[19] There the word of the Lord through the prophet promises to close eyes and ears to the things of God: "Make the mind of this people dull, and stop their ears, and shut their eyes" (6:10). Not unreasonably, Isaiah asks how long this must go on, to which God replies that it must be until the time when "the holy seed is its stump" (6:13). Whatever exactly this much contested phrase means, there is a link through to chapter 55 in which the word of the Lord "[gives] seed to the sower" (v. 10). The word of God in judgment set out in 6:9–13 now reveals its counterpoint in hope and comfort through the institution of the renewed covenant and the transformation that will flow from that covenant, all as a result of the word of God.

With that in mind we turn to the nature of God's word as it emerges in verses 10–11, before considering more of its effects in light of the surrounding material in Isa 55.

As the Rain and the Snow . . .

There is a clear poetic structure within verses 10–11. The start of each verse is around the grammatical structure: as . . . (v. 10), so . . . (v. 11). The process described in verse 11 thus mirrors that of verse 10. At the same time, each verse pivots on an important Hebrew particle *'im.* The term is represented by NRSV in verse 10 by "until" in the phrase "until they have watered the earth . . ." with the translators opting in verse 11 for "but" in the phrase "but it shall accomplish . . ." It is not an easy expression to capture exactly in English. The TNIV prefers "without"; "unless" is also a possibility. The TNIV and NRSV between them indicate the general conditional feel of the term. In any case, in each instance an agent is sent out, and is not permitted to return "unless/without/until" certain effects have occurred as a result of the agent's action. The structure of each of these two verses so closely reflects the other that the reader cannot help but read one in the light of the other. The "as . . . so . . ." scaffolding of the two verses also makes clear that the more abstract verse 11 is to be understood in the light of the picture taken from nature in verse 10. As with any reading of metaphor, the metaphor of rain and snow illumines that to which it is being likened, "[God's] word," and the text assumes some familiarity on the part of the reader with the metaphor itself.

So we turn to verse 10, a picture of precipitation which in its various forms causes the earth to sprout forth its vegetation for the benefit of

19. On this possibility, see Williamson, *Variations on a Theme*, 121–22.

humanity. The vegetables grow, the trees absorb the carbon dioxide, and the beauty of the world around is enhanced because the rains and the snows come in their seasons. In Auckland, where I am writing this, it is easy to take this miracle for granted, blessed as we are with plenty of rain and a green lush environment most of the year. But in many parts of the world, including in the Judean hills familiar to the earliest hearers of Isaiah's words, rain and snow are scarce and valuable commodities. They are eagerly awaited and carefully managed when they arrive. In such an environment agricultural and horticultural management centers around making the most of every drop of water that arrives.

When "the rain and the snow" do their work the effect is there for all to see. First of all, they "[water] the earth." The verb used (*rvh*) has the sense of abundance and plenty. The earth itself, not merely the foliage on it, receives the benefits of rains from the Lord's hands. The result is that it "bring[s] forth" (*hiphil* of *yld*), a word that explicitly concerns reproduction. And it also "sprout[s]" (*hiphil* of *tsmch*), a term that reinforces the sense of extravagance and abundance. Together "bring forth and sprout" speak of the self-sustaining fertility and fruitfulness of nature made possible through the watering of the earth.

The final two lines of verse 10 then point out the usefulness of all this fertility. The benefit is to those who depend on the fruitfulness of the earth for their well-being, and two kinds of dependence are highlighted. First, the well-watered earth provides the means for its own sustainability; there is "seed to the sower." Secondly, it provides sustenance for those who depend on it: "bread to the eater." These two aspects reflect the two verbs, "bring forth and sprout," both of which are in the causative form. The rains and snow cause the ground to reproduce, as a result of which its reproductive capacity is sustained in the form of seeds. At the same time, they cause the ground to produce extravagantly, thus providing "bread for the eater." It may not be pushing the metaphor too hard to note that, while the watering of the earth is something over which humanity has little control, the resulting fruitfulness comes about through human participation in the process.[20] Whether that particular point was intended by the prophet, it is part of the creation tradition shared by the early chapters of Genesis and these chapters of Isaiah. Therefore that the "sower" should appear in verse 10 echoes the commissioning of Adam and Eve to tend the garden and enable it to bear fruit (Gen 2:15).

---

20. There is a rich vein of reflection here on how God and humanity work together in the care of creation, but that is for another time.

. . . So Is God's Word

The word that goes out from God's mouth, the prophet says, may be understood in the same way. There are several key aspects of God's word that are treated in verse 11: it is effective; it does not return empty; it is sent forth with a purpose; and that purpose has to do with the will of God. This all sounds very abstract, but it achieves an immediacy when considered in light of the metaphor that has just preceded it.

Let us first think of one aspect of both the metaphor and what it illustrates not mentioned in the preceding section, namely, that it does not return without/unless it achieves that for which it is sent. The prophet was drawing on an established sense of the "word" of God as agent sent forth on a particular commission and then returning with that commission accomplished. By the time that these words were written there was an understanding of wisdom as the agent of God in the world (Prov 8:22–35), and the beginnings of an identification of the word of God, the *torah*, with this wisdom work of God in the world. Eldon Epp has demonstrated that "the two terms [Wisdom and Torah] were often interchangeable and . . . the writer or hearer of a Wisdom hymn could just as well be thinking of Torah."[21] Thus, when the prophet speaks of God's word "[accomplishing] that which [God] purpose[s]" or "[succeeding] in the thing for which [God] sent it" (v. 11), a sense of the word's activity on behalf of God is not far away.[22] In the same way, in the mind of the poet at this point, the rain once it has ceased may be thought of as having returned whence it came, the evidence of its effect remaining in the form of a fertile earth.

For a twenty-first century reader, with knowledge of the water cycle, the opposite effect is at work. The idea of water moving on once it has done its work helps to illuminate for us a sense of the word of God as effective agent that does its work, leaves its impact and then moves on.[23] And in both the metaphor and the actual reference the process is inevitable.

The phrasing adds an extra twist to that. Not only is there something inevitable about the process; there is also something persistent. The rains

21. Epp, "Wisdom, Torah, Word," 135.

22. See Baltzer, *Deutero-Isaiah*, 483, on the "personalization or even hypostatization of the word." Something of this sense is also captured by Jeremiah's vision of the almond blossom showing him that God is "watching to see that [God's] word is fulfilled" (Jer 1:11–12).

23. It has been pointed out that the prophet is unlikely to have had a scientific understanding of the precipitation cycle in speaking of the rain and snow returning to heaven once it has watered the earth. See Couroyer, "Note sur II Sam.," 512. Yet the metaphor is curiously in tune with the current state of science in a way that it could not have been for the earliest hearers.

and snow do not return whence they came "until" (v. 10) their task is completed, or "but" (v. 11) their task is completed. Likewise, the word of God persists until the desired effect is achieved. Every spring, when the rains come, the barren Judean wilderness blossoms briefly. It is impossible not to notice the effect. When God's word has been at work it is similarly evident, which in this context primarily reflects God's formation of covenant relationship with his people.

The role of God in this process is further illumined by a subtle difference between the nature metaphor in verse 10 and the "word" in verse 11. The language of verse 10 does not indicate any particular cause for the rain and snow, other than its source in "heaven."[24] The agents are the beneficiaries of the rain and snow, namely, the sower and the eater, each of whose task it is to appropriate the earth's abundance. Unlike in verse 10, the agent of God's word in verse 11 is the speaker: YHWH, from whose mouth the word "goes out." At the same time, the beneficiary of God's word is also YHWH in the sense both that the word is sent forth with a particular purpose in the divine mind and that the effect of the word is a cause of delight. While not so evident in the NRSV translation, the verb in the phrase "that which I purpose" (*chpts*) conveys a sense of divine delight in what is going on. By implication, just as the sower and eater benefit from the rains, so the Lord benefits from the word of God.

This is somewhat counter-intuitive in that we might have thought that humankind in some way would benefit. It is a remarkable emphasis that God benefits from the word of YHWH. However, the metaphor also allows for the possibility that humankind is the beneficiary also. The sower and the eater of verse 10 are likely to be identified in the mind of readers and hearers as people like themselves, therefore the effectiveness of the word of God that "shall not return to [God] empty" (v. 11) is assumed also to be of benefit to men and women who encounter it. Somehow the two things hold together in a way that reinforces the incarnational understanding of God that infuses the Old Testament Scriptures.[25] The equation of YHWH (v. 11) with the sower and eater (v. 10) is a subtle reminder that human beings are co-workers with God. God's purposes in verse 11 in some way relate to the response of the sower and eater of verse 10 in bringing into effect the purposes of God. The effect brings delight to YHWH. Something of the

---

24. Of course to the Hebrew mind, the source of all forces of nature is inescapably YHWH, but that is not the point being made here. Indeed, arguably by the time of this writing in the exilic period, "heaven" had come to be used as a shorthand for the God of heaven. See Collins, *Daniel*, 229–30.

25. For further on this see Meadowcroft, "Between Authorial Intent and Indeterminacy," 209, in which I reference also Pinnock, *Most Moved Mover*, esp. 88–104.

content of this delight emerges through the nature metaphor of verse 10 with its picture of extravagant fertility and joy in the delights of God's good creation.[26] The pleasure that the human experience of these things brings is akin to that felt by God at the effect of his word. At the same time, those on whom the word acts are similarly delighted both by its extravagant fruitfulness and by its self-sustaining possibility.

God's Word in the Call to Covenant

So far we have identified that God's word is effective. But what effect is in mind? Given that we are reading Isa 55 as a complete unit, these two verses on the word that goes out from God's mouth (vv. 10–11) respond to the key emphases that have been identified in the chapter as a whole. By working through each of those emphases, and the verses that articulate them, we may appreciate more fully the nature of the impact of God's word. Rain and snow are inherently interesting natural phenomena that may quite legitimately be described and experienced, but the poet in this context is less interested in doing that and more concerned with what happens as a result of the rain and snow. In the same way, the word of God may also be described and experienced for its own sake, but the prophet is more concerned with the impact of the word of God on that which it encounters.

And so to verses 1–5, which we have summarized as God's invitation into a renewed covenant. The metaphors chosen echo a link with creation but also sharpen the focus onto the covenant-making word of God. There are several aspects to this. First of all, it is a word that is spoken by direct address into the situation in which the people find themselves. The opening word in the Hebrew is an attention grabbing *hoy!* (v. 1, translated as "Ho" by NRSV). *Pay attention*, you who are thirsty and hungry and without the means to acquire food and drink! The covenant making word of God is for such as you, because the result is unimaginably "rich food" (v. 2). This message may be taken in both a spiritual and a "secular" sense. On the one hand, it recalls the metaphor of famine for those who are under the judgment of God desperately looking for a word from God (Amos 8:11–13). On the other, it foreshadows the later physical experience of those who returned from exile struggling to make ends meet like people whose wages are going

---

26. See Tull, "Persistent Vegetative States," 28, who comments with respect to the passage under discussion: "Attribution of human characteristics to plants, like the attribution of plant characteristics to people, affirms the critical ties binding humans to the landscape they depend upon, and evokes respect for the rights and dignity of nonhuman creation."

into a purse with holes (Hag 1:6). For them, the failings in their covenant relationship were being expressed physically. These words should not be read in a way that excludes a physical application of them. God speaks both for the poor and for the poor in spirit.[27] It has also been observed that the covenant making experience of the Exodus itself brings together both of those elements. It was a time of physical deliverance from oppression along with provision of food and water, but at the same time the broader canvas of the establishment of the people of God was always in view.[28]

And God speaks not only to alleviate the suffering and respond to the longings of individuals; he speaks also to bring a people into being. In the remarkable verse 3, the Lord through the prophet remembers the everlasting covenant made with King David (see 2 Sam 7), and effectively incorporates into that promise "all who would believe from all the nations."[29] To view the dynamic from a slightly different angle, "The covenant relationship David once enjoyed with God is now to be enjoyed by the nation as a whole."[30] God's effective word, like the snow and rain on a thirsty earth, enables the formation of a people of God; God's word comes to build communities of the faithful in cooperation with those same faithful.

To what end are these communities formed? To the end that their calling will be fulfilled as a people who draw other nations also into the covenant. The people are "glorified" (v. 5) so that the influence of the YHWH God, the Holy One of Israel might be evident. The involvement of the people of the covenant in the mission of God, which is hinted at regularly in Isa 40–55, is strongly and explicitly in evidence at this point.[31] The activity of the word of God speaks into being a people who then further the work of God in forming a people of faith. God's word comes to build communities of the faithful, so that those communities in their turn become agents in God's covenant making intention.[32] This reflects the dynamic that we noted in the metaphor of verse 10 that the rain and snow water the earth not only to provide bread for the hungry, but also to enable the sower to propagate

---

27. Compare the emphases of the Sermon on the Mount as recorded by Matthew (Matt 5:3) and the Sermon on the Plain recorded by Luke (Luke 6:29).

28. Knight, *Servant Theology*, 190. Much later, those who gathered around Jesus would hear him echo this invitation as he calls people to the "rivers of living water" (John 7:38). See Daise, "'If Anyone Thirsts,'" 687–99.

29. Kaiser, "The Unfailing Kindnesses," 97.

30. Williamson, *Variations on a Theme*, 118–19.

31. And is reflected in the LXX rendering of the last phrase of v. 11 as "I will prosper your ways and my commands," which on the face of it is interpretive of the purpose for which the word has been sent.

32. Wright, *The Mission of God*, 352.

and extend the fruitfulness of the earth. In the same way, the people spoken into being are also intended in some sense to be self-sustaining.

God's Word in the Appeal for a Response

Verses 6–9 have been characterized as an appeal to God's people to respond to God's words. In terms of our study of the effect of God's word, it demonstrates the effectiveness of God's instrumental word in drawing people into his covenant. In verse 6, much loved of evangelists, the English implies that God is only "near" and able to "be found" at particular moments, and that it is important to respond at those moments before the word recedes. This translation of the Hebrew preposition *b* as "while" does highlight the need for a response to God's word, and in that respect is in tune with what emerges in verses 7–8; a sense of urgency is not inappropriate to this theme. However, another possible translation of verse 6 reads as follows: "Seek YHWH in his being found; call on him in his being near." That translation has a less urgent ring about it, but it does draw out another likely intent of this verse, namely, that God's presence is not in doubt.[33] He is near and he is available to be found.[34] Therefore, harking back to the opening of this chapter, those who are thirsty and hungry and penniless can confidently come. This is assurance rather than threat. The word of God, which does not return without doing its work, is always at hand and always effective for those who seek and come.[35]

At the same time, there is a paradox inherent in the framing of this section. If God's immanence is expressed in verse 6, it is also the case that the difference between the "ways" and "thoughts" of YHWH and of the hearers of this message is as vast in scale as the difference between the "heavens" and the "earth" (v. 9). The Hebrew term translated as "thoughts" (*machsheboth*) has the sense of "device" or "plan." It has to do with all the factors at work that result in the formation of a person's intent, for good and ill. Then "ways" relates to the action or way of life that arises from the intention formed by the will. There are all sorts of limitations to the human heart and mind. God's will, however, is not bound by any of those limitations and as a result the actions undertaken by God are truly reliable and appropriate and good. Although God is always near, as verse 6 suggests, God is also always vastly different (v. 9).

33. Goldingay, *The Message of Isaiah 40–55*, 551.

34. It is no accident, then, that those who encountered the *Logos*, Jesus, were told that "the kingdom of God has come upon you" (Matt 12:29).

35. Deut 30:14 indicates that this is not only a New Testament concept.

Verse 7 sees the beginning of the alignment of the human will with that of God with a consequent alignment of the way of life with that of God.[36] The particular means by which this occurs in verse 7 is repentance and forgiveness. And this forgiveness is effected by God's word. The link emerges in the poetic shaping of verses 8–11. Each of verses 8–10 begins with the Hebrew particle *ki*, translated in each instance by NRSV as "for." There is a wide array of usage for this little word, but almost all of them come under the category of cause and effect linking in some form or other.[37] Grammarians will argue over the exact nuancing of this string of *ki* phrases, but it is sufficient for our purposes that they link the contents of those verses together and make them all consequent on the call to "seek the Lord . . ." in verses 6–7. Hence verse 8 reflects that the need for humanity to amend their ways and be pardoned arises from the difference between humanity's ways and God's ways. The scale of this difference is then further reinforced by the comparison with heaven and earth in verse 9. And then the *ki* at the start of verse 10 links the effective word of God all the way back to the substantive call to turn to YHWH and to be pardoned. By implication, the outcome is that the ways and thoughts of those who turn will more closely resemble those of YHWH who pardons. And this comes about through the word of God.

It is in God's speaking that the covenant people of God learn the thoughts or intentions of God, and so are enabled to live out the ways of God in situations in which they find themselves.

God's Word in Transformation

To conclude his reflection, the prophet reverts to the world of nature (vv. 12–13). This time, however, he goes far beyond the metaphor of the watering of the earth (v. 10). That was an everyday matter, albeit important and miraculous in its own way. Now the prophet does two further things with nature. First he evokes a sense of the whole of creation dancing for joy before its creator. The beauty and extravagance and differentiation of nature point us to God readily enough. But as humans we cannot ever enter into the experience of other parts of creation responding to God, although we

---

36. The effect of the incarnation is that this God enters into the world of humanity and enables the gap to be bridged. One outcome of this is that through the activity of God's word it becomes possible for humankind to begin to see the world through God's eyes, and so to begin to form ways of life that more adequately reflect the truth and goodness of God. See Oswalt, *Chapters 40–66*, 444.

37. Waltke, and O'Connor, *Biblical Hebrew Syntax*, 636–73.

can imagine that it might be so.[38] Verse 13a, however, seems to take us into the realm of the truly unimaginable. In such a place the thornbush becomes one of the plants of the cypress family,[39] and instead of briers a flowering myrtle. Transformation has taken place but in ways beyond our wildest dreams. Because God speaks.

But perhaps this vision of a transformed nature is not as beyond human ken as might be thought at first glance. The verb translated as "shall come up" (*'lh*, v. 13) is an extremely common word, which is often translated as "to go up." It is not unusual to find it being used, as here, of the cycles of plant and animal life, but it is a verb also occasionally used evocatively of the people of God. In yet another link back to chapter 40, the herald of Zion is enjoined to "get . . . up to a high mountain" (40:9), while the servant of chapter 53 "grew up . . . like a root out of dry ground" (53:2). Tellingly, amongst the so-called Songs of Ascent "the tribes go up" to Jerusalem (Ps 122:4). And so the people who "go out in joy" (v. 12), thus echoing the movement of the exodus, now go up as God's people to new possibility.[40] In this way the choice of vocabulary contains a giant hint that the transformation of nature is not only a sign of the cosmic influence of the word of God; it is also a pointer to the radical change in the people of God and their circumstances brought about by the effective word of God.[41] "You" (v. 12), the people of God, will do more than watch the mountains and hills dancing for joy.

For the active word of God will have transformed as truly as if a thornbush has turned into a juniper or briars into the myrtle. Once again, as a metaphor from nature illustrated the agency of God's word (v. 10), so now another metaphor from nature indicates the degree of transformation that God has in mind for the exiled people. In this way their imaginations are formed by God so that they can see beyond the limits of their current circumstances. In terms of our consideration of Isaiah and empire, an exilic perspective finds that "the year that King Uzziah died" (6:1) is not the end of the story; it is the start of a different story of possibility that is at least partly a re-building of the imperial tradition represented by Uzziah, but of course more importantly by David. From the perspective of a re-established

38. Northcott, *The Environment and Christian Ethics*, 181, argues that "in the Hebrew perspective humanity and the cosmos have moral significance, and both are required to make a moral response to the creator, a response to God which reflects his glory and offers the return of gratitude, praise and worship . . ."

39. Translated as "cypress" in NRSV and "juniper" in TNIV.

40. Brueggemann, *Isaiah 40–66*, 162.

41. See Goldingay, *The Message of Isaiah 40–55*, 557, on links drawn by early Jewish commentary between "the blossoming of the land" and "the community's spiritual transformation."

Palestinian community, this is leveraged to point towards a life that transcends the limitations of their Persian context. The "heritage" (54:17) of the people is one of joy and possibility, and it is a heritage that looks back across the experience of exile and forward into the rebuilt future.[42]

To return to the links made earlier between the Isaianic experience and that of the Western church, our heritage too is potentially formed by the active word of God into one of joy and possibility. It is one that looks back to a lost influence, but forward to renewed possibilities in a context in which imperial privilege may no longer be assumed. And it does so from the *turangawaewae* of being the covenant people of God.[43]

But, in either the ancient or the present-day context, it is important to remember that the transformation effected by the word of God is forged in the repentance and forgiveness of the people (vv. 6–9). The conundrum for the re-established province of Yehud was that the answer to hostile imperial context and lost empire has its roots in the empire that failed the people in the first place. In order for that failure not to be replicated, in order for it truly to become "an everlasting sign" (v. 13), in order that it "not be cut off" (v. 13), the humanity of empire must somehow remain in constant contact with the active word of God.

This is the same challenge facing the institutional church in the West, where the thirst for influence crouches constantly at the door.

---

42. Childs, *Isaiah*, 413, considers that "54:17b serves as an organic link to the ensuing chapters of Third Isaiah."

43. This is a Maori term meaning roughly "place where one has rights of residence and belonging through kinship and *whakapapa* [lineage]." See http://www.maoridictionary.co.nz/index.cfm?dictionary.

9

Isaiah 56–66

An Isaianic and a Postcolonial Reading[1]

JOHN GOLDINGAY

What Are Effective Approaches
to the Interpretation of Isaiah 56–66?

I start from the dominant critical view that these chapters form a coherent and relatively self-contained unit within the book of Isaiah, a collection of prophecies from the Second Temple period. It is also a widely-held view that the chapters are arranged as a chiasm, a concentric structure, and this is one evidence of their being a distinguishable unit within the book. Admittedly, Old Testament scholars can find chiasms under every bush, but this example looks more secure than most and in broad terms is more widely recognized than most, though there are differing views about the details and about its significance. I outline the chapters as follows.

---

1. An address to the conference of the Australian and New Zealand Association of Theological Schools in Brisbane, July 4, 2012. The first half of the paper takes up issues I discuss at greater length in "About Third Isaiah. . .," 375–89, and in "Poetry and Theology in Isaiah 56–66," 15–31.

A. 56:1–8 Preface: the place of foreigners in the service of YHWH

B. 56:9—59:8 YHWH's challenges concerning the Jerusalem community's life

C. 59:9–15a Prayers for YHWH's forgiveness and restoration

D. 59:15b–21 Vision of YHWH acting in judgment

E. 60:1–22 Vision of Jerusalem restored

F. 61:1–9 The prophet's commission

E^1. 61:10—62:12 Vision of Jerusalem restored

D^1. 63:1–6 Vision of YHWH acting in judgment

C^1. 63:7—64:11 Prayers for YHWH's forgiveness and restoration

B^1. 65:1—66:17 YHWH's challenges concerning the Jerusalem community's life

A^1. 66:18–24 Postscript: the place of foreigners in the service of YHWH

At the center is the prophet's account of his commission; in a chiasm there is a logic about its being located here, whereas in a more linear structure an equivalent account of a commission might come at the beginning, as it does in Jeremiah and Ezekiel (and Isa 40, I think). Outside that center are visions of the restored Jerusalem that repeat in more glorious technicolor the kind of promises that appeared in Isa 40–55, with their concomitant promise of YHWH's acting in judgment on the people's oppressors. Outside these visions are prayers that essentially plead with YHWH to do what the visions portray. Outside these prayers is a double series of challenges and warnings about the community's life in both its societal and worship aspects. Finally, the outer frame comprises more materials that are more miscellaneous but have in common a concern with the place of people from other nations in relation to Judah.

I will first say something about two approaches to the interpretation of the chapters that have dominated scholarly work for the past generation, then talk about two other approaches that seem to me to be more effective in opening up the chapters' interpretation.

A Redaction-Historical Reading and a Sociological Reading

The first of the dominant approaches is a redaction-critical reading, which seeks to trace the process whereby the chapters developed and reached the form they now have. The idea of tracing this process promises much insight, but the problem is that analysts who attempt it come to quite different conclusions.

In a number of these studies of the chapters a motif recurs. One could almost call it a *Gattung* or form, as in form-criticism; specifically, it is a subset of a salvation oracle. The form has three elements. First, there is a lament, at the scholarly impasse over dating the chapters. Second, there is a prophetic claim, that the key to understanding has now been revealed. Third, there is an oracle, announcing the true answer about dating. The trouble is that when each new scholar announces his oracle (I think each time it has been "he"), it has not been received with faith by subsequent scholar-prophets. One of them will then declare that the impasse persists and will present his own suggestion regarding the way through it. The persistence of this pattern in the recent history of the chapters' interpretation makes it seem unlikely that redaction-critical study will ever generate an interpretation of the chapters as a whole that carries conviction.

One fact underlying the impasse is that Isa 56–66 differs from the other major sections of the book in not referring to any specific people or events. Its comments on political and social conditions and on the religious situation could fit many contexts. While for the most part we can surely read the chapters against the background of the Persian period, we cannot read them on the basis of relating them to particular periods within these parameters. When we seek to set them in a more precise historical context, we are working against the grain of the material, which declines to provide the information that would enable us to do what we want to do. We do not know when the prophecies were uttered. This conclusion is not a gloomy admission of defeat but an acknowledgment that opens up the possibility of focusing study on questions that we might be able to answer.

Redaction-critical approaches commonly read Isa 56–66 in light of conflicts within the Second Temple community, and analysis of these conflicts has been a second dominant approach in studying these chapters. It has been an aspect of a sociological turn in the study of the Second Temple period over the past forty years.

The books of Ezra and Nehemiah make clear that there certainly were such conflicts within the Second Temple community, and Isa 56–66 gives considerable space to confronting other groups within the community. The scholarly world has generated two main accounts of the conflict. Morton Smith speaks of the two groups as the "Yahweh-alone party" and the "syncretistic party,"[2] and his understanding seems to me likely to be on the right lines. But more scholarly interest has attached to the work of Paul D. Hanson, who sees the conflict as involving prophets over against priests and/or people with some in power who believe that God is active in the

---

2. See Morton Smith, *Palestinian Politics*.

present over against people outside the power structure who can only look for God's action in the future.[3] Part of the background to Hanson's work is the fact that we have little by way of hard data on the socioeconomic and political situation of Judah during the Persian period. A sociological approach to the material aims to offer aid in precisely a situation when we lack concrete historical evidence, by beginning from modern sociological theory and looking at the text in light of it. In principle, this strategy is unexceptionable, but in the case of Hanson's theory the method seems to impose an alien interpretation on the text, which does not give an impression of representing the views of one sizeable group within the community set over against another sizeable group. It rather gives the same impression as the one suggested by pre-exilic prophecy, where a prophet and a small group of supporters stand over against the community as a whole. The thesis that the conflict involved prophets over against priests and/or people who believe God is active in the present over against people who can only look for God's action in the future does not very well correspond to data within the chapters. It is an imposed understanding of the conflict. Thus Hanson's thesis has led to lively discussion, but that is all.

An Isaianic Reading: The Interrelationship between Two Forms of Faithfulness

I come, then, to two approaches that have more potential for the interpretation of Isa 56–66. One I might call an Isaianic reading. I shall focus on a theological question raised by such a reading, the interrelationship between two forms of faithfulness.

Scholarly study has come to a renewed awareness that Isa 56–66 needs to be understood in relation to the rest of the book of Isaiah, notwithstanding its own careful arrangement and its substantially self-contained nature. The formal nature of Isa 56–66 as part of a larger whole, not a work standing on its own, is complemented by the more substantial point that it often takes up motifs, issues, and phrases from Isa 1–55. While it also has significant links with other prophetic material, particularly in Jeremiah, the fact that Isa 56–66 appears in the same work as Isa 1–55 gives an extra level of significance to its links with those chapters. Part of the meaning of Isa 56–66 lies in the way it takes up, affirms, modifies, supplements, and ignores earlier material in the book, in bringing the book itself to a close.[4]

---

3. See Hanson, *The Dawn of Apocalyptic.*
4. See, e.g., Sommer, *A Prophet Reads Scripture.*

Rolf Rendtorff put us on the track of the way the first verse in Isa 56–66 encapsulates much of the theological thrust of the chapters as a whole, and reflects their relationship to what precedes.[5] In the NRSV it reads, "Maintain justice, and do what is right, for soon my salvation will come, and my deliverance be revealed." The problem with that translation is that the word for "what is right" and for "deliverance" is the same word, *tsedaqah*. The Common English Bible thus has, "Do what is righteous, and my righteousness will be revealed," bringing out the repetition of the word *tsedaqah*. But this word is a tricky one to translate (hence most versions do give it different translations in the two lines), and "righteousness" does not work well as a translation. The idea of *tsedaqah* is of doing what is right to someone in light of your mutual commitment. It is nearer "faithfulness" than "righteousness."

To complicate things further, the word "salvation" has distinctive theological freight for Christian readers, which makes it a misleading translation of the word *yeshu'ah*. And finally, the word the NRSV translates "justice," *mishpat*, is another for which we do not have an English equivalent, but it is more a power word than a value word like "justice." The KJV has "judgment," and judgment can be right or wrong—hence the need to qualify *mishpat* by *tsedaqah*. More broadly, *mishpat* suggests the exercise of authority, the taking of decisions. The hendiadys *mishpat utsedaqah* commonly appears in English translations as "justice and righteousness." It has been described as the Hebrew equivalent of our expression "social justice,"[6] though in English "social justice" is itself a hazy expression, one commonly used without much reflection on its meaning or on the relationship of this meaning to that of the Hebrew expression. The expression *mishpat utsedaqah* means something like the taking of decisions and the exercise of authority in a way that involves people doing right by one another and living in a way that does right by YHWH. Such, then, is the biblical understanding of social justice, if *mishpat utsedaqah* is the Hebrew equivalent to social justice.

So one might try to bring out the meaning of the two lines in 56:1 as follows:

> Guard the exercise of authority, do what is faithful,
> because my deliverance is near coming, my faithfulness [is near]
> revealing itself.

These two lines summarize much of the thrust of Isa 1–39 and 40–55 respectively, and also encapsulate much of the theological thrust of Isa 56–66 itself. Isaiah 1–39 challenged the community to take *mishpat* and *tsedaqah*

---

5. Rendtorff, "Jesaja 56," 181–89.
6. See Weinfeld, *Social Justice*, 25.

more seriously (e.g., 1:17; 5:7; 28:17). The recurrence of the challenge here indicates that the exhortation still needs making. It was not so historically located that it ceased to be significant for later generations. On the contrary, its appearing in Isa 1–39 in written form enables it to address subsequent generations of Israel. It makes it both possible and necessary for future generations to heed the exhortation. Indeed, the fact that the earlier community did not heed this message (and paid the penalty) places a more demanding obligation on later communities to do so.

The second line with its promise that YHWH's deliverance is near coming, his faithfulness near revealing itself, sums up much of the thrust of Isa 40–55, chapters that promised the community in the exilic period that God would do right by it and deliver it (e.g., 45:8; 46:12–13; 51:6, 8). These notions, too, have not lost their importance. While Isa 56–66 may be responding to disappointment with the incomplete fulfillment of the promises in Isa 40–55, they give no indication of doing so. This is not merely an argument from silence, because Isa 40–55 and Isa 56–66 are capable of expressing in no uncertain terms their disappointment with YHWH's action, but this opening line does not. The statement about God's deliverance and faithfulness simply affirms God's promise.

As is typical with prophetic promises (and warnings), the promises in Isa 40–55 have in fact received some measure of implementing, but nothing like as radical an implementation as one might have expected. While YHWH has seen to the conquest of Babylon by Cyrus and to Cyrus's encouraging Judahites to return to rebuild the temple, Judah now lives under the dominion of another imperial power and the city still stands in a devastated state. As there is no indication that the people addressed by the prophecies felt that the prophecy given in the exile had failed, so there is no indication that the critique of the community that will follow in chapters 56–59 explains this failure. But in the circumstances, alongside the importance of repeating the challenge to "guard authority, act in faithfulness" it is important to repeat the promises, as will indeed happen in glorious technicolor in subsequent chapters. The promises' partial fulfillment makes their reaffirmation both necessary and possible.

The collocation of the two lines thus summarizes what has preceded and what will follow, but it also exposes an irresolvable question about the interrelationship of the points they make. The ambiguity compares with that in the summaries of Jesus' preaching in Matt 4:17, "Repent, because the reign of heaven has come near," and in Mark 1:14, "God's reign has come near; repent and believe in the good news" (strikingly lacking the "because"). These provoke reflection on the same question.

Is it the case that people must pay attention to *mishpat* and *tsedaqah* because YHWH is about to act in *yeshu'ah* and *tsedaqah*? In other words, will a life of *mishpat* and *tsedaqah* be a response to a divine commitment to *yeshu'ah* and *tsedaqah*? Or is it the case that people must pay attention to *mishpat* and *tsedaqah* because only then will YHWH act in *yeshu'ah* and *tsedaqah*? In other words, will YHWH's *yeshu'ah* and *tsedaqah* be a response to a human commitment to *mishpat* and *tsedaqah*? The consequences that follow from accepting either answer to the question show how important the answer is and also why the question is irresolvable. The first answer is open to implying that YHWH is committed to acting in *yeshu'ah* and *tsedaqah* irrespective of the community's attitude, which stands in tension with the indications that problems with the community's attitude are the reason why it needs deliverance. The second answer is open to implying that the community's *mishpat* and *tsedaqah* is the decisive consideration in determining whether YHWH acts in *yeshu'ah* and *tsedaqah*, so that the relationship between the people and YHWH becomes a transactional or contractual one.

At first sight it might seem that interposing the conjunction "because" between the imperatives and the declarations resolves the tension between these two stances, but it does not do so. The new statement could mean "Observe *mishpat*, do *tsedaqah*, because such action is necessary if I am to fulfill my promise, so that my *yeshu'ah* is near to coming, my *tsedaqah* to revealing itself." Obedience to the command is a condition of the fulfillment of the promise. Or it could mean "Observe *mishpat*, do *tsedaqah*, because such action is the only appropriate response to the fact that my *yeshu'ah* is near to coming, my *tsedaqah* to revealing itself." If we have to choose, then in light of broader theological considerations concerning the nature of the relationship between God and his people, the second understanding is more plausible. But there is indeed some ambiguity about the relationship between the imperatives and the declarations.

The two lines in the opening verse in Isa 56–66 do set agenda for the chapters that follow, and those chapters spell out this question further without resolving it. The chapters challenge the Judahite community to live in light of YHWH's promises concerning its coming restoration, which issue from YHWH's doing right by the community. They also challenge this community to do right in the way people live with one another. The double use of the word *tsedaqah*, both a description of what YHWH will do in restoring the community and a word for the way the community is challenged to live, helps to make the point, and to suggest a link between the divine act and the human act. The opening verse and the succeeding chapters thus hold together in necessary fashion God's promise and the need for the people's response, and make a theological point whose significance is not confined to their context. Indeed, the opening verse makes no mention of the Judahite community itself and thus sets a pattern for Isa 56–66 in suggesting that its exhortation applies to the people of God in any context.

We have noted that the material in Isa 56–66 incorporates no concrete historical references or dates. What is the significance of its being placed after the material that contains these? Isaiah 1–39 embodies YHWH's reaction to the situation in Judah in the eighth century and announces the divine intention regarding it, while Isa 40–55 embodies YHWH's reaction to the situation among Judahites in Jerusalem and/or Babylon in the mid-sixth century. (I do not imply that all the material comes from these two contexts, simply that these are the only contexts they refer to.) Located between the historical contexts to which these two blocks of material refer, the fall of Jerusalem and the exile to Babylon constitute both the solution to the problem set up by Isa 1–39 and the problem for which Isa 40–55 offers the solution. With Isa 55 the chapters thus come to a happy ending. The book could stop there. There is no need for anything else. Yet apparently there is. Historically we can properly interpret that need in light of Judah's experience in the Persian period and see Isa 56–66 as speaking to that context. But the chapters' lack of concrete reference raises the question whether there is more going on here. The chapters make a general point about the nature of YHWH's involvement in the world, about the nature of YHWH's people, and about the relationship between these two.

The chiastic arrangement of the chapters coheres with this notion and points to an understanding of the theological issues they raise. By its nature, a concentric structure has a different dynamic from a linear one like that of Isa 40–55. A concentric structure looks as if it is going somewhere but turns out to be doing something more ambiguous. Its second half may take the argument forward, as the second of two cola in a poetic line characteristically goes beyond the first in some way. There will thus be a little linearity about the structure; it is more like a spiral than a circle. But formally, Isa 56–66 ends up coming back to where it started. Like chapter 55, chapters 60–62 could seem the proper ending to the book of Isaiah; they resume and summarize the book's most central theme, Jerusalem and its destiny, and bring to a resolution problems and issues regarding the city's place among the nations of the world that occupy a central place in the book from the beginning. But the fact that the book of Isaiah does not end here, but continues as it does, constitutes a telling indication of the thesis that emerges from the book, and in particular from Isa 56–66. As Isa 1–55 and then the opening verse of the last eleven chapters announce, the book as a whole and these closing chapters expound two chief convictions, that Jerusalem needs to face YHWH's challenges about its life and that YHWH is committed to its glorious restoration. But the last eleven chapters, like their opening verse, do not establish the relationship between these two convictions. They simply juxtapose them. They do suggest that it is an oversimplification to say that the vital thing is for Jerusalem to clean up its act, and that its restoration will then follow. But they also suggest that neither is it the case that YHWH's act of restoration will take place irrespective of Jerusalem's stance in relation to YHWH.

As the genius of Isa 40–55 is to expound theological issues by means of a linear argument, the genius of Isa 56–66 is to expound theological issues by means of this chiasm. These strategies are contextual and not interchangeable. The thrust of Isa 40–55 could not be expressed as a chiasm, whereas the thrust of Isa 56–66 could not be expressed by a linear sequence. It expounds the irresolvable tensions between challenge, prayer, and promise, between an interest in the nations that focuses on their blessing and one that focuses on Israel's blessing, and between judgment and restoration. Such significance in a chiasm emerges when one contrasts it with a text open to deconstruction. There are texts that emphasize either divine action or human action, and it is not then surprising if readers can see the other emphasis lurking somewhere beneath the surface of the text. Indeed, this is so in Isa 40–55. The genius of a chiasm (or the cowardice of a chiasm) is to avoid deconstruction by being upfront with the two assertions that stand in tension with each other. While Isa 40–55 is amenable to deconstruction without overtly inviting it, Isa 56–66 wears its deconstruction on its sleeve.

The way Isa 56–66 unfolds thus underlines the ambiguity of its opening rather than resolving it. Chapters 56–59 are dominated by critique of the community and by the laying down of expectations, closing with a prayer that constitutes an acknowledgment to YHWH that this critique is fair. The expectations relate both to religious life and to ethical life. You could say that they are the outworking of what it means to observe *mishpat* and do *tsedaqah*. The central chapters of Isaiah 56–66 then constitute promises that YHWH intends to take action against his enemies, who are also Jerusalem's enemies, and to restore Jerusalem and make it the world's focus. When we reach the end of the central chapters, we might conclude that the ambiguity about the relationship of the imperatives and the declarations is solved. First put your life right; then the promises will be fulfilled. But it transpires that they are not the end of the book or of the section begun at 56:1, because there follows a further prayer that acknowledges the critique's fairness (though it goes on to ask YHWH to have mercy) and then two final chapters dominated by further critique of the community and by the laying down of expectations. Thus chapters 63–66 as a whole balance chapters 56–59, and dissolve any sense that the ambiguity of the opening verse has been resolved. The first and last major parts of Isa 56–66 stand in irresolvable tension with the central part. The first and last parts correspond to the thrust of Isa 1–39; the central part corresponds to the thrust of Isa 40–55. Isaiah 56–66 articulates the inherent tension between Isa 1–39 and Isa 40–55; it does not resolve it.

The chiastic structure of Isa 56–66 thereby makes a theological point. The material's omission to resolve the tension at issue is not a failure but a recognition of a question that cannot be resolved. It is not possible to say that Jerusalem's deliverance is conditional on its obedience or that YHWH is unconditionally committed to its deliverance. The legal or contractual framework for understanding the relationship does not work.

A more illuminating model for understanding the relationship implied by the book of Isaiah is that of marriage, at least as it is often understood in the West. When two people commit themselves to each other in marriage, their commitment presupposes that it is mutual. Yet we would not say either "I commit myself to you without knowing whether you are committing yourself to me" or "I commit myself to you on condition that you commit yourself to me," and if the couple think in terms of conditional commitment, they need to postpone the wedding to give them time to talk things through with a therapist. Rather the relationship is covenantal, and both parties make a commitment that presupposes the commitment of the other without being exactly dependent on it. The mutuality of commitment is a kind of logical necessity or a definitional necessity rather than a legal necessity. Such is also the nature of the relationship between YHWH and Israel (and between God and his church).

A Postcolonial Reading: God and Empire

My other way into a more effective reading of Isa 56–66 is postcolonial. I apologize for taking up this fashionable approach, which will be old hat in a decade or two like the hermeneutical fashions of the 1970s or 1980s, but like them may retain some significance even when it has ceased to be a scholarly fad.

An illuminating study of the book of Nahum, written (significantly) in South Africa, characterized that book as resistance literature, which as such compares with anti-apartheid literature.[7] Nahum invites people in Judah to believe that the Assyrian empire will fall. In the years after Assyria has done so, reading Nahum would invite subsequent generations to believe that the

7. See Wessels, "Nahum," 615–28.

same truth applies to Babylon, the empire of its own day, and Isa 40–55 picks up Nahum's promises in declaring that Babylon is indeed about to fall (see, e.g., Isa 40:9–11; 52:1, 7–10). The form of the prophecies in Nahum, with the paucity of their specific references to Nineveh or Assyria (modern translations are inclined to add to the allusions to Nineveh and Assyria to make their original reference more explicit), encourages this process of re-application. The paucity of specific references to Babylon in Isa 40–55 has the same effect on its reading. The entire absence of specific references in Isa 56–66 makes the point even more strongly. A pattern in YHWH's dealings with the world keeps asserting itself in these prophecies.

Western scholarship has regarded Nahum as unpleasantly national-istic, and one can see the ideological reasons why it has done so. Nahum's declarations about the empire's fate constitute a threat to the imperial pow-ers to which scholars in Britain and the United States belong. The same dynamics appear in scholarly study of Isa 56–66. Scholars like the "univer-salism" of passages such as chapter 56 with its reference to the temple as a place of prayer for all nations, but dislike the "nationalism" of passages such as chapter 60 with its picture of the nations bowing down to Jerusalem. They especially dislike the bloodthirsty nature of the visions of judgment in chapters 59 and 63.

In broad terms, one could describe Judah as a colonial entity for its entire life. It was always under some form of control by a bigger power. But in the Persian period it was more like a colony in a stricter sense. While it did not have a community of people from the imperial center living in its midst, it was a subordinate part of an empire that projected itself as benign and benevolent and allowed Judah to have some control of internal affairs, but Judah did not have its own king and it lived under the oversight of a governor responsible to the imperial administration, to which it paid taxes.

Like the rest of Isaiah, and like Nahum and other prophetic books, Isa 56–66 does not urge Judah to rebel against the superpower. One could call it quietist in stance. Further, whereas Isa 13 has spoken of the Medes bringing destruction upon Babylon, when Isa 56–66 speaks of the destruction of "the nations"—a term that commonly denotes the superpower of the day (e.g., 5:26; 8:9; 14:26; 17:12–13)[8]—it attributes the destruction to direct action by YHWH. YHWH is, indeed, aggrieved that there is no would-be next super-power itching to take Persia's place, which he can use as he used Assyria, Bab-ylon, and Persia itself (see 59:15b–19; 63:1–6). Whereas a prophet in the 540s had Cyrus to envisage as the means whereby YHWH's will could be fulfilled, and YHWH could work by means of him, there is no such power emerging

---

8. See Goldingay, *Israel's Faith*, 761.

in the period to which Isa 56–66 belongs. One should hardly see this prophet as inferior to his predecessor in this connection;[9] if there is no Cyrus to hand, this fact is God's responsibility, not that of God's representative. (For all the references to YHWH's raising up Assyria, Babylon, and Persia, their emergence is entirely explicable in historical terms; no supernatural intervention was involved. YHWH usually works via historical processes.)

YHWH promises a restoring of Jerusalem that will come about by YHWH's action. Like Nahum, Isa 56–66 aims at a process of conscientization, consciousness-raising, whereby the subordinate power can cut the imperial power down in its thinking, pending the day when YHWH cuts it down politically. One could say that all Isa 56–66 does is encourage hope and encourage prayer, but these are frightening actions. It would be easy for Judah to believe that YHWH had forgotten it and was not after all the kind of faithful God who puts things right in the world. Isaiah 56–66 declares that YHWH is that God. Unlike Nahum, it does not see Judah's imperial overlord as a great oppressor. Perhaps it recognizes the ambiguity of this overlord, in keeping with the overlord's shrewd policy. According to Ezra-Nehemiah, people in Judah did complain about the crippling tax burdens imposed by the imperial authorities, but it was those same imperial authorities that facilitated the return of Judahites to Jerusalem, the rebuilding of the temple, and the missions of Ezra and Nehemiah; they also supported Judah's independence over against surrounding provinces of the Persian Empire. The imperial policies of divide and rule and of playing both good cop and bad cop worked well.

The vision of the empire's future in Isa 56–66 thus has a different profile from that in Isa 1–55 or other prophets. In Isa 56–66 "The empire writes back," though not so much "with a vengeance" (the title of a famous article by Salman Rushdie in the London *Times*, July 3, 1982), as it does in Nahum. But like Nahum, Isa 56–66 does not write back "to the center" (as an adapted version of the phrase goes on), like an author such as Rushdie writing for British consumption. It writes for its own community. The chapters presuppose the classic colonial experiences of powerlessness and exaction of resources, and promise their community that these will not last forever. In doing so, the chapters decline to use the empire's language. As far as Persia is concerned, the province centering on Jerusalem is called Yehud, the name that appears in Hebrew on coins from the period[10] as well as in the Aramaic of Daniel and Ezra, and also in Western scholarly study[11] (which ironically

---

9. As Hanson implies: see, e.g., *The Dawn of Apocalyptic*, 1–31.

10. See, e.g., Carter, *The Emergence of Yehud*, 142, 268–69.

11. See, e.g., Edelman and Ben Zvi, eds., *The Production of Prophecy*; Cataldo, *A Theocratic Yehud?*

often shares criticism's instinct to "master" and "imperialize" rather than respecting otherness[12] even when it is being postcolonial). Isaiah 56–66 refers once to Judah, eleven times to Jerusalem, never to Yehud. The chapters hold onto the Judahites' own way of looking at Judah and Jerusalem.

The central chapters of Isa 56–66, especially chapter 60, illustrate how poetic form contributes to encouragement and consciousness-raising. Powerful poetry can emerge from a subject society, as happens in Nahum. The imagery and hyperbole of Isa 56–66 in describing Jerusalem's transformation and the reversal of positions between its people and its overlords creates before people's imagination a different world from the one people currently experience, and promises that this world will become a reality.

As well as containing no encouragement to rebellion, the chapters contain no exhortation to bring about the transformation of Jerusalem; they thus differ from Haggai and Nehemiah. They simply promise that what must have seemed impossible will become actual. Reliefs in the palace that Darius I began to build at his new capital, Persepolis, in the last decades of the sixth century portray peoples bringing tribute to the king, as Judah did.[13] The prophet declares that Persia is going to pay tribute to YHWH in Jerusalem. It is an aspect of the great reversal whereby the superpower and its kings turn from contempt to obeisance.

Isaiah 56–66 recognizes the tensions in perspective between different groups within the colonial entity.[14] In the twenty-first century world, people from former colonies all over the world (including many of their most able people) migrate to North America and Europe[15] and leave their home countries lacking the resources that could have contributed to their development. In addition, many of these postcolonial countries are riven by strife, partly issuing from divisions that go back to the work of the imperial powers that created artificial nations out of diverse groups. Isaiah 56–66 recognizes parallel realities. Many Judahites had not seized the opportunity to return to this backwater of the empire. Isaiah 60–62 promises that they will do so. Judah is riven by strife between people with different religious commitments; Isa 56–59 and 65–66 promises not that they will come to live in peace and tolerance but that this situation will not continue. The people it sees as compromised in their Yahwism will disappear; Judah will become a proper YHWH-worshiping community. This religious perspective links

---

12. Cf. Thiselton, *Thiselton on Hermeneutics*, e.g., 8.

13. See Strawn, "'A World under Control,'" 85–116.

14. These tensions are a focus of Lee's consideration of Isa 56–66 in his paper "Returning to China," 156–73.

15. And Australasia, I hypothesized in the oral version of this paper.

with another aspect of the vision of a restored Jerusalem. Resources come to the city not simply to beautify it as a city but to resource the worship of its temple, the worship of the true God.

Christian lectionaries set the beginning of Isa 60 for Epiphany and thus link the chapter with the story of eastern sages bringing Jesus gold, incense, and myrrh (Matt 2:1–12). Cyril of Alexandria waxes lyrical on the way "it is as though the promise that Israel will be saved had already been fulfilled" and adds that the prophet "all but says that Christ, who was long ago predicted by the law and the holy prophets, was already present among them and now at the end of the age has shone on all who dwell on earth."[16] While the recurrence of reference to gold and incense constitutes a verbal link between the two passages, there is insufficient correspondence between them for it to be possible to think of Isa 60 as a "prediction" of which the coming of the sages is the "fulfillment." The New Testament itself does not relate the prophecy and the event; it makes its link with Mic 5.

The subsequent explicit Christian juxtaposing of Isa 60 and Matt 2 does do justice to the nature of Isa 60 better than does a reading that envisages Isa 60 as essentially picturing the way a prophet expects political events to unfold at the end of the sixth century or in the fifth. For all the sense in which the chapters may be seen as resistance literature, they are poetic, lyrical, and hyperbolic in their language. Isaiah 60 is typical of Isa 56–66 in not relating its promises to specific political contexts or events. Like anything that anyone ever says or writes, it relates to a particular historical context in the sense that it emerges from such a context and reflects it. But both the attempt to see it as envisaging fulfillment in such a context and the understanding of it as a prediction of a particular event six centuries later miss the significance of its poetic nature.

In Isa 61, the central chapter of the central complex of chapters in Isa 56–66, the prophet declares himself to be someone "anointed" by YHWH. It is an unexpected expression, because anointing is a rite applied to kings and priests as holders of an office. Being a prophet is not an office, and prophets are not anointed (YHWH's commission of Elijah to anoint Elisha tests but does not disprove the rule). The only anointed king in Isaiah is Cyrus, and the prophet's claiming an anointing may thus constitute a "strong rereading"[17] of the commendation of Cyrus in Isaiah 40–55. This prophet has a part to play in the fulfilling of the role that was once destined for the Persian deliverer who has become the Persian overlord. He claims a commission to bring good news to people who are afflicted, broken in

16. As translated in Wilken, *Isaiah Interpreted*, 462.

17. Bloom's term in *The Anxiety of Influence*.

spirit, captives, prisoners, and who mourn Zion; they will have reason for joy. The commission is ambiguous about whether they are the people who will do the building of Jerusalem of which it speaks. The prophecy earlier envisaged foreigners doing this work (60:10), and perhaps its point is simply that some people will. The significant point is that the work will be done. Once again there is a link with Cyrus, who was earlier the person destined to do the work (45:13).

In the decades and centuries that followed, the people of YHWH did not see these promises much more fulfilled than they had been through the work of Cyrus, which was one reason why it was possible for Jesus to take up chapter 61, a favorite passage in his day. Pre-critical Christian commentaries naturally assume that Isa 61 is a prophecy of the Messiah; indeed, Jürgen Moltmann declares that here "Trito Isaiah, finally, sees the coming messiah as quintessential bearer of the Spirit."[18] Jesus indeed tells the people in the Nazareth synagogue that "today this scripture is fulfilled in your ears." But his statement is more suggestive and allusive than is often assumed. "Fulfilled" is *plēroō*, which is not a kind of technical term like the English word "fulfill" but the ordinary Greek word for "fill." While "filling" a passage of scripture might mean fulfilling it, it might also imply something like filling it out. The use of *plēroō* need not imply that the passage in question was a prediction or promise with a one-to-one relationship to a subsequent event. Indeed, what Jesus is doing with Isa 61 is something not unlike what Isa 61 was doing with passages from Isa 40–55. He is using scriptural material to interpret his own significance and to make a claim for that significance, at least as much as using his own significance to interpret Isa 61.

Jesus' ministry did not result in the fulfillment of these promises in Isa 60–62, and liberty of the kind that the prophet envisaged has no more been enjoyed by the church than it has been enjoyed by Israel. On the other hand, it is not the case that nothing of this kind took place in Second Temple Judaism and then during Jesus' ministry and in the life of the church. Here again we see the pattern whereby the proclamations of prophets do not find complete fulfillment but do find some fulfillment. Like other prophecies, Isa 61 represents a re-expression of God's ultimate purpose for Israel and for the world, for which the Judahites of the prophet's day could expect to see some fulfillment (as they did), but of which they might not be surprised to find they did not see the complete fulfillment.

Reading Isa 56–66 in light of Jesus thus illumines some aspects of the chapters, but encourages us to ignore many aspects of its inherent theological significance. A postcolonial reading brings out theological significance

---

18. *Der Geist des Lebens*, 66–67; ET *The Spirit of Life*, 53.

in the chapters that we might otherwise not note. It suggests insight on the relationship of colonial peoples to the imperial center and adds to the considerable material in the Old Testament that offers illumination on God's attitude to superpowers, a question that could have been of crucial importance to peoples such as Britain and the United States, but that Christian interpretation has grievously missed.

10

Imperial Imagination in Isaiah 56–66

MARK G. BRETT

UNLIKE THE VISIONARY EXHORTATIONS of Isa 40–55, which draw the eye of the audience to a glorious future, the conflict that surfaces within the final eleven chapters of the book of Isaiah seem to belong to a different world. Accordingly, as John Goldingay suggests, Isa 40–55 can be read as proposing a linear vision that contrasts strongly with the complex chiastic arrangement of textual elements in Isa 56–66. Chapter 55 might have offered an ideal ending to the Isaiah tradition, but the concentric structure that begins in chapter 56 eventually loops back, step by step, to where it started.[1] In addressing the literary complexity of the final eleven chapters I will argue, firstly, that there is nevertheless a significant continuity of imperial social imagination that imbues all of Isa 40–66, and secondly, that exegetes need to explore in greater depth the complex mix of mimicry and resistance within Third Isaiah. The Achaemenids sponsored the resettlement of Yehud, and a measure of collaboration with Persian administration was apparently necessary, but the Judean literature of the province exhibits its own imperial imagination.

Already in the visions of Second Isaiah we find the themes that are characteristic of imperial ideology: on the one hand, there is a universal offer of salvation in 45:20–25, and many nations are brought under YHWH's justice and torah (42:4; 51:4–6). On the other hand, some of the nations come to Israel in chains (45:14) and foreign kings lick the dust of Israel's feet (49:23). The submission of the nations therefore comes either by way of violence or by way of assimilation, dual options commonly provided by

---

1. Goldingay, "About Third Isaiah," 383–85.

imperial rule. Oppressors may either be bathed in blood (49:26) or join peacefully in the project of restoring Zion (49:22–23).

Harry Orlinsky argued long ago that we should see in Second Isaiah not universalism but a "nationalist-universalist" vision,[2] which we might otherwise term imperialism. Some scholars have not hesitated to use this term, for example in relation to Isa 2:2–4, where the nations stream up to Jerusalem in an eager quest for justice and reconciliation.[3] Participation in an imperial civilization can often be presented as an opportunity for liberation and justice, but opposition to this vision of life can at the same time be dealt with harshly. Accordingly, it appears that the justice presented in Second Isaiah implies a universal rule "which will mean salvation for Israel but submission for the other nations."[4]

Some of the tensions within Isa 40–55 are reiterated in chapters 56–66: the relatively irenic picture of the restored Jerusalem in Isa 60–62 stands in the center of the chiasm of chapters 56–66, with the options for violent judgment standing either side in 59:15b–21 and 63:1–6. With imperial expansiveness, the submission of foreign kings described in 49:23 is taken up again in chapter 60: "Nations shall come to your light, and kings to the brightness of your dawn," 60:3 suggests, and these foreigners bring both their labor and their wealth to contribute to the restored community (60:5, 9–12). In the central vision of Isa 61, a clear hierarchy is then established in this ideal society, which sets the holy people who are given sacred labor (cf. 62:12) over those who are given profane labor:

> 5 Strangers (*zarim*) shall stand and feed your flocks,
> foreigners (*bene nekar*) shall till your land and dress your vines;
> 6 but you shall be called priests of YHWH,
> you shall be named ministers (*mesharete*) of our God;
> you shall enjoy the wealth of the nations,
> and in their riches you shall glory. (61:5–6)

This stratification is somewhat deconstructed, however, in the "bookends" of 56:1–8 and 66:18–24, where even foreigners might enter the cultic service of YHWH. This can be illustrated by means of some minor adjustments to Goldingay's analysis in the previous chapter of the chiastic structure of Third Isaiah:[5]

2. Orlinsky, "Nationalism-Universalism and Internationalism in Ancient Israel," 206–36.

3. Roberts, "The End of War in the Zion Tradition," 119–28; cf. Fischer, "World Peace and Holy War," 151–65.

4. Whybray, *Isaiah 40–66*, 72.

5. To be clear, many of the chiasms proposed in biblical studies should probably

56:1–8 *Foreigners in sacred service*
 56:9—59:8 YHWH's challenges concerning the Jerusalem community's life
  59:9–15a Prayers for YHWH's forgiveness and restoration
  59:15b–21 Vision of YHWH acting in judgment
   60:1—61:4 Vision of Jerusalem restored
    61:5–6 *Foreigners in secular service*
   61:7—62:12 Vision of Jerusalem restored
  63:1–6 Vision of YHWH acting in judgment
  63:7—64:11 Prayers for YHWH's forgiveness and restoration
 65:1—66:17 YHWH's challenges concerning the Jerusalem community's life
66:18–24 *Foreigners in sacred service*

If the foreigners invited to enter the cult come from nations other than
Israel, then this is indeed a surprisingly extreme form of assimilation, which is
not explicitly contemplated in the hierarchical social vision in chapters 60–62.

Another familiar "colonial" theme appears in Isa 61:1–4, where it is
proclaimed that liberated captives, and those who mourn in Zion, will rebuild and "renew the ruined cities, the desolations of many generations"
(v. 4). This seems to imply that the land may lack political sovereignty and
therefore be available to the colonial imagination,[6] as perhaps already suggested by the reference to desolate towns in Second Isaiah:

> Enlarge the site of your tent,
> and let the curtains of your habitations be stretched out;
> do not hold back; lengthen your cords
> and strengthen your stakes.
> For you will spread out to the right and to the left,
> and your seed will possess the nations
> and will settle the desolate towns. (54:2–3)

Yet if the land is desolate, we may question where the foreign labor comes
from, e.g., in 60:10 and 61:5. Is there perhaps a joint enterprise of rebuilding
envisaged, which is to be led by *golah* returnees ("children of the exile") who
deem the Judeans who never went into exile to be foreigners and therefore

---

be regarded as heuristic fictions, which bring selected textual elements into focus. My
italics here do not imply that Goldingay has missed something crucial. Isaiah 56:6
interestingly deconstructs the hierarchy in 61:5–6 by proposing that some foreigners
(*bene nekar*) will "minister" to YHWH, using the same root *shrt* as in 61:6. Note that
if the "bookends" in 56:1–8 and 66:18–24 were the final additions to Third Isaiah, as
Claus Westermann suggested, then this chiasm is not likely to have been evident at
earlier stages of the book's development. Westermann, *Isaiah 40–66*, 307. Cf. Tiemeyer,
Priestly Rites and Prophetic Rage, 274–86.

 6. See the useful overview of the literature in Kessler, "Images of Exile," 309–51.

not central to the vision of restoration?[7] If this is the case, then some of the "foreigners" who are eventually invited to join the cult in 56:1–8 and 66:18–24 are likely to have been descendants of Jacob-Israel (which may also help to explain why cultic participation is not explicitly made conditional upon circumcision in 56:1–8, as it is in Exod 12:43–49, since they would already be circumcised).

Laying Claim to Abraham

Indications of intra-Israelite conflict between *golah* and remainee groups are evident in the occasional references to Abraham both in Isaiah and in Ezekiel. In Isa 63:16, the complaint that "Abraham does not know us" raises a difficult question about how to understand the social dynamics of this conflict. In the case of Ezek 33:24, it is clear that the remainee community lays claim to Abraham: "Mortal, the inhabitants of these waste places in the land of Israel keep saying, 'Abraham was only one person (*'ekhad*), yet he possessed the land; but we are many; the land is surely given us to possess'" (cf. Ezek 11:15). But the prophet goes on to condemn this logic in no uncertain terms, proclaiming yet more devastation. One line of interpretation suggests that Abraham is presumed by the remainees in Ezek 33:24 to be an indigenous figure, and that their claim on him would be undermined if Abraham were originally an immigrant from Mesopotamia.[8] But this argument seems to underestimate the significance of Abraham being rendered as only "one" person, a description that relates more directly to a lonely immigrant experience than to an autochthonous figure who would necessarily possess numerous kinship alliances. Ezek 33:24 makes clear that Abraham has been claimed by the remainees, whether or not he was earlier seen as an immigrant figure.

The case of Isa 51:1–3 is even more ambiguous. Here, Zion is urged to take courage from the story of Abraham—"the rock from which you were hewn"—who, although he was only "one" (again *'ekhad*), was blessed by YHWH with fecundity. If "Zion" refers here to a small and struggling community in Jerusalem who never went into exile, then these verses would be adopting a view of the remainees that is much more positive than the one in

---

7. For this interpretation of "foreigners" in the Persian period see especially Japhet, "People and Land in the Restoration Period," 112–16, reprinted in Japhet, *From the Rivers of Babylon*, 96–116; Eskenazi and Judd, "Marriage to a Stranger in Ezra 9–10," 266–85; Southwood, *Ethnicity and the Mixed Marriage Crisis in Ezra 9–10*, 191–211; "Hybridity and Return Migration."

8. Römer, "Abraham Traditions in the Hebrew Bible," 163, 178.

Ezekiel 33. Alternatively, Zion in Isa 51:1–3 might refer to the small, struggling *golah* community who returned to Judah after the rise of the Persian empire. Whichever view is adopted, it is evident that Abraham has been framed by an exilic identity already in Isa 41:

> But you, Israel, my servant,
> Jacob, whom I have chosen,
> the seed of Abraham, my friend;
> you whom I took from the ends of the earth,
> and called from its farthest corners,
> saying to you, "You are my servant,
> I have chosen you and not cast you off." (41:8–9)

Although the dating of the relevant texts is problematic, the complaint in Isa 63:16 raises the question whether the *golah* community has claimed Abraham *exclusively* for themselves and denied kinship connections with the remainees who give voice to this complaint. The verse is framed by the larger prayer in 63:7—64:11, which evidently comes from Yahwists who feel rejected both by God and by their wider community:

> For you are our father,
> though Abraham does not know us
> and Israel does not acknowledge us. (63:16)

If this text is read through the lens of the later exclusivist perspectives in Ezra 9 and Neh 9, then we might find already here in 63:16 some evidence that Abraham has indeed been claimed exclusively by the *golah* community, and consequently, the identity of Israel has been narrowed to "the children of the exile" (cf. Neh 9:7, which identifies Abraham as an immigrant from Ur of Chaldeans). The voice that speaks in Isa 63:7—64:11 responds to being disowned, having experienced the withholding of divine compassion (63:15 and 64:11), yet still laying claim to YHWH as father (63:16 and 64:7).

Clearly, there was more than one way to interpret the Abraham tradition. On the one hand, the seed of Abraham could be seen as holy in a narrowly ethnic sense, and this option was eventually taken up in the Ezra-Nehemiah traditions, ironically drawing in particular on Deuteronomy's national vision.[9] It has been suggested that because early post-exilic texts like Hag 2:4 and Zech 7:5 refer to "the people of the land" without any hint of Ezra's polemic against *'am ha'arets* we might infer that there was no such

---

9. See especially Japhet, "Periodization between History and Ideology II," 491–508; cf. Lipton, *Longing for Egypt*, 243: "Despite his obvious priestly associations, Ezra's model, both for marriage and for land, is rooted in the Deuteronomic worldview."

controversy in the early Persian period.[10] We might be tempted to conclude, perhaps, that a "holy seed" party had not yet risen to prominence. Yet Ezek 33:34 indicates that a polemic against remainees had begun already during the exile, so the neutral uses of the phrase 'am ha'arets in Hag 2:4 and Zech 7:5 reveal only that this was not yet a standard formula within the polemics that waxed and waned over time. And we can assume further that the issues at stake in these disputes would have been perceived differently by different groups, so a specialized terminology in Ezra need not be transferrable to other textual traditions. In particular, there are good reasons to think that Ezra's "holy seed" discourse should not be seen as part of priestly tradition. The phrase is not found there, and as we shall see, Abraham's "seed" was interpreted quite differently in P and in the subsequent revision of P undertaken by the Holiness School.

The Relationship between Isaiah 56–66 and the Holiness School (H)

For the purposes of the present discussion, it is not important to date the Holiness School tradition with any precision,[11] except to say that it is earlier than the current assemblage of Isa 56–66. The earliest edition of the Holiness Code in Lev 17–26 may well have been composed in the pre-exilic period, but even if it was edited during the Babylonian exile or Persian period, there is clear evidence that it was known to the authors of Isa 56–66, as we shall see. The extent of H editing outside of Leviticus is much disputed, although in one case that is important for our discussion below, there is substantial agreement that H can be identified in Exod 12:43–49, not least because the provision of "one law" for natives and immigrants in 12:49 corresponds to the wording of Lev 24:22.[12] Elsewhere, I have re-examined the case for seeing close affinities between Isa 61 and H's Jubilee legislation, and here we will expand on some of the implications of this argument within the larger context of Isa 56–66, considering also the resonances between Isa 56 and H's Sabbath law in Exod 31:13–14.[13]

10. Schramm, *The Opponents of Third Isaiah*, 63–64; cf. Fried, "The 'am ha'arets in Ezra 4.4."

11. The following discussion builds on the influential work of Knohl, *Sanctuary of Silence*.

12. See Nihan, *From Priestly Torah*, 566–67; Olyan, *Rites and Rank*, 69–70; Wöhrle, "The Integrative Function of the Law of Circumcision," 81–84.

13. Brett, "Unequal Terms." Cf. Himmelfarb, "A Kingdom of Priests."

The Priestly writers offered an "ecumenical" account of Abraham's genealogy even if, at the same time, they maintained narrowly defined strictures on cultic observance by Israelites. The promise of internationalism is embedded in the Priestly portrait of Abraham as the father of "many nations" (Gen 17:7) and Jacob as the father of an "assembly of nations" (*qehal goyim* in Gen 35:11; cf. Ps 47:9–10). Gen 12:2, on the other hand, speaks of a single "great nation," a phrase that is characteristic of Deuteronomy (4:6–7, 8, 38; 9:1; 11:23; 26:5). In contrast with Ezra-Nehemiah's Deuteronomic account of kinship, the Priestly picture of Abraham's seed has an imperial scope that is capable of absorbing more than one nation.[14] These differences between the national and "international" Abraham are quite clear, whether or not we can reconstruct a history of disagreements between the later exponents of the Deuteronomistic and Priestly traditions.

From the perspective of the Holiness School, the opportunity for non-Israelites to join the cult is clearly laid out in Exod 12:43–49, which provides that *gerim* may worship YHWH in the Passover celebrations on the condition that males are circumcised (their uncircumcised state providing in this case a clear indication of their foreignness). According to Exod 12:48–49, these *gerim* can become "like a native of the land" and a single legal system can be applied to native and the immigrant alike. Those who were originally not kin, who were not among the descendants of Abraham, could now be treated *as* kin when their males are circumcised.

As we have already seen, Isa 61:5–6 proposes poetically that the whole people can be considered "priests" and "ministers," a democratization of holiness that is characteristic of H rather than P; such an expansion of holiness is evident especially in Lev 19:2, which exhorts the whole assembly to be holy, not just the priests and sanctuary as in P. I want to explore further the deep agreements between Trito-Isaiah and the greater priestly tradition, acknowledging that the "bookends" of Isa 56:1–8 and 66:18–24 seem to exceed even the imagination of H's version of inclusive hierarchy. The imperial vision of Isa 56–66 overlaps considerably with what we find in P and H, but it seems to differ in at least two respects: first, the greater opportunities for assimilation into sacred service in Isa 66:18–24, and secondly, the prominence given to the idea of justice as something that reaches beyond even the divinely given statutory laws in the Holiness Code.

---

14. See further Brett, "Permutations of Sovereignty in the Priestly Tradition."

Colonial Vs. Nativist Imaginaries

Before we examine the significance of these differences, however, it will be necessary to distinguish my account of Isaiah's imperial social vision from Francesca Stavrakopoulou's recent argument that Isa 56:1–8 possesses a kind of "colonial" force. She suggests that the inclusion of foreigners in an immigrant community's claim to land can serve to dispossess existing claims to land, especially those claims that stem from genealogical connections with the ancestral dead. There is no difficulty with Stavrakopoulou's suggestion that the phrase "memorial and name" (*yad weshem*) in 56:5 is terminology derived from ancestral mortuary cults, and that this terminology plays a role in land claims.[15] In this respect, Isa 56:1–8 belongs to the discourse of land claims just as surely as 57:13 does: "But whoever seeks refuge in me shall inherit (*nchl*) the land, and possess (*yrsh*) my holy mountain" (cf. 49:8b).[16] Similarly, the preservation of a *shem* has a role in reference to land holdings in Num 26:53–62; 27:3–4 and Ruth 4:10, although in these cases without clear links to mortuary cults.[17] Having reviewed the diversity of land claim terminologies, Stavrakopoulou interprets Trito-Isaiah as presenting a colonial ideology that joins the *golah* community and selected foreigners in common cause against indigenous claims, including the claims of the indigenous dead.[18] Contrary to the customary reading of Isa 56:1–8 as an inclusive text, she suggests that "this portrayal of the reconstituting of the temple-city's community seems designed to exclude the living descendants of the local dead, the dead through whom claim to that place can no longer be made."[19]

---

15. Stavrakopoulou, *Land of Our Fathers*, 124, building on Loretz, "Stelen und Sohnespflichten Totenkult Kanaans und Israels," and van Winkle, "The Meaning of *yad wašem* in Isaiah LVI 5." Jacob Wright and Michael Chan have proposed a related thesis that Isa 56:3–5 addresses the situation of imperial eunuchs, assuring them of honor beyond death. In effect, the absolute devotion to empire which is symbolized by eunuch administrators is here transferred to YHWH's empire, and the temple supersedes the king's palace as the centre of sovereignty. Wright and Chan, "King and Eunuch."

16. Stavrakopoulou (*Land of Our Fathers*, 126) also finds a semantic link or wordplay between the "gathered ones" in Isa 57:13 and the gathered (*qbts*) in Isa 56:8, suggesting that the newly gathered from exile supplant the ancestral dead who are the focus of the polemic in 57:13. She points out that *qbts* and *'sph* belong to the same semantic field in Ezek 29:5. The theme of idolatry permeates Isa 57, and it is linked specifically to land holdings (*chlq*) in verse 6. See *Land of Our Fathers*, 116; cf. Blenkinsopp, *Isaiah 56–66*, 152–54, 158.

17. On the use of *shem* in Deuteronomic land claims, see Morrow, "'To Set the Name,'" and Richter, *The Deuteronomistic History and the Name Theology*.

18. See for example the references to "colonial" discourse in Stavrakopoulou, *Land of Our Fathers*, 17, 73, 140. Cf. Niehr, "The Changed Status of the Dead in Yehud."

19. Stavrakopoulou, *Land of Our Fathers*, 128.

This hypothesis reaches well beyond the evidence of non-Yahwist mortuary cults in Isa 57. Even in Neh 2:20, where foreigners are denied any legitimate rights in land, the claim is presented in nativist rather than colonial terms.

> The God of Heaven will give us success; we his servants shall arise and build; but you have no portion (*chlq*), or right (*tsdqh*), or memorial (*zkrwn*) in Jerusalem.[20]

This exclusivist declaration from Nehemiah is "nativist" in the sense that it lays claim to an authentic indigenous tradition, which excludes alternatives that are perceived to be syncretistic.[21] And this claim is asserted precisely through demonstrating proper connection with the dead, as revealed in Neh 2:5, where Nehemiah seeks permission from the Persian king to go "to the city in Judah where my fathers are buried." Nehemiah thereby claims that the dead are his own.[22]

Nativist Vs. Imperial Social Imagination

My proposal is that Trio-Isaiah opposes this nativist discourse both by defending the land rights of non-*golah* "foreigners" descended from Abraham and, in addition, by offering the possibility of cultic inclusion to uncircumcised foreigners who have no lineage connected to Abraham. In other words, all these people are to be "added" together (as the use of *'wd* in Isa 56:8 seems to imply). In the case of Isa 61:8–9, the inclusive vision is forged by means of vocabulary drawn from P's Abrahamic covenant in Gen 17:

> 8b I will cut an eternal covenant (*bryt 'wlm*) with them.
> 9 And their seed (*zr'*) will be known among the nations
> and their descendants amidst the peoples;

20. Translation from Stavrakopoulou, *Land of Our Fathers*, 127. A comparison between Neh 2, 5 and 13 would suggest that the Judean nobility have brokered alliances with the nobility surrounding Yehud. Accordingly, Nehemiah's exclusivism seems to have an egalitarian impulse, as suggested by Eskenazi, "The Missions of Ezra and Nehemiah."

21. Brett, *Decolonizing God*, 112–31, esp. 129–31. To clarify my earlier arguments, I would certainly agree that Ezra-Nehemiah's nativism is more ambivalent about Persian imperialism than is characteristic of modern nativist nationalisms, where the debts to imperial models are more systematically obscured by anti-colonial discourse. But the *appearance* of deference to empire is not always evidence of actual deference; sly civility may simply be one among many complex strategies for survival. Cf. Smith-Christopher, *A Biblical Theology of Exile*, 38–49.

22. Kessler also acknowledges this point, but he deflects it as a minor qualification to his theory that the Golah returnees can be compared with the modern colonial "Charter Group." See Kessler, "Persia's Loyal Yahwists."

All who see them will know them,
that they are the seed whom YHWH has blessed.

The discourse of the "eternal" covenants belongs especially to priestly tradition, both P and H (reinterpreting the Davidic covenant?).[23] As we have already noted, the Abrahamic seed are dispersed among the nations in P, notably in Gen 17:7 and 35:11, rather than gathered within a single nation. So when these descendents gather in the restored Jerusalem, they bring together the many branches of Abrahamic genealogy,[24] and in line with the teaching of the Holiness School, this assembly might also include even those who were formerly uncircumcised.

Isaiah 56:1–8, however, refers not to circumcision but to Sabbath observance, using specific terminology derived from H's conception of the Sabbath covenant in Exod 31:13–14.[25] The verbal correspondences are quite clear when the texts are set out in parallel:

You yourself are to speak to the Israelites: "You shall observe my Sabbaths, (*et-shbbtty tshmrw*) for this is a sign between me and you throughout your generations, given in order that you may know that I, YHWH, sanctify you. You shall observe the Sabbath, because it is holy for you; everyone who profanes it shall be put to death; whoever does any work on it shall be cut off (*krt*) from among his people." (Exod 31:13–14)

56:4 For thus says YHWH:
To the eunuchs who observe my Sabbaths (*ywhmrw et-shbbtwty*),
who choose the things that please me
and hold fast my covenant,
5 I shall give them, in my house and within my walls,
a memorial and a name
better than sons and daughters;

23. Olyan, for example, sees the *berit 'olam* in Gen 17:13b as H (Olyan, *Rites and Rank*, 154–55, n23). Similarly, Wöhrle sees the phrase *berit 'olam* in both the P and H layers of Gen 17, in Wöhrle, "The Integrative Function of the Law of Circumcision," 71–87.

24. Brett, "Unequal Terms," outlines this argument in relation to Isa 61, but cf. also Römer's suggestion that Isa 51 seems designed to "overcome the conflict between the inhabitants of the land and the exiles" in that verse 3 comforts Zion and verse 11 the exiles. Römer, "Abraham Traditions," 167.

25. Olyan divides Exod 31:12–17 into two layers, assigning verses 12–15 to H and verses 16–17 to P, in Olyan, "Exodus 31:12–17." This division is disputed by Nihan, *From Priestly Torah*, 568, who reaffirms the position that all of 31:12–17 is H. The clause "be cut off (*krt*) from among his people" corresponds closely to Lev 17:10; 18:29; 19:8; 20:6; 23:29 in the Holiness Code. See also Milgrom, *Leviticus 1–16*, 457–60. On the sanctification of the people in the Holiness Code, see especially Lev 20:8; 21:8, 13, 15; 22:9, 16, 32.

I shall give them an everlasting name
which will not be cut off (*l' ykrt*).
6 And the foreigners who join themselves to YHWH,
to minister to him, to love the name of YHWH,
and to be his servants,
all who observe the Sabbath, and do not profane it,
and hold fast my covenant,
7 these I will bring to my holy mountain,
and make them joyful in my house of prayer;
their burnt-offerings and their sacrifices
will be accepted on my altar;
for my house shall be called a house of prayer for all peoples
(*'mym*).

Adding weight to this linking of Isa 56 with the Holiness School's discourse is the observation that the distinctive phrase "observe my Sabbaths" found in Exod 31:13 and Isa 56:4 reappears in Lev 19:3, 30 and 26:2, within the Holiness Code itself.[26] The plural "Sabbaths" likely refers not just to the weekly observance but to the Sabbath year and the "Sabbath of Sabbath years" in the Jubilee.

The proclamation of a "release" (*deror* in Isa 61:1) in the early Persian period has been seen by some scholars as an attempt to legitimate the claims of returnees over against those who had remained in the land during the Babylonian exile.[27] This hypothesis might be seen as another version of nativism in that it envisages the restoration of ancestral land. However, if the *deror* of 61:1 is in fact an allusion to the *deror* of the Holiness Code's Jubilee legislation,[28] then it would be necessary to consider the wider framework of H's ethics which clearly allow for the integration of foreigners in the cult (notably in Exod 12:43–49), and even for the

26. Cf. Levenson, "The Temple and the World," 291–97; Schramm, *Opponents*, 121.

27. See the overview of recent discussions in Bergsma, "The Jubilee: A Post-exilic Priestly Attempt to Reclaim Lands?"; *The Jubilee*. It is notable that Neh 5 makes no attempt to relate debt problems to the Jubilee, although it might well be assuming the *shemittah* debt release of Deut 15 (as is Jer 34:12–20).

28. Collins denies that *deror* in Isa 61:1–3 is an allusion to the Jubilee of Lev 25, but he illustrates how later Jewish literature makes this connection. See Collins, "A Herald of Good Tidings." There are, however, a number of verbal correspondences with the Holiness Code, and Collins' skepticism on this point is not warranted. See the uses of *g'l* in 60:16 and 62:12 and *nqm* in Isa 59:17, 61:2 and 63:4 (*nqm* appears in Lev 26:25). While the reference to "favour" in 61:2 could well be alluding to Isa 49:8, *rtswn* is part of the Holiness Code's vocabulary in Lev 19:5; 22:19, 20, 21; 22:29; 23:11. It also appears in Isa 56:7.

legitimacy of some foreigners' land rights—at least to the extent that such foreigners can claim Abrahamic descent.[29]

Contrary to the view that divine justice in Isa 40–66 is entirely ethnocentric and "will mean salvation for Israel but submission for the other nations," the combination of Isa 56:1–8 and 61:1–11 may imply that divine justice can include both the redemption of families to their ancestral country *and* an invitation to the Gentiles to be part of this imperial order. Isaiah 56:1–8 exhibits a bolder universalism than what we find in priestly traditions, or in Isa 60–62, but even the boldest inclusivism in Trito-Isaiah is not entirely incompatible with the hierarchical inclusivism found in priestly material. On the issue of intermarriage, the Holiness Code's prohibition in Lev 21:14 binds only the high priest, and in relation to priests more generally, Lev 21:7 does not mention any *ethnic* criteria constraining marriage. Gen 17:12 affirms that males within the household who are "not of your seed (*zr'*)" may be circumcised as a sign of Abraham's eternal covenant (*bryt 'wlm*), and interestingly, this implies that the foreign slaves (Lev 25:44–45) could potentially join the worshipping assembly.[30]

The possession of land seems to be envisaged as a benefit for all of Abraham's descendants in P, regardless of whether they belong to the elect or to the non-elect.[31] This may also be inferred from the reference to Esau's "holding" (*'chzh*) in Gen 36:43.[32] In agreement with Isa 56:3–4, non-Israelites must actively be "joined" to YHWH, to "keep Sabbaths," if they are to be part of the worshipping assembly (*qhl*). But whether they are joined in this cultic way or not, they may still enjoy the blessings that belong to Abraham's *goyim* (Gen 17:8) and to Jacob/Israel's assembly of *goyim* (Gen 35:11), including the possession of land. P's social imagination in this respect borrows the imperial logic that incorporates the nations, while relinquishing Deuteronomy's emphasis on national sovereignty. In substantial agreement with Isa 40–66, the priestly tradition envisages an Abrahamic

29. The details of this argument are provided in Brett, "Natives and Immigrants."

30. See further Levinson, "The Manumission of Hermeneutics." Given the circumcision provision for foreign slaves, it is not quite accurate to describe these non-Israelites simply as an "out-group," as Levinson does on 314. Nevertheless, his suggestion that the holding of foreign slaves would have been a "utopian" legal fiction in the Persian period, bearing no relation to social reality, is instructive. It might also apply, *mutatis mutandis*, to Trito-Isaiah's utopian visions of foreign labor enriching Jerusalem, which inverts much of Israelite experience.

31. Cf. de Pury, "Abraham," 172–75, who draws attention to the land promise in Gen. 17:8; "Der priesterschriftliche Umgang," 52–54.

32. See Köckert, "Das Land in der priesterlichen Komposition," 155; Nihan, *From Priestly Torah*, 68.

"counter-empire," whose land is owned by God alone and leased with conditions to each generation who keeps the law of the land.

A further implication of this "inclusivist" reading of priestly tradition has been drawn out by Jakob Wöhrle, who takes up the recent suggestions that P has deliberately reshaped Abraham as the ideal *golah* immigrant, even beginning his journey from the anachronistically named "Ur of Chaldeans," i.e., from an area where Judean exiles themselves resided from the days of the Chaldean empire. The ideal ancestor arrives to find that the promised land is inhabited, and according to priestly tradition, these "people of the land" are to be respected (cf. Gen 23:7). "The land is given to the ancestors not instead of the people of the land, but in *addition* to these people."[33] As in the case of Isa 56, Wöhrle's reading of P proposes that the various groups can be reconciled rather than opposed to each other.

Indeed, H's notion that natives and immigrants (*gerim*) should be governed by "one law," and that theologically speaking all Israelites are *gerim* (Lev 25:23), seems to have been applied even to the equalizing of legislation relating to the possession of the promised land. According to the Holiness Code, all occupants of Canaan, past and present, are bound by essentially the same ethical code when it comes to land allocations, and breaches of this code will have the consequence that the land "vomit" them out (Lev 18:26–28).[34] Instead of seeing the prior inhabitants of Canaan as uniformly devoted to destruction, as in Deuteronomic literature, here they are seen to have been driven out for specific acts of defilement. Whether committed by a native or an immigrant, cultic impurity is subject to a death penalty in Lev 20:2–5, but interestingly, it is precisely the "people of the land" (*'am ha'arets*) who are called on to execute judgment in this case.[35]

In short, the Holiness traditions provide both harsh judgments for cultic impurity and opportunities for including strangers in cultic activities. These twin options can also be found in Isa 56–66, along with very specific verbal correspondences with the Holiness Code. Both H and Isaiah avoid a binary opposition between a *golah* community and the "people of the land," providing instead a conception of holiness that is based on behavior rather than ethnicity.

Even the awkward reference to judgment in Isa 61:2 can be read as qualifying a narrowly ethnic interpretation of the prophet's declaration of liberty and restoration: "to proclaim the year of YHWH's favour and the day of vengeance (*nqm*) of our God" might be taken, ostensibly, as a word

---

33. Wöhrle, "The Un-Empty Land," 204; *Fremdlinge im eigenen Land,* 215–22.

34. See Schwartz, "Reexamining the Fate of the 'Canaanites' in the Torah Traditions."

35. See further Brett, "Natives and Immigrants."

of judgment against foreign nations. But if we can detect here an allusion to the *nqm* of Lev 26:25, then Isa 61 is re-asserting a key claim in the Holiness Code that the divine landowner will exercise sovereignty in relation to land justice, whether in restoration or in judgment against Israel. This claim to sovereignty, which can cut both ways, arguably takes up a similar issue from the earlier Isaiah tradition where, for example, Isa 5:1–10 condemns Judeans themselves for the misappropriation of land.

The declaration of *deror* in Isa 61:1, which releases people from debts and restores traditional land, is exclusively the preserve of monarchs in the ancient Near East,[36] so the ambiguity about who exactly it is that makes this declaration in Isa 61:1–9 is interesting. We might have expected that Cyrus, having been designated the "anointed one" in Isa 44:28—45:1 would again be the one anointed to proclaim the release in Isa 61:1. Yet it is only YHWH who ultimately has the power to declare liberty in Isa 61, as in Lev 25, so the authority of Cyrus is thereby put into perspective (cf. Isa 41:21; 43:15; 44:6 where YHWH is clearly identified as Israel's "king"). Whatever the ambiguities of the poetry in Isa 61:1–3, the underlying claim of YHWH's divine sovereignty is absolutely clear: contrary to imagination of the Achaemenid administration, it is YHWH's empire that has jurisdiction in Yehud.

So instead of seeing prophetic and priestly groups pitted against each other in Isa 56–66, it is more plausible to see a range of prophetic and priestly groups each expressing in their own ways the sovereignty of YHWH over against the pretentions of Persian power. Ironically, the articulation of this resistance has actually mimicked imperial symbolism, a mimetic dynamic that is commonly found both in modern colonial history as well as in the ancient unfolding of biblical theology in the tides of successive empires.[37]

Where the Holiness School and Isa 56–66 finally part company is perhaps in the details of their vocabulary relating to justice. The common parallelism of *mishpat* and *tsedaqah* in the prophetic tradition ("justice" and "righteousness" in most English translations) is not to be found in priestly literature. In the Holiness Code, for example, the *mishpat* is overwhelmingly a "statute" or "regulation" standing in parallel with *chuqah* (e.g., Lev 18:4, 5, 26; 19:37; 20:22; 25:18; 26:15, 43, 46). Similarly, the requirement that there be "one law" (*mishpat*) covering both native and immigrant in Lev 24:22 (cf. Exod 12:49 and Num 15:15–16, 29) is best understood as a single regime of statutes. Only in Lev 19:15 and 35 does *mishpat* carry the connotation of

36. Weinfeld, *Social Justice*. The Hebrew terminology corresponds to the Akkadian *andurarum*, meaning literally "return to the mother." Weinfeld, *Social Justice*, 79; cf. Bergsma, *The Jubilee*, 20–26.

37. See, e.g., Strawn, "A World under Control"; Sparks, "*Enuma Elish* and Priestly Mimesis"; Brett, "Genocide in Deuteronomy"; Morrow, "To Set the Name."

"judgement," since in both these cases the possibility of rendering an *unfair* judgment (*mishpat*) is acknowledged.

The case of Lev 19:15 comes closest to the prophetic parallelism of "justice and righteousness":

> You shall not render an unfair judgment (*mishpat*); do not favor the poor or show deference to the rich. With righteousness (*tsedeq*), you will judge your kin.

This example intersects with the many others in non-priestly tradition where *mishpat* exceeds merely statutory law to include the just rulings of a monarch or a judge. And among those just rulings would be included a king's declaration of the *deror* when he first ascends the throne. In the ancient Near Eastern examples, this redemptive initiative of the king is seen as an exception to the quotidian patterns of debt and alienation from traditional land. In Isa 61 this sense of a gracious sovereign prerogative returns.

In conclusion, we have seen how Isa 56–66 envisages the imperial jurisdiction of YHWH, which implicitly contests the authority of other empires. The justice of this divine empire is inclusive only in the sense that it offers different options for assimilation to YHWH's rule. Isaiah 56–66 looks ultimately to divine initiative for the consummation of a just society, and within that society, a new form of hybrid social redemption is expected, deconstructing the opposition between natives and immigrants.[38]

---

38. Cf. the discussion in Mamdani, "Beyond Settler and Native as Political Identities."

1 1

Redeeming the Earth

Imagining the Folk Songs

Malcolm Mac MacDonald

Israel has experienced not only the despair that follows a crushing defeat, but also the hopelessness of exile, and now they've got the post-exilic blues. The truth is hard to bear; foreign gods are far more powerful than YHWH. There is much fear, grave doubt, and it's hard, too hard to be bothered about anything. What can be done, and if there is something, who can do it?

This is the moment of a particular calling, a time for those who explore the realm of the emotions, the sensitive ones, those who see the spirit of the people and feel their collective despair. These are the days of the poet and the bard, those who make the implicit explicit through the arts of poetry, lyric, melody, and rhythm, and there's a lot of this going on. The pastoral responsibility to help the people process the exile has fallen to them unofficially and by default. But they have not yet found the key to unlock the stronghold that continues to imprison the hearts of the people.[1]

Benji's quietly twiddling on an old beat up lute that could do with some new strings. He's thinking about the song Granddad wrote back there in Babylon—the one about YHWH allowing Jacob to be gathered up as booty and Israel to be plundered (42:24). "Why couldn't Granddad be like everyone else and accept that YHWH was humiliated by Marduk?[2] Why

---

1. For Quinn-Miscall, "Israel is in despair and doubts the Lord's ability to save them." (*Reading Isaiah*, 35). Brueggemann believes that what is required is a kind of therapy, a process therapy to help people re-enter exile, to be in exile and to depart out of exile (*Hopeful Imagination*, 1).

2. According to Heaton, Israel "thought they had been defeated by the more powerful gods of Babylon" ("Isaiah 40–55," 53).

did he have to try to justify the unjustifiable? And why did Granddad say it was all because of sin (22:14)? Everyone knows sacrifices take care of that."

"Hang on though, didn't Joey say just yesterday, that at the beginning of all of this, Isaiah of Jerusalem condemned offerings and sacrifices as meaningless" (1:13)?

"Crikey," said Benji to no one in particular, "what if the old crooner was right?"

"Ya reckon?" came the counter argument. "He could only be right if YHWH was the God of everywhere, not just Israel, but he isn't." Right there and then, it was as if someone had lit a candle in his head, at last, a tiny light amid the darkness. "What if he was? What if YHWH was the God of everywhere? What if it wasn't Marduk who killed Tiamat like the Babylonians said, what if it was YHWH? What if it was YHWH who separated the land from the watery chaos and brought order to the world? Maybe it was him who made the beginning—whatever that was."[3] His imagination popped out a picture of Granddad having a bit of a chuckle at his thoughts and giving him a wink. "Well, if you're right old fella, it has to mean that YHWH is the boss and he can do what he wants." At that point he sensed Granddad give him the "thumbs up." His shoulders did a wee dance as he laughed in response. "I tell ya what young son," he said to himself, "that means when YHWH does want to fix us up, he'll do it. And what's more, nothing can stop him 'cause he's actually running the whole damn show!"

A surge of faith welled up causing him to stand. He turned towards the empire and its seat of power in the north-east, and gave it the appropriate internationally recognized gesture with the index finger of his left hand.[4] Then he sat down again and spent some time mulling over the ins and outs of his moment of inspiration. Gradually he figured out how he might make something of it.

He experimented on his lute until he worked out a pattern and picked up a feel. Then he started writing his song. It took him a couple of days and when he got it as right as he was ever going to, he went round to Dizzy Izzie's where every Thursday Deb and Dave ran what amounted to an open mike night, and there he sang it. You could have heard a pin drop. The gist of it

---

3. Throughout most of this essay I promote the view that creation was generally thought of as order being applied to chaos. Obviously for there to be a necessity for such action, somehow chaos came into being in the first place and we see this hinted at in Gen 1:1. Therefore with George Landes, I believe that there were some of Israel who took a both/and approach. YHWH created, and he brought order to his creation. So there is an aspect of creation, as Landes puts it, that was "not a liberating act, it was wholly creative" ("Creation and Liberation," 138).

4. See chapter 47 on Babylon's humiliation for the canonical version.

went something like this: On the one hand they may still be in subjection to imperial forces, but indeed, so also is the seat of the empire itself subject to forces greater than itself—YHWH himself! What YHWH has started, he will finish. What he has created, he will redeem. And, he will redeem not to the old, but to a whole new creation with Jerusalem, not merely as Israel's centre, but as the glorious heart of the entire earth. Their suffering has been a price worth paying for the glory that is to come. It was YHWH, you see, who defeated chaos in the first place.[5] He is its master and has of late been using it as Israel's teacher, first through Babylon and then Persia, to prepare the way for a new era of unsurpassed greatness for Israel. Israel is still YHWH's darling, but YHWH is not only the God of Israel, he is in fact, the one sovereign Lord over the whole world! Benji "nails" it. The response is deafening. For the first time in living memory the village goes into unrestrained party mode.

The following week a couple of poets presented similar material. The week after that it was clear that nearly everyone had "jumped onto the chariot." Benji had started something. While not entirely new, for creative folk the change in perspective was tremendously attractive.[6] In the end, partly because they were so catchy, and more importantly because they were "so powerful, so unsettling, and so buoyant,"[7] the songs and poems began to catch on among the populace at large. The capacity and boldness of the material to speak about the great loss enabled the people "to face the nullification wrought by God"[8] on the one hand, and brought a glimpse of hope through the vision of a new world on the other. Though times remained tough, even survival was a challenge for some, it had just got a little bit easier. The songs and chants about YHWH the Creator-Redeemer now told of his universal sovereignty. Thus, for the first time they could begin to make

---

5. McCarthy believes that notions of the beginning of creation in the Hebrew sense were not so much a concern for the origin of the world. "All the interest is directed toward good ordering. . . . The longing for order in human and natural affairs is characteristic of the laments of the ancient world, including Israel, and the praise of it (order) rings out in the Psalter (e.g., Ps 8: 10)" ("Creation Motifs," 84). However, Ps 104 hints at creation and ordering as separate events. If we are willing to note a parallel between "ordering" and "redemption," and remain open to the idea of the presence in biblical thought of initial creation, though maybe not as an emphasis, then the idea of a linking creation and redemption has potential. The imperial context is providing opportunity for the Isaianic poets to think about this as we shall shortly see.

6. Brueggemann suggests that the new approach was first of all only discernable to those who possessed enormous prophetic imagination (*Hopeful Imagination*, 2).

7. Ibid.

8. Ibid.

sense of the imperial situation.[9] It gave them hope. In fact, they began to believe they were more special than ever. This engendered faith, and faith began to redeem them, for redemption meant healing from a broken heart.

This hope is locked in as wordsmith after wordsmith adds yet another hue to the grand vision of a remnant of Israel fully redeemed, on centre stage in a new creation, to whom the rest of the world come to experience redemption as well.[10] The poets and bards did a fine job. Faith welled up in the hearts of at least a remnant of the remnant.

⁓⚬⁓

Our short story could be described as an imaginative possibility, illustrative of the folk origins of the creation and redemption songs and poems found in Isaiah, predominantly but not only, in chapters 40–55. My point is that once the creation-redemption-new creation concept got its first clumsy public airing, because of the power of its therapeutic effect, it more than likely opened the gates of the imagination for all manner of creative folk, releasing a flood of material which tumbled out in response to a variety of contexts within the exilic and post exilic situations before any formally worked theological framework was established. Part of the therapy would have involved processing the decay portion of the concept, situated between creation and redemption (decay is obviously prerequisite for redemption). However, it is not a matter of focus in this essay and as a notation is generally absent in what is often referred to as the "creation-redemption-new creation continuum." Nevertheless, it has an assumed presence.

Brueggemann sheds light on the canonical purpose for the inclusion of some of the best of these songs and poems in the book of Isaiah:

> The disordered mass of material has been subject to a long editorial process which eventuated in the canonical shape of the material as we have it. That editorial process has served to order and thematize the material. While the intentionality of the order is not always clear to us, we can identify the thematization which is behind the editorial process. The literature as it has now been

---

9. Or as Brueggemann puts it: "New poetic imagination evoked new realities in the community" (ibid.).

10. Schmid reminds us that it has long been realized that there is a close relation between views of creation and consummation. This expected salvation corresponds to what the entire ancient Near East considered to be an orderly world ("Creation, Righteousness and Salvation," 110). In the Isaianic context, I would suggest that universalized new creation is what emerged from the consummation of creation and redemption. After all, universalized new creation can only be the result of universal redemption. This will become clear as we proceed.

> shaped is intended to help the community of faith make two
> crucial and difficult moves, relinquishment and receiving.[11]

For example, 587 B.C.E. is "the end of the known world and its relinquishment."[12] The challenge is to let it go. The new world is an imperial one which they did not believe possible, and have not chosen. So 587 is also the beginning of "the reception of a new world given by God through these poets."[13] The challenge is to accept it. Critical to this is the development of theology that has enough of the old to give it legitimacy, while at the same time providing sufficient newness to allow the national culture (from the Yahwistic perspective) to flourish rather than founder in the new international environment which now dominates.

What I want to attempt in this essay is to describe how the separate concepts of creation and redemption may have been deliberately combined to contribute to a new constellation: creation-redemption-new creation. This became necessary in order to rescue the local national deity, YHWH, from the threat of extinction (the result of his apparent defeat at the hands of other more powerful gods). By recreating him as a universally sovereign deity while still maintaining Israel's relative particularity, a radically nuanced faith specific to the demands of the imperial context then became possible.

I will be referring to all those who in any way are responsible for the book of Isaiah as we now have it, as "the poet."

The poet reminds Israel that YHWH formed them as a community to worship him (43:21). But times have changed and the old notions of worship require modernizing. The poet's rationale works along the lines that now YHWH is creating something new.

> Do not remember the former things,
> Or consider the things of old.
> I am about to do a new thing;
> Now it springs forth, do you not perceive it?
> I will make a way in the wilderness
> And rivers in the desert (43:18–19).[14]

Watts believes reference to the "new thing" (43:19) concerns the real goal of YHWH's use of Persian political and military power.[15] The emphasis on "a

---

11. Brueggemann, *Hopeful Imagination*, 3.

12. Ibid., 4.

13. Ibid., 4.

14. Quotations from the Bible are from the NIV in this essay, unless otherwise noted.

15. Watts, *Isaiah 34–66*, 676–77. Goldingay and Payne's thinking is along similar lines (*Isaiah 40–55*, 298).

way in the wilderness" and "rivers in a wasteland" is in deliberate contrast to the predictions of wasteland (5:5–19; 6:11) and exile (5:13; 6:12) according to Watts, which had become reality for Israel.[16] However, even though wilderness and desert continue to exist, there is a way through and the joy of life will return once more to sustain them. On what basis is the poet able to say this? On the basis that YHWH the Creator of Israel (43:15) formed her for the task of serving him (43:10) by "declaring his praise" (43:21). Therefore he has a vested interest in their redemption. This will come about in a way never seen before because they are in a situation they have never been in before. However, the people need to be brought into a state of mind and heart that enables them to receive this. So a convincing case has to be built in order to make this happen. This occurs in the following fashion.

First, YHWH's incomparability is argued solely on the basis that he alone is the creator. He alone formed the cosmos, and he alone maintains order in the cosmos:

> To whom will you compare me,
> Or who is my equal? says the Holy One.
> Lift up your eyes on high and see:
> Who created these?
> He who brings out their host and numbers them,
> Calling them all by name;
> Because he is great in strength,
> Mighty in power,
> Not one is missing (40:25–26).

What is striking in this passage, is that although there is no reference to the exodus tradition (also 42:5–9, 12–13, 18; 48:12–13), and YHWH's uniqueness is explained only on the basis of his cosmic creation, the passage is not about creation *per se*. Israel's understanding is that YHWH can't see their plight, or that he may have overlooked them because of more pressing commitments (40:27–28). Gerhard von Rad believes that here the poet is struggling against unbelief.[17] Therefore to engender confidence in YHWH's might, he points to the creation of the world as the foundation for belief. At no point does creation in the whole of Deutero-Isaiah appear as a subject in itself. Its function, von Rad says, is to support the message of redemption, "in that it stimulates faith."[18] Bernhard Anderson agrees. The poet promotes YHWH's power as creator to awaken a greatly disheartened Israel. The goal, he asserts, is to move the people to belief that they do have a future in God's

---

16. Watts, *Isaiah 34–66*, 676–77.

17. Von Rad, "Theological Problem," 56.

18. Ibid.

divine purpose.[19] So, although in this passage (40:25–26) there is not an explicit link between creation and redemption, it is certainly where the link has its beginning. How so? Because creation points to sovereignty, revelations of sovereignty inspire hope, and faith results in redemption.

Proceeding to the next stage in the argument however, the juxtaposition of creation and redemption in the opening words of some of the prophetic oracles is very explicit:

> But now thus says the Lord, who created you, O Jacob,
> He who formed you, O Israel;
> Do not fear, for I have redeemed you;
> I have called you by name and you are mine (43:1).

And

> Thus says YHWH, your Redeemer,
> Who formed you in the womb:
> I am YHWH who made all things,
> who alone stretched out the heavens,
> who by myself spread out the earth (44:24).

Because the poet is so intentional about putting the two concepts together, it would seem that the reader is meant to understand them as symbiotic contributions to one concept of broader width and greater depth than either is able to contribute in isolation. That is, no longer are we talking about creation and redemption as if one does not need the other, we are now talking creation-redemption in an intrinsically linked manner specifically relative to purpose. What YHWH has set in motion, he will redeem when necessary, in order for his creation to complete the task for which it was formed. It turns out that this duality has always been a key contributor to the relationship between Israel and YHWH since the relationship's inception.[20] This will become clearer still once the theology to inform the "new thing" is fully rolled out.

19. Anderson, "Introduction," 19–20.

20. Motyer provides some depth to my assertion. "The biblical use of 'create' points to such an act as must be ascribed to God, proceeding from his free determination that it should be so. In creation itself, the Lord originates, maintains, controls, directs (37:15); his relationship to his people is the same. 'Formed' is more intimate (Gen 2:7), indicating painstaking care whereby every circumstance of life is weighed and measured to give exactly the right pressure to the potter's hand so that the finished vessel will match his specifications. More intimate still is 'redeemed' (35:9; 41:14), the Lord's deliberate acceptance of all the rights of next of kin, making the needs of his helpless relative his own. Finally, in a crowning intimacy, there is naming; to call by name (40:26) is a direct personal relationship involving a specific plan and place for the one named" (*The Prophecy of Isaiah*, 330–31).

The momentum builds as YHWH's inaugurator of the "new thing," is named. This agent is not one of the elect in the traditional sense. In fact, he is not a part of Israel at all. This helps to explain, in part, why the universal idea of creation rather than the particular theology of Israel's election has to be linked to redemption, for it becomes necessary to develop a rationale from a perspective wider than traditional notions of election, if you want to number a foreign ruler among YHWH's servants:

> I am YHWH, who made all things,
> who alone stretched out the heavens,
> who by myself spread out the earth; . . .
> . . . who says to the deep, "Be dry . . ."
> . . . who says of Cyrus, "He is my shepherd,
> and he shall carry out all my purpose";
> and who says of Jerusalem, "It shall be rebuilt,"
> and of the temple, "Your foundation shall be laid (44:24, 28).

The linking of creation and redemption together, in so far as they contribute to a single symbiotic concept, is about to reach maturity in Deutero-Isaiah. "Yahweh the creator," says von Rad, "who raised up the world out of chaos, will not leave Jerusalem in chaos; he who dried up the elemental waters will also raise up Jerusalem anew."[21] However, this time he uses a human agent to achieve this, for it is the decree of Cyrus that begins to restore order to the chaos of captivity. In order to reinforce YHWH's sovereignty over the matter, that indeed Cyrus is merely acting as YHWH's servant, notice is given that YHWH is in fact, the God of order. How so? On the basis that he brought order to the chaos of original beginnings:

> For thus says the Lord,
> Who created the heavens
> (he is God!)
> Who formed the earth and made it
> (he established it;
> he did not create it a chaos,
> he formed it to be inhabited):
> I am YHWH and there is no other (45:18).

Then with an exceedingly deft stroke of genius, the poet brings Israel's election into the creation-redemption element of the emerging constellation to provide it with a recognizable and accepted theological underpinning. This locks what were two separate concepts together in such a way that

---

21. Von Rad, "The Theological Problem," 57.

it becomes impossible to pry them apart. We could say that complete union has been achieved and it occurred in the following manner:

> Awake, awake, put on strength,
> O arm of YHWH!
> Awake as in days of old,
> the generations of long ago!
> Was it not you who cut Rahab in pieces,
> Who pierced the dragon?
> Was it not you who dried up the sea,
> the waters of the great deep;
> who made the depths of the sea a way
> for the redeemed to cross over (51:9–10)?

The Babylonian creation myth is co-opted into the argument and this is made possible by a very simple cut and paste approach. Marduk is cut out and YHWH is pasted in, in Marduk's place.[22] The myth is then brought into direct contact with YHWH's miraculous act of deliverance of Israel that took place at the Red Sea in a way that renders the passage of time irrelevant. The two events are now entwined to become one in YHWH's battle with the primeval dragon. Von Rad interprets this as meaning that "the doctrine of creation has been fully absorbed into the complex of soteriological belief."[23] He closes his argument with 54:5: "Your Maker is your husband . . . the Holy One of Israel is your Redeemer," which he cites as "a particularly good example of this complete absorption of the doctrine of creation into the prophetic doctrine of salvation."[24] However, I do not believe this to be

22. See Dalley, *Myths from Mesopotamia*, 228–77. Furthermore, Gunkel suggests dependence by Gen 1 on the Babylonian account (*Israel and Babylon*, 43).

23. Von Rad, "The Theological Problem," 58.

24. Ibid. Stuhlmueller is of a similar ilk. Creation in Second Isaiah is "an aspect or characteristic subordinate to the work of redemption" (*Creative Redemption*, 1, 9). Eichrodt appears to support von Rad when he describes "the salvation . . . bestowed by God as superior to all the majesty of creation" based on 51:6–8 ("In the Beginning," 70). However, Westermann believes that creation has a universal dimension of its own which originated in early traditions handed down through the generations and which precede recognition of YHWH as savior. Therefore, creation is not a subset of redemption ("Das Reden," 238–44, cited by Marlow, *Biblical Prophets*, 117). Rendtorff goes even further by promoting creation as the key element in the faith matrix: "Faith in God the Creator was perceived and experienced as the all-embracing framework, as the fundamental, all underlying premise for any talk about God, the world, Israel, and the individual" (*Canon and Theology*, 107–8). In my opinion though, the poet is here utilizing a strategy to emphasize the critical benefit of linking creation and redemption together as a single event (or continuum). After all, you can't have salvation without creation having first taken place, and without redemption creation would cease to exist. Therefore it seems illogical to view one as more important than the other. Landes also believes they belong together.

the case. It seems to me that von Rad is over emphasizing redemption in the creation-redemption link. My suggestion is that the poet has taken a "both/and" approach in which creation and redemption are fused to form part of what becomes an uninterrupted continuum running from creation to redemption, and as we shall shortly see, to new creation. What gives the poet license to do this is the implied presence of the predestined election of Israel within the redemptive defeat of Rahab at creation which is illustrated by the Red Sea crossing.

Von Rad does not recognize this implied inclusion of election though. He believes election is not present at all in 51:9–10, and neither is it in Deutero-Isaiah overall, in stark contrast to the earlier prophets. However, he does wisely note that though Deutero-Isaiah is basing his argument on creation rather than election, there is no fundamental theological change for he does not actually dispense with the doctrine of election.[25] He is right to argue that the poet has not rejected election, but is remiss to suggest that it is not present at all, since without election there are no grounds for Israel's redemption. Therefore election, though not called upon explicitly, must be charging the atmosphere to enable the concepts of creation and redemption to be brought together in the first place. What has transpired is that a wider perspective than merely election became necessary to provide justification for the use of Cyrus as YHWH's servant on the one hand,[26] and the ongoing lack of national sovereignty on the other.

Brueggemann lends some support to this position. There are new actions of God taking place and these need explaining. But, they have to be explained from the old tradition in order to enjoy credibility. Therefore, the poet presents a new reading of the old tradition. This, in fact, has always been available, but is fully present only now because it could only come out of the new creativity a new situation demanded. The poet has probed and mined the tradition "in ways that articulate a newness."[27]

He lists many examples from Hebrew tradition where YHWH's acts of deliverance are depicted as utilizing the forces and elements of creation such as the plagues against the Egyptian oppressors, the parting of the Red Sea, the sending of the manna, quails and water, separating the waters of the Jordan, making the sun and moon stand still for Joshua. "Thus for Israel, Yahweh's creation power in history was the same as his liberation power, and they must be held together" ("Creation and Liberation," 137).

25. Von Rad, "The Theological Problem," 58.

26. Quinn-Miscall also senses an initial objection to notions that Cyrus might be acting as YHWH's agent (*Reading Isaiah*, 36). So although Cyrus is referred to as the Lord's shepherd (44:28), a term normally associated with a Davidic king, these descriptors are not compelling enough because Cyrus is clearly not of the Davidic line. Therefore, a step back has to be taken, to allow the broader perspective of creation to come into play.

27. Brueggemann, *Hopeful Imagination*, 2.

The new theological concept of creation-redemption as a continuous event not only makes it possible to embrace Cyrus as YHWH's servant and to begin to make sense of foreign rule without any threat to the notion of Israel's election, it also has a natural flow on effect; if YHWH is "Universal Creator" he must also be "Universal Redeemer":

> Turn to me and be saved,
> all the ends of the earth!
> For I am God, and there is no other (45:22).

In Isa 65:17–25, a vision is proffered of the new creation Israel is being redeemed to. With the addition of "new creation," the emerging idea now consists of a threefold symbiosis; creation-redemption-new creation as an integral continuum, is now complete. It was said earlier that the joining of creation and redemption in Isaiah was purpose driven. By the time one arrives at 66:22–23 this is supremely evident. Finally, the purpose for YHWH's creation and redemption of Israel is revealed. "All flesh" is gloriously redeemed into new heavens and a new earth, and at the epicenter is Jerusalem resplendent, the religious capital of the entire world where every nation comes to offer its praise to YHWH.

We are reminded at this point, of the assertion from von Rad, that the goal of all this was to provide a foundation for faith.[28] The recreation of YHWH will not bear fruit until both YHWH and his worshippers have been redeemed by the faith the new formulation is intended to foster. The new emphasis contains enough elements from the old, in particular the nation's ongoing state of election which maintains the very appealing intimate sense of being special, to give it continuity. This smoothes the way for Bruggemann's "relinquishment" and "receiving" suggestion. Relinquishment involves acceptance; accepting that the old concept of a national identity centered round a local national deity is no longer realistic. Receiving also involves acceptance; accepting the new concept of an international identity centered round an internationally sovereign deity who offers a glorious hope for the future. Once the new theology is first understood and then owned—as cognitive permission for faith— then YHWH is redeemed in the heart of the worshipper.

In short, one could say that creation asserts sovereignty, sovereignty gives hope, hope births faith, and out of faith comes redemption. Redemption here involves the rebuilding of the nation's identity around the now internationally sovereign YHWH and his cult—a far cry from early redemptive songs and poems.

28. Von Rad, "The Theological Problem," 56.

I have attempted to describe how Israel's theology may have evolved in order to meet the challenge of providing meaning for the new situation. That is, by way of a symbiotic reconstruction that integrated what were previously separate conceptual orders into a new constellation: the creation-redemption-new creation continuum. This not only had the potential to rescue YHWH from the scrap heap of defunct national deities by recreating him as the one and only internationally sovereign Lord, it also opened up space for what was possibly an entirely new development in Israel—the worship of YHWH alone.

⁓⌇⌇⁓

Kate is twiddling on her guitar, seeking solace in the harmony created by its resonations as she grieves over the future facing her sleeping little ones and their unborn children. The air is being poisoned, so is the soil and the sea. Should this continue, and she is unaware of any serious moves by the biggest polluters to bring it to a halt, the earth's naturally balanced systems may malfunction to such an extent that current rates of food production will be impossible to maintain, resulting in chronic shortages and widespread chaos.[29] She has read reports prepared by experts warning that there are roughly only fifty years left to turn things around.[30] If insufficient human involvement is brought to bear on salvific processes that reintroduce pure air, pristine water and naturally fruitful pastures, then the earth of the Cenozoic age will not be redeemed and the existence of many of the higher life forms, including humans, may gradually come to an ignominious end.[31]

---

29. Gottlieb speaks of the possibility of the earth becoming a "ruin." "The environmental crisis is a crisis of our entire civilization. It casts doubt on our political, economic, and technological systems, on theoretical science and Western philosophy, on how we consume or eat. Corporate greed, nationalistic aggression, obsessions with technological 'development,' philosophical attitudes privileging 'man's' reason above the natural world, addictive consumerism . . . all these collaborate in the emerging ruin of the earth" (*This Sacred Earth*, 8).

30. Professor Sir John Lawton, in 2005 at a presentation of the Millennium Ecosystem Assessment (MEA) described the report as "profoundly worrying" and announced that "we have about fifty years to change things." Transcribed verbatim from a speech at the MEA launch, Royal Society, London, March 31, 2005; quoted in Bookless, "A Famine of Hope," i.

31. This extinction spasm is likely to produce "the greatest single setback to life's abundance and diversity since the first flicker of life almost four billion years ago" (Myers, "The Biodiversity Crisis," 37–47). Leakey and Lewin argue that the scale of extinctions could be similar to the previous five mega events when at least 65 percent of marine species disappeared (Leakey and Lewin, *The Sixth Extinction*, 45). Even by 1996, some 20 percent of all vertebrate species were in danger of extinction. See Brown, Flavin, and Kane, *Vital Signs, 1998–99*, 128.

There is little comfort to be had in the version of the Christian tradition she has been brought up in. "What's the point of looking to the salvation of the earth as some sort of big dramatic event in the future that will happen who knows when?" she asks herself. "Who cares about new heavens, a new earth, and the perfection of everything later on? How can that help the kids, and their kids, and the world they'll be living in? The Earth needs saving now for goodness sake!"

"At least it can give them something to look forward to when everything else has turned to custard," came the internal reply. "Sure, but why settle for custard in the first place? What if the idea of fulfillment as the final destiny of history was the core of the problem? Could the notion of anything and everything eventually being sorted out by technological progress actually be fuelled by the ongoing lack of fulfillment of literal interpretations of the biblical big picture?"

In Kate's opinion, it has been the industrialization of technological processes by commercial interests in the name of progress that is primarily responsible for the degradation of the earth and its systems.[32] She sees this as a rampant kind of imperialism driven by multinational corporations. What makes it possible, and indeed for the most part acceptable, is belief in the efficacy of the myth of progress so widely held amongst the general population of the world.

Her meditation continued . . . "Is that where technology gets its grand sense of meaning—as the conduit through which new creation really does find form? Did this perception develop because hope in the literal return of Christ to usher in the new creation proved fruitless? Is that why the hope of salvation ended up in the myth of progress instead?"[33]

32. In terms of the technological contribution to this degradation, Berry believes this to have begun at the end of the nineteenth century when there was an abandonment of the human role "in an ever-renewing, organic, agricultural economy in favor of an industrial, extractive economy. This development decisively moved the scientific and technological might of the modern world into a merciless program of disruption of the organic function of the planet. . . . It became an object of *use*, of exploitation. Engineers took over—the mechanical, the electronic, the chemical, and now the genetic engineers. These persons flaunted their technical competence and asserted their intellectual arrogance in assuming the planet would be better off under their control than under the primordial control of those forces that first brought Earth into being and guided its development down through the ages" (*The Christian Future*, 63).

33. Berry offers the following thought: "The course of the human community seems to be determined by the more intense technological forces within the community. The causes of this go back to the millennial expectations of Western society that have been communicated to the human community on a wide scale . . . Since this new Earth has not come down to us from heaven, then we must bring this new age into being by violent efforts directed to seizing control of the deepest genetic as well as the most

"The irony is" she thought, with a touch of bitterness, "the biblical creation-redemption-new creation idea is essentially correct. What's wrong is its trajectory. Science confirms that life in the universe is expressed via creation and decay, redemption and new creation, but it is within a spiraling cycle going round and round on a journey towards increasing complexity, rather than journeying along a historical straight line, at the end of which is a perfect universe."

As she gazed out of her front window, not focusing on anything in particular, a flash of insight illuminated her consciousness and brought the church across the street into sharp relief in the same instant. "You people need to get real!" Without realizing it, she was actually speaking out loud, a well and truly riled up mother imaginatively protecting her children, waggling her finger at the absent parishioners of the somewhat dilapidated building. "Because you have not updated the Christian myth in a way that has the potential to nullify the progress myth, you guys are now helping to provide legitimacy for the ongoing rape of the planet, and may be numbered among the agents of destruction that are wreaking havoc on the wider Earth community!"

She paused in the delivery of her angry tirade to fit in a much needed breath. That briefest of moments was just enough time for the spirit of nurture to very gently conceive something new in Kate. But, right there and then, she was unaware of it, though it immediately softened her tone. Gradually, concern and kindness began to clothe her words in warmth and empathy. "Do you think it would be helpful to the world we live in today, if the Christian story was rewritten a bit, like the Jews did when their world fell apart, when they could no longer tell who they were or where they fitted in? Those desperate days necessitated desperate measures so they imported a creation story foreign to their own tradition into the theological mix. The broader perspective provided an opportunity to forge a new sense of identity relative to the new world that had enveloped them against their will. In fact, the new theology that emerged actually evoked so much meaning it eventually sprouted two more dynamic religions, Christianity and Islam."

"Do you think it might be time to import a new creation myth into the Christian tradition, one not limited to ancient theology but which makes use of scientific theories of beginnings and the developmental processes of biological evolution unknown in antiquity? Could, as in those days of old, the broader perspective produce sufficient nuance for Christianity to finally offer a positive, vibrant, sacramental contribution, rather than continuing

---

powerful physical forces within the phenomenal world. Here then is the dominant source of Western aggressiveness that is manifested . . . against the natural world itself in a technological conquest that will enable us to exploit the inner constitution of things in a tyrannical manner" (*The Sacred Universe*, 63–64).

to emphasize the same old covenantal one of a transcendent monarchical deity and a rebellious human race who can only get on together because of a gruesome human sacrifice that took place two thousand years ago?[34] Why can't you see how powerless the current formula is to meet the ecological challenge of an entire planet under grave threat in the twenty-first century?"

She imagined herself inside the church, pleading on behalf of wee ones yet to be born. "Surely it is obvious that the Earth is groaning with desire for spiritual change. Is it not time to abandon the destructive human/divine approach which at this time is contributing to the decay of the world? Is not the time ripe for embracing a compassionate eco/divine approach to worship in the hope that it may contribute to the redemption of all life on Earth, including humans? Science tells us that everything is made up of the same atomic material; the dust of exploded supernovae (apart from hydrogen and most helium), and all life forms are genetically linked—every form of life is cousin to every other life form.[35] Humans exist within this matrix, not outside it. What if the Universe Story and the Christian Story could become so intimately entwined that they produced a symbiosis of science and mythical meaning of sufficient magnitude to engender a new integral sense of belonging to the world, where it is recognized that nothing exists in isolation, but everything is intrinsically contributing to one gigantic unity. From the Christian perspective, this could be helped along by expanding the metaphor of "the body of Christ" from a referent to merely human Christian believers, to a descriptor of the entire universe. After all, does not scripture declare that in Christ all things hold together (Col 1:17b). So if everything is in one way or another contributing to the totality that is the body of the Cosmic Christ, then it follows that everything must be viewed as sacred and needs to be treated as such.[36] Do you think development down this track might transmit enough meaning to the twenty-first century context to produce genuine hope for the Earth going forward? If so, would not this provide the opportunity for a new kind of faith to find expression—the kind of faith that enables the relinquishment of an anthropocentric orientation to life and the reception of an ecocentric orientation instead? Surely this would be the right kind of faith for motivating the right kind of action before it is too late."

That brought her back, back to the guitar cradled in her arms. As she looked at it she realized that there were grounds for hope. That hope gave

34. Anecdotal evidence suggests that this view of the new covenant is often the result of hearing a literal, rather than mythical and/or metaphorical telling of the story.

35. See Dowd, *Thank God for Evolution*, 53. Also Christian, *Maps of Time*, 49–52, 92.

36. Berry argues that, by necessity, the Body of Christ must equate to the entire universe for redemption to be complete. Berry, *The Christian Future*, 11. McFague also recommends viewing the entire universe as the body of God (*The Body of God*).

her faith. She had a job to do, her little bit. She could feel new life stirring within, a song, and it needed her help to enter the world. So she worked out a pattern and picked up a feel. The Earth is in mourning; . . . her heart is broken; . . . she yearns for healing . . .

12

Responses

MARK G. BRETT AND JOHN GOLDINGAY

Negotiating the Tides of Empire

MARK G. BRETT

THIS VOLUME BEGINS WITH the insight that archaeologists can tell us a great deal about the historical events in Judah at the end of the eighth century, more indeed than what the Bible does. David Ussishkin unveils this history with more reserve than does the archaeologist William Dever, who suggests in his recent work *The Lives of Ordinary People* that the biblical writers from Jerusalem were "simply oblivious" to the suffering endured at this time in Lachish, barely forty miles distant from the capital of Judah. "Not only is this horrifyingly callous, but it disqualifies these writers as anything like reliable historians."[1] The parallel accounts in 2 Kgs 18–20 and Isa 36–39 mention Lachish in passing, but the Bible does not dwell on the slaughter of men, women, and children that took place there. The book of Isaiah is focused on Jerusalem. By contrast, back in Nineveh, Sennacherib devoted about 27 meters of his palace walls to carved depictions of his victory at Lachish. History, it is often said, is written by the winners, but there is also something very instructive about the contrast between victory written on Sennacherib's walls and defeat written on the scroll of Isaiah.

From the point of view of biblical writers, the loss of Lachish and other Judean towns served mainly to demonstrate the sovereignty of YHWH, who protected Jerusalem from destruction. Like Dever, many ethicists today

1. Dever, *The Lives of Ordinary People*, 367.

would question whether this divine pedagogy can be aligned with any modern principles of justice. Indeed, there was no biblical lament for Lachish, but neither do we find lament for the Phoenician and Philistine lives lost under the Assyrian tsunami as it rolled brutally southward in 701, relentlessly through towns and cities, regardless of their ethnicity. Isaiah presents no general defense of human rights, conceived in a worldview within which all humanity is born equal. On the contrary, as the book unfolds, the text embodies the conflict of Judean social groups as they struggle to discern what their God might be saying about their own responsibilities, the justice deserved by imperial invaders, and the scope of hospitality for strangers who might one day live peaceably as neighbors.

Yet perhaps more fundamental than these familiar themes, as Andrew Abernethy reminds us, is the struggle simply to eat. For Isaiah, the key questions turn more specifically on commensality: who does Israel eat with, who provides the food and drink, and what obligations arise from the repast? Abernethy's argument illuminates the broader covenantal dimensions of a social identity constituted by choices around eating. We know from Assyrian records and reliefs that the feasting that followed victory in war was a means to demonstrate the king's power. The choices proposed by the Rabshakeh in Isa 36:12–18, and in the parallel text in 2 Kgs 18:27–33, throw light on another dimension of economic ideology—the suggestion that everyone benefits from an imperial *pax*.

The Assyrian emissary conjures up the agrarian ideal within which each family owns their own vine, fig tree and cistern "until I come and take you away to a land *like* your own land." In this imperial imaginary, as has often been the case, one portion of land is indistinguishable in its value from any other, especially at the peripheries, as long as the economic outcomes benefit the center (cf. Isa 10:9 for Assyria's rhetorical questions: "Is not Calno like Carchemish? Is not Hamath like Arpad? Is not Samaria like Damascus?"). Isaiah and the Deuteronomists dissent from this vision: if the people choose to "make their blessing" with Assyria (Isa 36:16//2 Kgs 18:31), the outcome will be death, as Christopher Hays argues in his contribution to this volume.

Hays takes up earlier suggestions that postcolonial studies can illuminate the study of biblical literature, focusing in particular on the work of Frantz Fanon. The analogies are suggestive, although we should note that Fanon was more an anti-colonial writer than a postcolonial one; his binary distinction between colonizer and colonized is replaced in postcolonial theory by more complex accounts of resistance characterized by cultural hybridity. This theoretical shift might perhaps elicit the question whether the Deuteronomic literature is more hybrid in its borrowing of Assyrian genres (treaties and loyalties oaths) than what we find in Isaiah of Jerusalem. In some respects, Isaiah simply deflected the Assyrian "cultural bombs,"[2] and was never in this respect a colonized poet, although the presence of Persia later in the book presents a different, and more ambiguous, picture.

Jerusalem itself survived for around a century after the crisis of 701, but the encounter with brutal imperial economies left their mark in the re-shaping of Israel's hope. The scroll of Isaiah falls into a loud silence after the Babylonians eventually destroyed Jerusalem, with a painful historical gap between chapters 39 and 40. There may be hints of Zion's lamenting voice left here and there, Judith McKinlay suggests, and perhaps the "comfort" proclaimed in Isa 40 answers Zion's cry of "no comfort" in Lamentations. Or should we rather ask, with John Goldingay, whether by assuming "the right to declare God's response" in Isa 40, an exilic prophet is, in effect, lay-ing "claim to power in the future Jerusalem community"?[3] Lena-Sofia Tie-meyer's work, in this volume and elsewhere, presents yet a third possibility that the entire Isaiah tradition has been composed in Jerusalem, and that in Isa 40–55, the Judeans who never went into exile look forward to the return of her scattered children. This view is therefore opposed to the common suggestion that Isa 40–55 represents the social interests and perspectives of an exilic group of Yahwists. The antagonism expressed towards the cul-tic leadership in Isa 56–66 is just that, in Tiemeyer's view, an antagonism towards the leadership in Yehud, and not, in the first instance at least, an expression of conflict between the *golah* identity and remainees.

Whatever the compositional possibilities, we can see that after chap-ter 39 Zion-Jerusalem swiftly returns in literary triumph as the very focus of redemption from chapter 40 onwards. This is particularly evident in Isa 60–62, where it is the foreigners who bring their wealth to Jerusalem, in-verting the customary economic flow of empires—notably superseding the old domestic image of utopia within which each family's "vine and fig tree" supplies the production sufficient for their own needs. Despite the preten-sions of Assyria, Babylon, and Persia, we discover that it is YHWH who has always been in control: "I will not again give your grain as food to your enemies, and the children of the foreigner shall not drink the new wine for which you toiled" (Isa 62:8).

Following up on this agrarian theme, Tim Meadowcroft's essay medi-tates on the metaphor of the divine word as a "seed" in 55:10–11. The word *zr'* appears some twenty-eight times throughout Isaiah, taking on various connotations, but in 55:10–11 it becomes the verbal seed of divine purpose,

---

2. Ngugi, *Decolonizing the Mind*, 3, quoted in Hays.

3. Goldingay, "Isaiah 40–55 in the 1990s," 244.

or rather, divine desire (*chpts*).[4] Meadowcroft suggests that "God's effective word, like the snow and rain on a thirsty earth, enables the formation of a people of God." However comforting this theology might be, the claim also has an abstractness about it that belies the social history of the Isaiah tradition. In the Persian period, the question of who belonged to this seed-people became hotly disputed. In the course of time, the "children of the *golah*" in Ezra-Nehemiah were conceived as a "holy seed," perhaps alluding to the use of this phrase in Isa 6:13, but in Isa 56–66 this holy people were seen very differently. I have argued that the Abrahamic seed reflected in 61:8–9 would necessarily include descent groups beyond the borders of Yehud, beyond the genealogical borders of Jacob-Israel, and thus beyond the narrowed circle of holiness in Ezra-Nehemiah.[5] The "bookends" of Isa 56 and 66 go further to contemplate even the prospect of holy foreigners within YHWH's empire.

The repeated assertions that YHWH is the creator, found throughout Isa 40–66, seem to have possessed a counter-imperial motivation, as does the Priestly narrative of creation.[6] Creation theology and monotheism can be seen as two sides of the same coin in the later parts of Isaiah, each making universal or global claims for YHWH's jurisdiction. As Tim Bulkeley's contribution shows, however, this universal model of sovereignty differs from the kind that makes only local assertions, even when these local assertions contest an imperial claim made on the same territory.

While Joy Hooker tells the story of Zion symbolism in a more comprehensive way than Bulkeley, her essay tends to conflate the concepts of local and global sovereignty, and thereby raises the question whether her "symbolic" method has had the effect of blurring the contours of quite different discourses. Bulkeley's essay helpfully draws us back to the details of the text, and points up the need to move beyond generic invocations of divine sovereignty. Closer attention to such nuances in different biblical traditions, we may note, could well inform a critique of the hermeneutics of medieval Christendom and modern, settler colonialism.[7]

Although some of the symbolism of Christendom was indeed based on biblical foundations, it is worth remembering that the book of Isaiah was produced in social contexts that were peripheral to the Assyrian, Babylonian and Persian empires. Indeed, even to speak of the "Persian colony" of

---

4. Cf. the new name for Zion in Isa 62:4 "*chptsi bah*," and the marriage of "*chptsi bah*" and her land in 62:1–5.

5. Brett, "Unequal Terms."

6. Cf. Sparks, "*Enuma Elish* and Priestly Mimesis."

7. Among many other works, see Smith, *Chosen Peoples*. For an early dissenting view, see Chamerovzow, *The New Zealand Question and the Rights of Aborigines*.

Yehud is potentially confusing, since as Jacob Wright points out, "colonies are established by non-natives."[8] From the point of view of Persian interests, Yehud is better understood as an imperial territory from which resources are extracted, rather than a "settler colonial" territory that might, in the course of time, assert its own sovereignty over against the empire. If anything, the books of Ezra and Nehemiah represent nativist traditions, not the settler colonialism of Charter Groups in the modern period.[9] If postcolonial studies of the ancient world are to be coherent, their use of modern analogies will need to be more nuanced than has been the case in some recent biblical studies. The examples provided in this volume will hopefully provide some food for thought in this regard, whether or not they are read as contributions to a particular school of criticism, which, as Goldingay complains, might be regarded as faddish (and indeed, already fading from glory in cultural studies).

My own view is that postcolonial studies have barely begun to show their potential in biblical studies, in part because some postcolonial commentators have expressed their emancipatory interests in truncated and preemptive hermeneutics. We also have numerous hermeneutical gestures that give priority to the discourse of liberation within academic conversation, rather than to the complex practice of politics outside the academy. This set of priorities may have had the desirable effect of promoting diaspora intellectuals within English speaking schools of religion and theology (notably, we have no Maori, Aboriginal Australians or Pacific Islanders contributing to our collection of essays), but academic politics are of limited value if they remain focused on the health of the profession to the expense of public engagement and social transformation.

Reflecting on Goldingay's characterization of Isa 56–66, a key question would be how the lyrical and hyperbolic "quietism" of the divine counterempire, could so easily be turned to the violent purposes of Christendom in later centuries. Several critics, myself included, have suggested that because the idiom of resistance to successive empires often borrowed from imperial language and ideas, the Bible could become a source of sanctions for legitimating later Christian regimes. While there is no doubt an element of truth to this suggestion, it runs the risk of distracting us from the other ingredients that shaped the conditions of modern colonialism and imperialism in their various guises.

---

8. Wright, "Continuing these Conversations," 163.

9. Contra Kessler, "Persia's Loyal Yahwists," who finds analogies between the leadership of Yehud and the non-indigenous elites of modern settler colonialism.

The transnational and "deterritorializing" forces of financial markets today, for example, and their effects on our global environment, are hardly the product of biblical interpretation. Contrary to the ritual denunciation of Gen 1 in introductory textbooks on ecology, the dominance of nature that began with the industrial revolution cannot be sheeted home to the Priestly writer. The biblical imagination of economics, which moves between the domestic utopia of "vine and fig tree" to the grand imperial vision centered on Jerusalem, are economic options at home in the ancient world. The practices of empire today present a different set challenges, and these differences require careful analysis if biblical criticism is to make a credible (and therefore modest) contribution to public ethics. Our ecological predicaments, for example, are unlikely to be resolved by recommending a return to the agrarian utopias of biblical Israel.[10]

Malcolm MacDonald's contribution to this volume provokes further reflection on these issues. He begins by imagining the folk singers who first gave voice to the loss of Jerusalem and the national vision that went with it—in essence, the Deuteronomist vision. In its place rose not a doctrine of creation conceived in autonomous theological reasoning, but therapeutic songs, which sought to ground the enduring life of Israel in the seasonal pulse of creation. (This same task, we should note in passing, was taken up in the Priestly tradition.) These songs, and then perhaps liturgy, relinquished the sovereignty of the Judean state, and replaced it with the sovereignty of the Creator. In establishing the continuity necessary for Israel's redemption, Isa 45:18 emphasizes that the Judean YHWH is none other than the 'elohim who is named as the Creator of the world in Gen 1. Isaiah 45:22 adopts another Priestly name for God to make essentially the same point: "I am El, and there is no other." There is evidently more than one way to name this Creator, but in the final analysis there is only a single divine sovereignty that sustains the earth and all its creatures, human and non-human.

Looking back on these biblical visions of hope from the point of view of postmodern conditions, MacDonald rightly asks whether we can relinquish not only national identities (transnational capitalism has already made significant progress on that), but also our anthropocentric orientation to life. What might the Priestly covenant with Noah mean today, binding 'elohim with "every living creature on the earth"? Beyond the ritual denunciation of Genesis 1 in academic seminars the world over, what substantial contribution can biblical scholars make?

---

10. The otherwise admirable work of Davis, *Scripture, Culture, and Agriculture*, runs this risk.

A professional Hebrew Bible scholar might, for example, begin by interrogating the idea of "subduing the earth" and its links to the national imagination in the book of Joshua, or alternatively perhaps, emphasize that the canonical Torah relinquishes land possession as a fundamental marker of Jewish identity.[11] Or more specifically in relation to the Isaiah tradition, we might say that the relinquishing of national sovereignty gave rise to a creation-shaped hope that grounded Israel's identity so deeply in the order of things that even the great floods of empire could not assail it. For both Isaiah and the Priestly tradition, the seasonal pulse of creation was reflected in YHWH's cult, particularly in the Sabbath, which could be observed wherever diaspora conditions of life prevailed.[12] Yet as MacDonald rightly suggests, even creation now feels like a less secure basis for faith. Living under postmodern conditions, is there sufficient reason to think that concerted human attempts to limit climate change will be more successful than the human agency that constructed national identities and borders?

Whatever approaches might be taken in addressing our contemporary malaises, a new solidarity of folk singers and biblical scholars is not likely to take us very far. Biblical hermeneutics will need to move beyond the model of sweeping generalizations appended to studies of exegetical complexity. More effective would be active collaborations between economists, policy makers, faith-based organizations, and labor unions until sustainability is written into the fabric of every major corporation.[13] And even if this scale of solidarity were achieved, we would still be left I think with the kind of paradoxical juxtaposition of human and divine agency that we find at the beginning of Isa 56: Do justice, because divine justice is yet to be revealed. The ethical traditions of the Hebrew Bible, both the Law and the Prophets, continue to hold both kinds of agency in tension, without giving license to the Protestant version of quietism that allows faith to veto works.

11. Boorer, "The Envisioning of the Land in the Priestly Material."

12. See further Calaway, "Heavenly Sabbath, Heavenly Sanctuary."

13. See especially the pioneering work of Jackson, *Prosperity without Growth*.

Four Reflections
on Isaiah and Imperial Context

John Goldingay

I have enjoyed and been informed and stimulated by this collection of papers. I emerge from reading them with four sets of reflections or questions.

(1) The experience of being a subaltern people is an illuminating context for studying the book of Isaiah, and indeed the Old Testament as a whole. It's worth noting that a people doesn't have to be a colony or ex-colony to benefit from postcolonial thinking. Israel was never a colony in the sense of having in its midst a significant settlement of people from the imperial center who controlled its affairs on behalf of the imperial center. On the other hand, Israel was regularly subject to the domination of an imperial power within the region. The title of this collection thus usefully refers to Judah's living in an imperial context rather than its being a colony or a postcolonial entity.

My colleague Christopher Hays notes that lay readers of the Old Testament are conditioned to understand ancient Israel as an imperial power, and the same is true of scholars. Most scholarly Old Testament interpretation from the renaissance onwards (and much of it before) has been undertaken by Christians belonging to European powers and then to the United States. Even in this volume, the contributors from Australia and New Zealand are people of European background. David Ussishkin is the nearest to a non-Westerner. The natural instinct of such scholars has been to identify with Israel. Yet Israel was never an imperial power, except perhaps for a short period in the tenth century. Even the book of Joshua, which provided European settlers with a model for looking at their takeover of land in North America and South Africa, does not portray the Israelite invasion of Canaan as the act of an imperial power. Then and later, Israel was nearly always in the position of less powerful peoples such as Sri Lanka, Algeria, Haiti, and Mexico. But the political position of most scholars and ordinary people, who wanted to identify with Israel, led us to see Israel as a nation like ours. In due course that dynamic backfired, when Old Testament Israel came to be subject to critique on the assumption that it was a major power, even a quasi-imperial power.

When biblical criticism was invented, its concern was to critique the church's tradition of biblical interpretation so that the text could speak for itself, but it rapidly became critique of the text and not merely of its interpretation. There is a parallel ambiguity about postcolonial criticism. On one hand, it aims to unmask imperial interpretation. On the other, it aims to unmask imperial instincts within the text, on the basis of the dictum that Judith McKinlay quotes from R. S. Sugirtharajah:

> Anyone who engages with texts knows that they are not innocent and that they reflect the cultural, religious, political, and ideological interests and contexts out of which they emerge. What postcolonialism does is to highlight and scrutinize the ideologies these texts embody and that are entrenched in them as they relate to the fact of colonialism.

Something paradoxical issues: even the writings of the colonized are affected by imperial thinking. Mark Brett's chapter embodies this conviction, illustrating issues on which Mark Brett and I have engaged in friendly discussion in the past. One unease I have is that Mark Brett is inclined to a suspicious reading of the text where its ambiguity makes such a reading possible but not necessary. An example is his comment about Isa 63:16, where he simply assumes the view that "Abraham" stands for a group within the community that does not recognize the group to which the prophet belongs. This is neither a necessary understanding, nor (I think) the majority scholarly understanding, but it suits a reading that is looking for social conflict in the text. Likewise it's not self-evident that the work of Gentiles on the farm is inferior to the work of Israelites in the temple or that Isa 60–62 thus implies a hierarchy in which Israel is above the Gentiles. Actually it puts Gentiles into what the Torah sees as the same position as the eleven other clans over against Levi as the priestly clan. Their "profane" labor isn't inferior to "sacred" labor.

My related unease concerns the basis for critique of the biblical text. For postcolonial criticism, postcolonialism provides the key framework for thinking about texts (or other things). This framework provides the norm for truth and the basis for deciding between good and bad. It thus parallels convictions (one might say ideologies) such as those of feminism. There are feminist Christians and Christian feminists. Feminist Christians are people for whom Christian faith is their fundamental commitment; feminism nourishes or nuances their Christian faith. Christian feminists are people for whom feminism is their fundamental commitment and Christian faith nourishes or nuances their feminism. In a similar way there are scholars for whom the Bible is fundamental and postcolonial insight is a means of resourcing biblical study and critiquing our understanding of the Bible, and scholars for whom postcolonial insight is fundamental and the Bible is a means of resourcing postcolonial commitment. In the work of many people who are especially committed to postcolonial biblical scholarship I don't see much evidence of the Bible being allowed to answer back. To put it another way, postcolonial scholarship easily takes an imperial stance in relation to the Bible, harnessing it to its own concerns without letting the Bible have a voice of its own.

(2) The papers imply some unresolved questions about the significance of questions concerning the historical origin and reference of the material in Isaiah. Lena-Sofia Tiemeyer, for instance, notes how thin is the explicit evidence for assuming that the Judahites addressed in Isa 40–55 are in Babylon. The issue is not merely what are the right answers to these questions, but whether and how the answers matter. David Ussishkin illustrates how external data can illumine texts. The point is not that they prove the Bible right nor that they clarify the text's meaning but that they enable readers to know more of what the text refers to and of what might have been taken for granted by the author and first audience.

The contributors assume the classic critical conviction that the book of Isaiah reflects both the work and words of Isaiah ben Amoz and also the ministry of later figures in the context of the exile and the Second Temple period. Further, they accept the current critical conviction that the book's three main parts are not separate units glued together; they are part of something that is in some sense a coherent whole. That assumption raises intriguing questions about the interpretation of individual units in the book. Andrew Abernethy comments that the foreigners in Isa 1 are surely the Assyrians, but that leaving them unnamed "facilitates the chapter's function as an introduction to the entire book and the identifying of the foreigners with later attackers." Given that Isa 40–55 makes its spectacular references to Cyrus, it was strange that Brevard Childs said that the concrete historical references had been eliminated from the chapters to facilitate their application beyond the exilic context.[14] But the lack of concrete historical reference in Isa 1 does have that effect, as is the case in Isa 56–66 (I prefer to speak of effect rather than intention, because convictions about intention would have to be more hypothetical). That comment on Isa 1 thus encourages a reading of the passage at two levels. Tim Meadowcroft raises the same question in noting how

14. Childs, *Introduction to the Old Testament as Scripture*, 325–27.

55:10–11 with its origin in the exile is set in the context of a book that came into being in the Second Temple period, when the community's relationship with the imperial power is different both from that which obtained before the exile and that which obtained at the time this prophecy was uttered.

Judith McKinlay comments that someone in Babylon publishing poems like the ones in Isa 40–55 would be both unsafe and unwise. Yet the way the chapters unfold suggests that the poet did operate in this unsafe and unwise fashion. That is why the poet was flogged and shamed (50:4–9), and despised, persecuted, and threatened by death if not actually killed (52:13—53:12) (I take it that the poet-prophet speaks in 49:1–6 and is the subject of 52:13—53:12 but other interpretations need not make a difference to the fact that persecution of an "unwise" speaker lies behind the passages; and prophets were inclined to be unsafe and unwise). The chapters imply that the poet's ministry issued in opposition from the Judahite community itself and not just the imperial authorities, so it doesn't look as if the poet could assume membership of a "self-trusting community." It seems that the poet did not heed the wise principles about public and hidden transcripts articulated by James Scott. The chapters are not a "hidden transcript." The significance of postcolonial theory at this point is then to bring out the distinctiveness of the text by contrast with what the theory would make one expect.

Judith McKinlay comments that Isa 40–55 is clearly a political text, which "exists in the service of a particular sociohistorical context" (Tod Linafelt). But like Lena-Sofia Tiemeyer, she also notes that we can't be sure of the particular sociohistorical context. As a consequence, interpreters may fill in the gap by utilizing modern sociological or anthropological theories, and this may be effective, but it risks circular argument. Further, while Isa 40–55 may have been a political text in origin (though the idea that these chapters ever existed as a discrete entity is contested), in the context of the book of Isaiah it is not so obvious that Isa 40–55 invites a political reading. Admittedly, we know even less about how the complete book of Isaiah might have functioned politically than what we might infer about the material in chapters 40–55 in their exilic context. But for people in late Second Temple times the book of Isaiah was at least as much a religious text, designed to tell them about God and to resource their relationship with God, and it is a plausible view that it came into being at least as much for religious purposes as for political ones. It would be anachronistic to separate the political and religious as if Judah not only believed in the separation of church and state but practiced that separation, but it is equally misleading to assume that religious motivations can be ignored in favor of the political. Postcolonialism's suspicion of religion thus limits its capacity to read the text.

(3) Several papers bring out or hint at our modern unease about violence. One striking aspect of David Ussishkin's paper was its portrait of the harsh reality of an event such as the siege of Lachish. Over the past century, the cultural circles within which most of us belong as scholars have become uneasy about violence, and this fact is reflected in scholarly work. The way "cultures have their own orthodoxies that inhibit questioning" (Hays) affects postcolonial thinking as well as imperial thinking; in our context, it is countenancing violence that is "*heterodox*, and indeed *heretical*." People who are interested in non-violence are partial to Isaiah because it shows less interest in encouraging Israel's violence and more interest in peace than some other books. But if we want to learn from the Old Testament, we will not just want to learn from Isaiah because it may resource convictions we already have and function in a proof-texting manner. We will want to learn from (say) Deuteronomy and Joshua when their thinking is scandalous. The same point emerges from Joy Hooker's consideration of divine sovereignty, conflict, and order. I do not see the Old Testament as so different from other aspects of ancient near Eastern thinking on this subject. Its difference lies in saying that if there is anyone who acts violently to achieve order, it is YHWH rather than other so-called gods.

The nature of the exercise of violence in our context may mean we have good reason for our unease (if, for instance, war is more horrific than it was in the ancient Near East, though my point about Ussishkin's paper qualifies that possibility). But our understanding of violence has become undifferentiated. The *Oxford English Dictionary* defines violence as "the exercise of physical force so as to inflict injury on, or cause damage to, persons or property." This definition does not carry moral connotations. It implies that there can be proper violence and improper violence (as there can be proper mercy and improper mercy). In the cultural circles to which most of us belong as scholars, the idea of proper violence is more likely to seem odd than was once the case. Yet paradoxically, our belonging to democratic war-making nations means that we are complicit in war-making to a greater extent than our forebears. These cultural factors affect our approach to the Old Testament and threaten to skew our understanding of it.

One way they do so is in making us write as if violence is an issue in Isaiah as it is for us, when this is not so. The Hebrew word most often translated *violence* is *chamas*, which does carry moral connotations; it refers to improper violence, though its meaning overlaps with that of violation. Neither the noun nor the related verb come in Isa 1–39, though the noun does occur in 53:9; 59:6; 60:18. Yet Isa 1–39 is clearly against *chamas*, though not against violence when exercised by YHWH either on Israel or on other peoples. The fact that Isaiah speaks of YHWH exercising violence on Israel because of its internal violence puts a question mark by the idea that Isaiah adopts "a perspective that identifies 'Israel' as 'us' and 'Assyria' as 'them'" (Hays). Its assumption that Israel is subject to, deserving of, and victim of Yhwh's violence indicates that in this sense Isaiah does not go in for "othering."

In Isaiah there is indeed virtually no reference to or encouragement of violence on the part of the people of God. The nearest (Andrew Abernethy notes in a comment that didn't make it into the book) is 11:14–15, though even there the violence is a matter of plundering rather than (say) killing, and even there the reference presupposes a repointing of MT (see BHS and Wildberger's comments).[15] The chains in 45:14 may be imposed by the Judahites, but the context points rather to Cyrus (45:13), and the point about the chains is to indicate that the rulers' sovereignty is over. The book of Isaiah is then intriguingly similar to the book of Psalms. Psalms protest long and often about the human violence of which the community and individuals are victims and keep urging YHWH to act against attackers and to do so violently, but they never imply that the protestors are to take any action (except in some royal psalms) until the very penultimate psalm which declares that Israel is to wield a sword to implement redress on the nations and bind their rulers in chains—again to indicate that their sovereignty is over.

I myself find it theologically and ethically significant that while the book of Isaiah speaks approvingly about violence on YHWH's part it does not speak approvingly about violence on Israel's part. Yet I am not sure that the difference in attitude to divine and human violence is important for the book of Isaiah in the way that it is for me. While there is a difference in attitudes to divine and human violence in the book, when we focus on this difference, we do so because of the importance of the issue to us (the situation is the same with appeals to Jesus' non-violence, in my view, but that's another story). The book's own category is different. The issue in Isa 1–39, at least, is lack of trust, not violence. The key verbs are 'aman and batach, not chamas. "Trust me, don't trust YHWH" is the Assyrian king's challenge (Abernethy). The point links with Joy Hooker's comment that one of the ways Isaiah uses Zion symbolism is to present a concept of God's sovereignty and order that challenges the ancient Near Eastern concept of empire as the primary understanding of reality for the ordering of society.

Judah is to refrain from military activity not because violence is wrong but because this refraining leaves the action (and thus incidentally the violence) to YHWH. Part of the background is that very fact that Judah is a little, quasi-colonial people, not a big, imperial power. Its vocation is not to enter into covenant relations with big powers in order to safeguard

15. Wildberger, *Isaiah 1–12*, 487.

its freedom but to rely on its covenant relationship with YHWH (compare comments on covenant by Abernethy, Hays, and Hooker). The difference in position between an ancient Judahite and a modern Westerner again becomes significant here. Our membership of powerful nations that choose their own governments gives us a different relationship with our nations' decision to engage in violence.

It also means I am not clear that we can view ourselves as "in exile," the idea Tim Meadowcroft takes up. The contributors to this volume, like most biblical scholars, are citizens of democratic nations, most of us with an imperial present or an imperial past. We are not in exile; we are simply people who have been outvoted, literally and/or metaphorically. Exile happens to people who are not citizens and not members of imperial powers. We can't use the image of exile to let ourselves off the hook of responsibility for the violence our nations undertake. Further, it's surely not the case that most Christians see themselves as increasingly on the edge, at odds with the empire, or in exile from their culture—you might even suggest that the problem lies in our not seeing ourselves thus. I don't think that most Christians in (say) Uganda or the United States think in that way. Further, while Europe and countries such as Australia, New Zealand, and Canada are post-Christian, most of Africa and the rest of the colonial/postcolonial world are not, and neither is the United States (which is of course a postcolonial entity, with the appropriate love-hate relationship with its European forebears). In the United States, I like to say we are living in the time of Josiah, not the exile.

(4) I am similarly intrigued by the question of the relationship between divine sovereignty and human decision-making. Andrew Abernethy notes that Isa 1 counters the Assyrian assumption that the Assyrian king is sovereign over land and food resources by presenting YHWH as sovereignly using Assyria's imperial tactics of food confiscation and destruction to punish the people, while also asserting himself as the one who can provide them with food if they obey. Admittedly, Sennacherib's provision will not be as generous as the one he enjoys himself. The inequality he presupposes is one accepted by Israelite kings, and also by most if not all the contributors to this volume, who live better than other people in their country and certainly better than people in the colonial world that we supposedly care about.

Tim Bulkeley interestingly demonstrates the prominence in Isaiah of the description of YHWH as "Lord," which is easy to miss because we're used to substituting the word *Lord* for the name *YHWH*. The importance of this divine lordship is also expressed in the claims in Isa 41 concerning YHWH's arousing the conqueror from the east and the claim that YHWH thereby manifests a sovereignty that other deities cannot manifest. Yet Judith McKinlay notes in connection with Lamentations that while it is accepted that YHWH is behind the disaster that has happened to Jerusalem, and while the city's cries rise up to heaven imploring YHWH to look and see the city's misery, it was the Babylonian army that actually caused the mayhem, acting with devastating brutality. Likewise it is Cyrus the Persian whose army will take Babylon and commission the Judahites to go home to build the temple. Malcolm MacDonald comments that the linking of creation and redemption together, in so far as they contribute to a single symbiotic concept, reaches maturity in Isa 40–55. But a big difference between creation and redemption is that YHWH created the world without anyone's help (as 44:24 points out), whereas redemption would not have happened without Cyrus.

It might be logical to infer with Judith MacKinlay that the challenging question is, do we thus get led to praxis? Yet Isaiah points us to another paradox in this connection. It believes in the significance of human action and sees YHWH working through human action. But the people who undertake the human action through which God works don't do so deliberately and don't know that this is what they're doing (in Cyrus's case, at least, YHWH hopes that Cyrus will recognize YHWH as a result of being conscripted into YHWH's service, but he doesn't recognize YHWH at the time). In Isaiah, the people who acknowledge YHWH aren't people who are called to do anything, with two exceptions. One is to put their own lives right, which again issues a challenge to people like us scholars who occupy privileged positions in privileged nations. The other is to proclaim or explain what YHWH is doing, in the manner of the servant figure in Isa 42 and the prophetic speaker in Isa 61 (neither of whom *do* anything but speak); or perhaps to sing (MacDonald).

Bibliography

Abernethy, Andrew T. "'My Servants Shall Eat': The Prospect of Eating in the Book of Isaiah." PhD diss., Trinity Evangelical Divinity School, 2012.

Aharoni, Y. *Investigations at Lachish; The Sanctuary and the Residency (Lachish V)*. Tel Aviv: Gateway, 1975.

Anderson, Bernhard W. "Introduction: Mythopoeic and Theological Dimensions of Biblical Creation Faith." In *Creation in the Old Testament*, edited by Bernhard W. Anderson, 1–24. Philadelphia: Fortress, 1984.

Asen, Bernhard A. "The Garlands of Ephraim: Isaiah 28:1–6 and the Marzēah." *Journal for the Study of the Old Testament* 71 (1996) 73–87.

Ashcroft, Bill, Gareth Griffiths, and Helen Tiffin. *The Empire Writes Back: Theory and Practice in Post-Colonial Literatures*. 2nd ed. London: Routledge, 2002.

Aster, Shawn Zelig. "The Image of Assyria in Isaiah 2:5–22: The Campaign Motif Reversed." *Journal of American Oriental Studies* 127 (2007) 249–78.

Avigad, N. *Discovering Jerusalem*. Nashville, TN: Thomas Nelson, 1983.

Bagg, Ariel. *Die Orts- und Gewässernamen der neuassyrischen Zeit*. Vol. 7. Répertoire Géographique des Textes Cunéiformes. Wiesbaden: Reichert, 2007.

Baldwin, Joyce G. "Tsemach as a Technical Term in the Prophets." *Vetus Testamentum* 14 (1964) 93–97.

Baltzer, K. *Deutero-Isaiah: A Commentary on Isaiah 40–55*. Edited by P. Machinist, translated by M. Kohl. Hermeneia. Minneapolis: Fortress, 2001.

Barnett, R. D. "The Siege of Lachish." *Israel Exploration Journal* 8 (1958) 161–64.

Barr, J. *Comparative Philology and the Text of the Old Testament*. Oxford: Clarendon, 1968.

Barré, Michael L. *The Lord Has Saved Me: A Study of the Psalm of Hezekiah [Isaiah 38:9–20]*. Washington, DC: Catholic Biblical Association of America, 2005.

Barstad, H. M. "Akkadian 'Loanwords' in Isaiah 40–55 and the Question of the Babylonian Origin of Deutero-Isaiah." In *Text and Theology*, Studies in Honour of Prof. Dr. Theol. Magne Sæbø, edited by A. Tångberg, 36–48. Oslo: Verbum, 1994.

———. "Lebte Deuterojesaja in Judäa?" *Veterotestamentica Norsk Teologisk Tidsskrift* 83.2 (1982) 77–87.

———. *The Myth of the Empty Land: A Study in the History and Archaeology of Judah during the "Exilic" Period*. Oslo: Scandinavian University Press, 1996.

———. "On the So-Called Babylonian Influence in Second Isaiah." *Journal for the Study of the Old Testament* 2 (1987) 99–100.

Bibliography

Bartholomew, Craig, Colin Greene, and Karl Möller, editors. *After Pentecost: Language and Biblical Interpretation*. Scripture and Hermeneutics vol. 2. Carlisle, UK: Paternoster, 2001.

Beaulieu, Paul-Alain. *The Pantheon of Uruk during the Neo-Babylonian Period*. Leiden: Brill, 2003.

Begrich, J. *Studien zu Deuterojesaja*. 1938. Reprint. Munich: Kaiser, 1969.

Behr, J. W. *The Writings of Deutero-Isaiah and the Neo-Babylonian Royal Inscriptions: A Comparison of the Language and Style*. Issue 3 of Publications of the University of Pretoria. Series III: Arts No. 3. Pretoria: Rubinstein, 1937.

Ben-Dov, M. *Historical Atlas of Jerusalem*. New York: Continuum, 2002.

Ben Zvi, Ehud. "Isaiah 1:4–9, Isaiah, and the Events of 701 B.C.E. in Judah: A Question of Premise and Evidence." *Scandinavian Journal of the Old Testament* 1 (1991) 95–111.

Berges, Ulrich. *Deutero-Jesaja (Jes 40–48)*. Freiburg: Herder, 2007.

———. "Personifications and Prophetic Voices of Zion in Isaiah and Beyond." In *The Elusive Prophet: The Prophet as a Historical Person, Literary Character and Anonymous Artist*, edited by Johannes Moor, 54–82. Leiden: Brill, 2001.

Bergsma, John. "The Jubilee: A Post-exilic Priestly Attempt to Reclaim Lands?" *Biblica* 84 (2003) 225–46.

———. *The Jubilee from Leviticus to Qumran: A History of Interpretation*. Leiden: Brill, 2007.

Berquist, Jon L. "Postcolonialism and Imperial Motives for Canonization." *Semeia* 75 (1996) 15–36.

———. "Resistance and Accommodation in the Persian Empire." In *In the Shadow of Empire: Reclaiming the Bible as a History of Faithful Resistance*, edited by Richard A. Horsley, 41–58. Louisville: Westminster John Knox, 2008.

Berry, Thomas. *The Christian Future and the Fate of the Earth*. Edited by Mary Evelyn Tucker and John Grim. New York: Orbis, 2009.

———. *The Sacred Universe: Earth, Spirituality, and Religion in the Twenty-First Century*. Edited by Mary Evelyn Tucker. New York: Columbia University Press, 2009.

Beuken, Willem A. M. *Isaiah II: Isaiah 28–39*. Leuven: Peeters, 2000.

Biddle, Mark E. "The Figure of Lady Jerusalem: Identification, Deification and Personification of Cities in the Ancient Near East." In *The Biblical Canon in Comparative Perspective*, edited by K. Lawson Younger, William W. Hallo, and Bernard F. Batto, 173–94. New York: Mellen, 1991.

Binney, Judith. *The Encircled Lands: Te Urewera, 1820–1921*. Wellington, NZ: Williams, 2009.

Bleibtreu, Erika. "Five Ways to Conquer a City." *Biblical Archaeology Review* 16.3 (1990) 37–44.

Blenkinsopp, Joseph. *A History of Prophecy in Israel*. Rev. ed. Louisville, KY: Westminster John Knox, 1996.

———. *Isaiah 1–39: A New Translation with Introduction and Commentary*. New York: Doubleday, 2000.

———. *Isaiah 40–55*. New York: Doubleday, 2000.

———. "Review of John Goldingay and David Payne, *Isaiah 40–55*." *Catholic Biblical Quarterly* 70 (2008) 341–43.

Bloom, Harold. *The Anxiety of Influence*. Rev. ed. Oxford: Oxford University Press, 1997.

Bookless, Dave. "A Famine of Hope: Christian Mission and the Search for a Sustainable Future." *Global Connections Occasional Paper* 26 (2007) i–iv.

Boorer, Suzanne. "The Envisioning of the Land in the Priestly Material: Fulfilled Promise or Future Hope?" In *Pentateuch, Hexateuch, or Enneateuch? Identifying Literary Works in Genesis through Kings*, edited by T. B. Dozeman, T. Römer, and K. Schmid, 99–125. Atlanta: SBL, 2011.

Bourdieu, Pierre. *Outline of a Theory of Practice*. Translated by Richard Nice. Cambridge: Cambridge University Press, 1977.

Boyce, R. N. "Isaiah 55:6–13." *Interpretation* 44 (1990) 56–60.

Brekelmans, C. "Deuteronomistic Influence in Isaiah 1–12." In *Book of Isaiah-Le livre d'Isaie*, edited by J. Vermeylen, 167–76. Leuven: Leuven University Press, 1989.

Brett, Mark G. *Decolonizing God: The Bible in the Tides of Empire*. Sheffield, UK: Sheffield Phoenix, 2008.

———. "Genocide in Deuteronomy: Postcolonial Variations on Mimetic Desire." In *Seeing Signals, Reading Signs: The Art of Exegesis*, edited by M. O'Brien and H. Wallace, 76–90. London: T. & T. Clark, 2004.

———. "Natives and Immigrants in the Social Imagination of the Holiness School." In *Imagining the Other and Constructing Israelite Identity in the Early Second Temple Period*, edited by E. Ben Zvi, and D. Edelman. London: T. & T. Clark, forthcoming.

———. "Permutations of Sovereignty in the Priestly Tradition." *Vetus Testamentum*, 63 (2013) 383–392.

———. "Unequal Terms: A Postcolonial Approach to Isaiah 61." In *Biblical Interpretation and Method: Essays in Honour of Professor John Barton*, edited by K. Dell, and P. Joyce, 243–256. Oxford: Oxford University Press, 2013.

Bright, John. *A History of Israel*. London: SCM, 1960.

Brown, Lester R., Christopher Flavin, and Hal Kane, *Vital Signs, 1998–99: The Trends That Are Shaping Our Future*, edited by Linda Starke. London: Earthscan, 1998.

Brueggemann, Walter. *Hopeful Imagination: Prophetic Voices in Exile*. Philadelphia: Fortress, 1986.

———. *Isaiah 1–39*. Louisville, KY: Westminster John Knox, 1998.

———. *Isaiah 40–66*. Louisville, KY: Westminster John Knox, 1998.

———. "Isaiah 55 and Deuteronomic Theology." *Zeitschrift für die alttestamentliche Wissenschaft* 80 (1968) 191–203.

———. *Out of Babylon*. Nashville: Abingdon, 2010.

———. "Unity and Dynamic in the Isaiah Tradition." *Journal for the Study of the Old Testament* 29 (1984) 89–107.

Budde, Karl. *Jesaja's erleben: eine gemeinverständliche auslegung der denkschrift des propheten (kap. 6, 1–9, 6)*. Gotha, Germany: Klotz, 1928.

Bultmann, Rudolf. "New Testament and Mythology." In *Kerygma and Myth: By Rudolf Bultmann and Five Critics*, edited by Hans Werner Bartsch, 1–44. New York: Harper & Row, 1961.

Caird, G. B. *The Language and Imagery of the Bible*. London: Duckworth, 1980.

Calaway, Jared C. "Heavenly Sabbath, Heavenly Sanctuary: The Transformation of Priestly Sacred Space and Sacred Time in the Songs of the Sabbath Sacrifice and the Epistle to the Hebrews." PhD diss., Columbia University (New York), 2010.

Camp, Claudia V. "Understanding a Patriarchy: Women in Second-Century Jerusalem through the Eyes of Ben Sira." In *"Women Like This": New Perspectives on Jewish Women in the Greco-Roman World*, edited by Amy-Jill Levine, 1–40. Atlanta: Scholars, 1991.

Carroll, Robert P. "YHWH's Sour Grapes: Images of Food and Drink in the Prophetic Discourses of the Hebrew Bible." *Semeia* 86 (1999) 113–31.

Carter, Charles E. *The Emergence of Yehud in the Persian Period*. Sheffield, UK: Sheffield Academic Press, 1999.

Carter, Warren. *John and Empire: Initial Explorations*. London: T. & T. Clark, 2008.

Cataldo, Jeremiah W. *A Theocratic Yehud?* London: T. & T. Clark, 2009.

Chamerovzow, Louis A. *The New Zealand Question and the Rights of Aborigines*. London: Newby, 1848.

Chan, Michael. "Rhetorical Reversal and Usurpation: Isaiah 10:5–34 and the Use of Neo-Assyrian Royal Idiom in the Construction of an Anti-Assyrian Theology." *Journal of Biblical Literature* 128 (2009) 717–33.

Childs, Brevard S. *Introduction to the Old Testament as Scripture*. Philadelphia: Fortress, 1979.

———. *Isaiah*. Louisville, KY: Westminster John Knox, 2001.

———. *Isaiah and the Assyrian Crisis*. Naperville, IL: Alenson, 1967.

———. *Myth and Reality in the Old Testament*. London: SCM, 1960.

Christian, David. *Maps of Time: An Introduction to Big History*. Berkeley, CA: University of California Press, 2011.

Claassen, W. T. "Linguistic Arguments and the Dating of Isaiah 1:4–9." *Journal of Northwest Semitic Languages* 3 (1974) 1–18.

Claassens, L. Juliana M. *The God Who Provides: Biblical Images of Divine Nourishment*. Nashville: Abingdon, 2004.

Clements, R. E. "Beyond Tradition-History: Deutero-Isaianic Development of First Isaiah's Themes." *Journal for the Study of the Old Testament* 31 (1985) 95–113.

———. *Isaiah and the Deliverance of Jerusalem: A Study of the Interpretation of Prophecy in the Old Testament*. Sheffield, UK: JSOT, 1980.

———. "The Unity of the Book of Isaiah." *Interpretation* 36 (1982) 117–29.

———. "Zion as Symbol and Political Reality: A Central Isaianic Quest." In *Studies in the Book of Isaiah: Festschrift Willem A. M. Beuken*, edited by J. Van Ruiten, and M. Vervenne, 4–17. Leuven: Leuven University Press, 1997.

Clifford, Richard J. "Isaiah 55: Invitation to a Feast." In *The Word of the Lord Shall Go Forth: Essays in Honor of David Noel Freedman in Celebration of His Sixtieth Birthday*, edited by Carol L. Meyers, and M. O'Connor, 27–35. Winona Lake, IN: Eisenbrauns, 1983.

Cogan, Mordechai. *Imperialism and Religion: Assyria, Judah, and Israel in the Eighth and Seventh Centuries B.C.E.* Atlanta: Scholars, 1973.

———. "Into Exile: From the Assyrian conquest of Israel to the Fall of Babylon." In *The Oxford History of the Biblical World*, edited by Michael David Coogan, 242–75. New York: Oxford University Press, 2001.

———. "Sennacherib's First Campaign: Against Merodach-baladan (2.119A)." In *The Context of Scripture*, Vol. 2, edited by William W. Hallo and K. L. Younger, 300–302. Leiden: Brill, 1997.

Coggins, Richard, Anthony Phillips, and Michael Knibb, editors. *Israel's Prophetic Tradition: Essays in Honour of Peter R. Ackroyd.* Cambridge: Cambridge University Press, 1982.

Cohen, Chaim. "Neo-Assyrian Elements in the First Speech of the Biblical Rab-Šāqê." *Israel Oriental Studies* 9 (1979) 32–48.

Cohen, H. R. *Biblical Hapax Legonema in the Light of Akkadian and Ugaritic.* Ann Arbor, MI: Scholars, 1978.

Cohn, Robert L. "The Mountains and Mount Zion." *Judaism* 26 (1977) 97–116.

Cole, Steven W. "The Destruction of Orchards in Assyrian Warfare." In *Assyria 1995,* edited by S. Parpola, and R. M. Whiting, 29–40. Helsinki: University of Helsinki Press, 1997.

Collins, John J. *Daniel.* Hermeneia. Minneapolis: Fortress, 1993.

———. "A Herald of Good Tidings: Isaiah 61:1–3 and Its Actualization in the Dead Sea Scrolls." In *The Quest for Content and Meaning,* edited by C. Evans, and S. Talmon, 225–40. Leiden: Brill, 1997.

Conrad, Edgar W. *Reading Isaiah.* Minneapolis: Fortress, 1991.

———. "The Royal Narratives and the Structure of the Book of Isaiah." *Journal for the Study of the Old Testament* 13 (1988) 67–81.

Conway, Colleen M. "There and Back Again: Johannine History on the Other Side of Literary Criticism." In *Anatomies of Narrative Criticism: The Past, Present and Future of the Fourth Gospel as Literature,* edited by Tom Thatcher, and Stephen D. Moore, 77–91. Atlanta: Society of Biblical Literature, 2008.

Couroyer, B. "Note sur II Sam., et Is., LV, 10–11." *Révue Biblique* 88 (1981) 505–14.

Dahood, M. "Phoenician Elements in Isaiah 52:13—53:12." In *Near Eastern Studies in Honor of William Foxwell Albright,* edited by H. Goedicke, 63–73. Baltimore, MD: Johns Hopkins University Press, 1971.

Daise, M. A. "'If Anyone Thirsts, Let That One Come to Me and Drink': The Literary Texture of John 7:37b–38a." *Journal of Biblical Literature* 122 (2003) 687–99.

Dalley, Stephanie, translator. *Myths from Mesopotamia: Creation, The Flood, Gilgamesh, and Others.* Oxford: Oxford University Press, 2008.

Danker, Frederick William. *A Greek-English Lexicon of the New Testament and Other Christian Literature.* Chicago: Chicago University Press, 2000.

Davies, W. D. *The Gospel and the Land: Early Christianity and Jewish Territorial Doctrine.* Berkeley, CA: University of California Press, 1974.

Davis, Ellen F. *Scripture, Culture, and Agriculture: An Agrarian Reading of the Bible.* Cambridge: Cambridge University Press, 2009.

Day, John. "God and Leviathan in Isaiah 27:1." *Bibliotheca Sacra* 155 (1998) 423–36.

———. *God's Conflict with the Dragon and the Sea: Echoes of a Canaanite Myth in the Old Testament.* Cambridge: Cambridge University Press, 1985.

Dekker, Jaap. *Zion's Rock-Solid Foundations: An Exegetical Study of the Zion Text in Isaiah 28:16.* Leiden: Brill, 2007.

Delitzsch, Franz. *Biblical Commentary on the Prophecies of Isaiah.* 4th ed. Edinburgh: T. & T. Clark, 1892.

———. "Der priesterschriftliche Umgang mit der Jakobsgeschichte." In *Schriftauslegung in der Schrift,* edited by R. G. Kratz, T. Krüger, and K. Schmid, 33–60. Berlin: de Gruyter, 2000.

Dever, William. *The Lives of Ordinary People in Ancient Israel: Where Archaeology and the Bible Intersect.* Grand Rapids: Eerdmans, 2012.

Bibliography

Diesel, A. A. »*Ich bin Jahwe*«: *Der Aufstieg der Ich-bin-Jahwe-Aussage zum Schlüsselwort des alttestamentlichen Monotheismus*. Neukirchen-Vluyn: Neukirchener, 2006.

Dion, H. M. "Le genre littéraire sumérien de l'hymne à soi-même' et quelques passages du Deutéro-Isaïe." *Révue Biblique* 74 (1967) 215–34.

Dobbs-Allsopp, Frederick W. *Lamentations*. Louisville, KY: John Knox, 2002.

———. *Weep, O Daughter of Zion: A Study of the City-Lament Genre in the Hebrew Bible*. Rome: Pontifical Biblical Institute, 1993.

Douglas, Mary "One God, No Ancestors, in a World Renewed." In *Jacob's Tears: The Priestly Work of Reconciliation*, 176–95. Oxford: Oxford University Press, 2004.

Dowd, Michael. *Thank God for Evolution*. New York: Penguin, 2009.

Duhm, B. *Das Buch Jesaia*. Handbuch zum Alten Testament III/1. Göttingen: Vandenhoeck & Ruprecht, 1892.

Edelman, Diana V., and Ehud Ben Zvi, editors. *The Production of Prophecy: Constructing Prophecy and Prophets in Yehud*. Oakville, CT: Equinox, 2009.

Eichrodt, Walter. "In the Beginning." In *Creation in the Old Testament*, edited by Bernhard W. Anderson, 65–73. Philadelphia: Fortress, 1984.

Eidevall, Göran. *Prophecy and Propaganda: Images of Enemies in the Book of Isaiah*. Winona Lake, IN: Eisenbrauns, 2009.

Eph'al, Israel. "Ways and Means to Conquer a City, Based on Assyrian Queries to the Sungod." In *Assyria 1995*. Neo-Assyrian Text Corpus Project, 49–53. Helsinki: University of Helsinki Press, 1997.

Epp, E. J. "Wisdom, Torah, Word: The Johannine Prologue and the Purpose of the Fourth Gospel." In *Current Issues in Biblical and Patristic Interpretation*, edited by G. F. Hawthorne, 128–46. Grand Rapids: Eerdmans, 1975.

Eskenazi, Tamara. "The Missions of Ezra and Nehemiah." In *Judah and the Judeans in the Persian Period*, edited by O. Lipschits, and M. Oeming, 509–29. Winona Lake, IN: Eisenbrauns, 2006.

Eskanazi, Tamara, and E. P. Judd. "Marriage to a Stranger in Ezra 1–9." In *Second Temple Studies*, vol. 2, *Temple and Community in the Persian Period*, edited by T. Eskenazi and K. Richards, 266–85. Sheffield, UK: JSOT, 1994.

Fales, F. M. *Aramaic Epigraphs on Clay Tablets of the Neo-Assyrian Period*. Materiali per il lessico aramaico 1. Studi semitici nuova ser., 2. Roma: Università degli studi "La sapienza," 1986.

———. "Grain Reserves, Daily Rations, and the Size of the Assyrian Army: A Quantitative Study." *State Archives of Assyria Bulletin* 4 (1990) 23–34.

———. "The Rural Landscape of the Neo-Assyrian Empire: A Survey." *State Archives of Assyria Bulletin* 4 (1990) 81–142.

Fanon, Frantz. *Black Skin, White Masks*. Translated by C. L. Markmann. New York: Grove, 1967.

———. *Toward the African Revolution: Political Essays*. New York: Grove, 1969.

———. *The Wretched of the Earth*. Translated by Richard Philcox. New York: Grove, 2004.

Fischer, Irmtraud. "World Peace and Holy War—Two Sides of the Same Theological Concept: YHWH as Sole Divine Power. A Canonical-Intertextual Reading of Isaiah 2:1–5, Joel 4:9–21 and Micah 4:1–5." In *Isaiah's Vision of Peace in Biblical and Modern International Relations*, edited by R. Cohen, and R. Westbrook, 151–65. New York: Palgrave MacMillan, 2008.

Fishbane, Michael. *Text and Texture: Close Readings of Selected Biblical Texts.* New York: Schocken, 1979.

Fohrer, Georg. "Jesaja 1 als Zusammenfassung der Verkündigung Jesajas." *Zeitschrift für die alttestamentliche Wissenschaft* 74 (1962) 251–68.

Franke, C. A. "The Function of the Satiric Lament over Babylon in Second Isaiah (xlvii)." *Vetus Testamentum* 41 (1991) 408–18.

Fried, Lisbeth. "The 'am ha'ares in Ezra 4.4 and Persian Imperial Administration." In *Judah and the Judeans in the Persian Period,* edited by O. Lipschits, and M. Oeming, 123–45. Winona Lake, IN: Eisenbrauns, 2006.

Garnsey, D. A., and C. R. Whitaker, editors. *Imperialism and the Ancient World: The Cambridge University Research Seminar in Ancient History.* Cambridge: Cambridge University Press, 1978.

Gates, H. L. Jr. "Critical Fanonism." In *Rethinking Fanon: The Continuing Dialogue,* edited by Nigel C. Gibson, 251–68. Amherst, NY: Humanity, 1999.

George, A. "Babylonian and Assyrian: A History of Akkadian." In *The Languages of Iraq, Ancient and Modern,* edited by J. N. Postgate, 31–71. Baghdad: The British School of Archaeology in Iraq, 2007.

Goldingay, John. "About Third Isaiah." In *On Stone and Scroll: Essays in Honour of Graham Ivor Davies,* edited by J. K. Aitken, K. J. Dell, and B. A. Mastin, 375–89. Berlin: de Gruyter, 2011.

———. *Isaiah.* NIBC. Peabody, MA: Hendrickson, 2001.

———. "Isaiah 40–55 in the 1990s: Among Other Things, Deconstructing, Mystifying, Intertextual, Socio-Critical, and Hearer-Involving." *Biblical Interpretation* 5 (1997) 225–46.

———. *The Message of Isaiah 40–55: A Literary-Theological Commentary.* London: T. & T. Clark, 2005.

———. *Old Testament Theology. Volume Two: Israel's Faith.* Downers Grove, IL: InterVarsity, 2006.

———. "Poetry and Theology in Isaiah 56–66." In *Horizons in Hermeneutics,* edited by Stanley E. Porter and Matthew R. Malcolm, 15–31. Grand Rapids: Eerdmans, 2013.

———. "The Theology of Isaiah." In *Interpreting Isaiah: Issues and Approaches,* edited by David G. Firth, and H. G. M. Williamson, 169–90. Downers Grove, IL: InterVarsity, 2009.

Goldingay, John, and David Payne. *Isaiah 40–55 Volume 1.* London: T. & T. Clark, 2006.

Gordon, Robert P. *Holy Land Holy City: Sacred Geography and the Interpretation of the Bible.* Carlisle, UK: Paternoster, 2004.

Gottlieb, Roger S. *This Sacred Earth: Religion, Nature, Environment.* New York: Routledge, 2004.

Gottwald, Norman K, "Social Class and Ideology: An Eagletonian Reading." *Semeia* 69 (1992) 43–57.

Gray, George Buchanan. *A Critical and Exegetical Commentary on The Book of Isaiah I–XXXIX.* New York: Scribner's Sons, 1912.

Grayson, A. K. "Assyrian Rule of Conquered Territory in Ancient Western Asia." In *Civilizations of the Ancient Near East,* edited by Jack M. Sasson, John Baines, Gary M. Beckman, and Karen Sydney Robinson, 959–68. Peabody, MT: Hendrickson, 2000.

Bibliography

———. "Assyria: Sennacherib and Esarhaddon (704–669 B.C.)." In *The Cambridge Ancient History*, edited by John Boardman, I. E. S. Edwards, E. Sollberger, and N. G. L. Hammond, 103–41. Cambridge: Cambridge University Press, 1992.

———. *Assyrian Rulers of the Early First Millennium BC I (1114–859 BC)*. The Royal Inscriptions of Mesopotamia Assyrian Periods 2. Toronto: University of Toronto, 1991.

Gruber, Mayer I. "The Motherhood of God in Second Isaiah." *Révue Biblique* 90 (1983) 351–59.

Gunkel, Hermann. *Israel and Babylon: The Babylonian Influence on Israelite Religion*, edited by K. C. Hanson. Eugene, OR: Cascade, 2009.

———. *The Legends of Genesis: The Biblical Saga and History*. New York: Schoken, 1964.

Hagelia, Hallvard. "Meal on Mount Zion—Does Isa 25:6–8 Describe a Covenant Meal?" *SEÅ* 68 (2003) 73–95.

Hägglund, F. *Isaiah 53 in the Light of Homecoming after Exile*. Forschungen zum Alten Testament II/31. Tübingen: Mohr Siebeck, 2008.

Halpern, Baruch. *From Gods to God: The Dynamics of Iron Age Cosmologies*. Tübingen: Mohr Siebeck, 2009.

———. "Jerusalem and the Lineages in the Seventh Century B.C.E.: Kingship and the Rise of Individual Moral Liability." In *Law and Ideology in Monarchic Israel*, 11–107. Sheffield, UK: JSOT, 1991.

Hansen, Emmanuel. "Portrait of a Revolutionary." In *Rethinking Fanon: The Continuing Dialogue*, edited by Nigel C. Gibson, 49–83. Amherst, NY: Humanity, 1999.

Hanson, Paul D. *The Dawn of Apocalyptic*. Philadelphia: Fortress, 1975.

Hasel, Michael G. *Military Practice and Polemic: Israel's Laws of Warfare in Near Eastern Perspective*. Berrien Springs, MI: Andrews University, 2005.

Hayes, John. "The Tradition of Zion's Inviolability." *Journal of Biblical Literature* 82 (1963) 419–26.

Hays, Christopher B. "The Covenant with Mut." *Vetus Testamentum* 60 (2010) 212–40.

———. *Death in the Iron Age II and in First Isaiah*. Tübingen: Mohr Siebeck, 2011.

———. "How Shall We Sing?: Psalm 137 in Historical and Canonical Context." *Horizons in Biblical Theology* 27 (2005) 35–55.

Heaton, Eric. "Isaiah 40–55." In *Prophets & Poets*, edited by Grace Emmerson, 53–80. London: SPCK, 1994.

Hess, Richard S. *Israelite Religions: An Archaeological and Biblical Survey*. Nottingham, UK: Apollos, 2007.

Himmelfarb, Martha. "'A Kingdom of Priests': The Democratization of the Priesthood in the Literature of Second Temple Judaism." *Journal of Jewish Thought and Philosophy* 6 (1997) 89–104.

Hom, Mary Katherine. "The Characterization of the Assyrians in Isaiah: Synchronic and Diachronic Perspectives." *Tyndale Bulletin* 60 (2009) 316–18.

Horowitz, W., and T. Oshima, with S. Sanders. *Cuneiform in Canaan: Cuneiform Sources from the Land of Israel in Ancient Times*. Jerusalem: Israel Exploration Society/The Hebrew University of Jerusalem, 2006.

Horsley, Richard A., editor. *In the Shadow of Empire: Reclaiming the Bible as a History of Faithful Resistance*. Louisville, KY: Westminster John Knox, 2008.

———. *Revolt of the Scribes: Resistance and Apocalyptic Origins*. Minneapolis: Fortress, 2010.

Horvath, Ronald J. "A Definition of Colonialism." *Current Anthropology* 13 (1972) 45–57.

Howard-Brook, Wes, and Anthony Gwyther. *Unveiling Empire: Reading Revelation Then and Now.* Maryknoll, NY: Orbis, 1999.

Ingham, Patricia Clare, and Michelle R. Warren, editors. *Postcolonial Moves: Medieval through Modern.* New York: Palgrave MacMillan, 2003.

Jackson, Tim. *Prosperity without Growth: Economics for a Finite Planet.* London: Routledge, 2009.

Jacoby, R. "The Representation and Identification of Cities on Assyrian Reliefs." *Israel Exploration Journal* 41 (1991) 112–31.

Jameson, Fredric. *The Political Unconscious: Narrative as a Socially Symbolic Act.* London: Methuen, 1981.

Janzen, Gerald J. "On the Moral Nature of God's Power: Yahweh and the Sea in Job and Deutero-Isaiah." *Catholic Biblical Quarterly* 56 (1994) 458–78.

Japhet, Sara. *From the Rivers of Babylon to the Highlands of Judah.* Winona Lake, IN: Eisenbrauns, 2006.

———. "Periodization between History and Ideology II: Chronology and Ideology in Ezra–Nehemiah." In *Judah and Judeans in the Persian Period*, edited by O. Lipschits, and M. Oeming, 491–508. Winona Lake, IN: Eisenbrauns, 2006.

Jeppesen, Knud. "Myth in the Prophetic Literature." In *Myths in the Old Testament*, edited by Benedikt Otzen, Hans Gottlieb, and Knud Jeppesen, 94–123. London: SCM, 1980.

Johnson, Dan G. *From Chaos to Restoration: An Integrative Reading of Isaiah 24–27.* Sheffield, UK: JSOT, 1988.

Jong, M. J. de. *Isaiah among the Ancient Near Eastern Prophets: A Comparative Study of the Earliest Stages of the Isaiah Tradition and the Neo-Assyrian Prophecies.* Leiden: Brill, 2007.

Kaiser, Otto. *Das Buch des Propheten Jesaja.* 5th ed. Gottingen: Vandenhoeck & Ruprecht, 1981.

———. *Isaiah 1–12: A Commentary.* Translated by John Bowden. Philadelphia: Westminster, 1972

Kaiser, W. C. "The Unfailing Kindnesses Promised to David: Isaiah 55:3." *Journal for the Study of the Old Testament* 45 (1989) 91–98.

Kapelrud, A. S. *Et folk på hjemferd: "Trøstepropfeten"—den annen Jesaja—og hans budskap.* Oslo: Universitetsforlaget, 1964.

Kenyon, K. M. *Digging Up Jerusalem.* Tonbridge, UK: Been, 1974.

Kessler, John. "Images of Exile: Representations of the 'Exile' and 'Empty Land' in Sixth to Fourth Century B.C.E. Yehudite Literature." In *The Concept of Exile in Ancient Israel and its Historical Contexts*, edited by E. Ben Zvi, and C. Levin, 309–51. Berlin: de Gruyter, 2010.

———. "Persia's Loyal Yahwists: Power, Identity and Ethnicity in Achaemenid Yehud." In *Judah and the Judeans in the Persian Period*, edited by O. Lipschits, and M. Oeming, 91–121. Winona Lake, IN: Eisenbrauns, 2006.

———. "Reconstructing Haggai's Jerusalem: Demographic and Sociological Considerations and the Search for an Adequate Methodological Point of Departure." In *"Every City Shall Be Forsaken": Urbanism and Prophecy in Ancient Israel and the Near East*, edited by L. L. Grabbe, and R. D. Haak, 137–58. Sheffield, UK: Sheffield Academic Press, 2001.

Kessler, Martin. "The Scaffolding of the Book of Jeremiah." In *Reading the Book of Jeremiah: A Search for Coherence*, edited by Martin Kessler, 57–66. Winona Lake, IN: Eisenbrauns, 2004.

Killebrew, Ann E. *Biblical Peoples and Ethnicity: An Archaeological Study of Egyptians, Canaanites, Philistines, and Early Israel (ca. 1300–1100 B.C.E.)*. Atlanta: SBL, 2005.

Kimuhu, Johnson M. *Leviticus: The Priestly Laws and Prohibitions from the Perspective of Ancient Near East and Africa*. New York: Lang, 2008.

Kittel, R. "Cyrus und Deuterojesaja." *Zeitschrift für die alttestamentliche Wissenschaft* 18 (1898) 149–62.

Knight, G. A. F. *Servant Theology: A Commentary on the Book of Isaiah 40–55*. Grand Rapids: Eerdmans, 1984.

Knohl, Israel. *The Sanctuary of Silence: The Priestly Torah and the Holiness School*. Minneapolis: Fortress, 1995.

Knudsen, R. D. "Symbol." In *New Dictionary of Theology*, edited by Sinclair B. Ferguson, and David F. Wright, 669–70. Leicester, UK: InterVarsity, 1988.

Köckert, Matthias. "Das Land in der priesterlichen Komposition des Pentateuch." In *Von Gott reden: Beiträge zur Theologie und Exegese des Alten Testaments*, edited by D. Vieweger, and E. J. Waschke, 148–62. Neukirchen-Vluyn: Neukirchener, 1995.

Koester, Craig R. *Symbolism in the Fourth Gospel: Meaning, Mystery, Community*. Minneapolis: Augsburg Fortress, 2003.

Koole, J. L. *Isaiah. Part 3, Volume 1: Isaiah 40–48*. Kampen: Peeters, 1997.

Korpel, Marjo C. A. "Metaphors in Isaiah LV." *Vetus Testamentum* 46 (1996) 43–55.

———. "Second Isaiah's Coping with the Religious Crisis: Reading Isaiah 40 and 55." In *The Crisis of Israelite Religion*, edited by Bob Becking, and Marjo C. A. Korpel, 90–105. Leiden: Brill, 1999.

Kramer, S. N. *The Sumerians: Their History, Culture, and Character*. Chicago: The University of Chicago Press, 1963.

Laato, Antti. *'About Zion I Will Not Be Silent': The Book of Isaiah as an Ideological Unity*. Stockholm: Almqvist & Wiksell, 1998.

Laberge, L. "Is 30, 19–26: A Deuteronomic Text?" *Église et théologie* 2 (1971) 35–54.

Lack, Rémi. *La symbolique du Livre d'Isaïe: Essai sur l'image littéraire comme élément de structuration*. Rome: Biblical Institute, 1973.

Landes, George M. "Creation and Liberation." In *Creation in the Old Testament*, edited by Bernhard W. Anderson, 135–51. Philadelphia: Fortress, 1984.

Leakey, Richard, and Roger Lewin. *The Sixth Extinction: Patterns of Life and the Future of Mankind*. New York: Doubleday, 1995.

Lee, Chi Chung Archie. "Returning to China: Biblical Interpretation in Postcolonial Hong Kong." *Biblical Interpretation* 7 (1999) 156–73.

Lesko, Barbara S. *The Great Goddesses of Egypt*. Norman, OK: University of Oklahoma Press, 1999.

Levenson, Jon D. *Creation and the Persistence of Evil: The Jewish Drama of Divine Omnipotence*. Princeton: Princeton University Press, 1994.

———. *Sinai and Zion: An Entry into the Jewish Bible*. Minneapolis: Winston, 1985.

———. "The Temple and the World." *Journal of Religion* 64 (1984) 275–98.

Levine, Baruch A. "Assyrian Ideology and Biblical Monotheism." *Iraq* 67 (2005) 411–27.

Levinson, Bernard. "The Manumission of Hermeneutics." In *Congress Volume Leiden*, edited by A. Lemaire, 281–324. Leiden: Brill, 2006.

Liebreich, Leon J. "The Compilation of the Book of Isaiah (Part I)." *Jewish Quarterly Review* 46 (1956) 259–77.

———. "The Compilation of the Book of Isaiah (Part II)." *Jewish Quarterly Review* 47 (1956) 114–38.

Linafelt, Tod. *Surviving Lamentations: Catastrophe, Lament, and Protest in the Afterlife of a Biblical Book*. Chicago: University of Chicago Press, 2000.

Lind, Millard C. "Monotheism, Power and Justice (Isaiah 40–55)." *Catholic Biblical Quarterly* 46 (1984) 432–46.

Lipton, Diana. *Longing for Egypt and Other Unexpected Biblical Tales*. Sheffield, UK: Sheffield Phoenix, 2008.

Liverani, Mario. "The Ideology of the Assyrian Empire." In *Power and Propaganda. A Symposium on Ancient Empires*, 297–317. Copenhagen: Akademisk Forlag, 1979.

Livingstone, Alasdair. "New Dimensions in the Study of Assyrian Religion." In *Assyria 1995*, edited by S. Parpola, and R. M. Whiting, 165–77. Helsinki: The Neo-Assyrian Text Corpus Project, 1997.

Loretz, Oswald. "Stelen und Sohnespflichten Totenkult Kanaans und Israels: *skn* (KTU 1.17 I 26) und *jd* (Jes 56,5)." *Ugarit-Forschungen* 21 (1989) 241–46.

Lust, Johan. "The Divine Title האדון and אדני in Proto-Isaiah and Ezekiel." In *Isaiah in Context: Studies in Honour of Arie van der Kooij on the Occasion of His Sixty-Fifth Birthday*, edited by Arie van der Kooij, Michaël N. van der Meer, P. S. F. van Keulen, W. Th. van Peursen, and R. B. ter Haar Romeny, 131–49. Leiden: Brill, 2010.

MacDonald, Nathan. "Monotheism and Isaiah." In *Interpreting Isaiah: Issues and Approaches*, edited by David G. Firth, and H. G. M. Williamson, 42–61. Leicester, UK: InterVarsity, 2009.

———. *Not Bread Alone: The Uses of Food in the Old Testament*. Oxford: Oxford University Press, 2008.

Macey, David. *Frantz Fanon: A Biography*. New York: Picador, 2000.

Machinist, Peter. "Assyria and Its Image in the First Isaiah." *Journal of American Oriental Studies* 103 (1983) 719–37.

Macky, Peter. *The Centrality of Metaphors to Biblical Thought: A Method for Interpreting the Bible*. Lewiston, NY: Mellen, 1990.

———. "The Ræb Šaqeh at the Wall of Jerusalem: Israelite Identity in the Face of the Assyrian 'Other.'" *Hebrew Studies* 41 (2000) 151–68.

Maier, Christl M. *Daughter Zion, Mother Zion: Gender, Space, and the Sacred in Ancient Israel*. Minneapolis: Fortress, 2008.

Mamdani, Mahmood. "Beyond Settler and Native as Political Identities: Overcoming the Political Legacy of Colonialism." *Comparative Studies in Society and History* 43 (2001) 651–64.

Mandolfo, Carleen R. *Daughter Zion Talks Back to the Prophets: A Dialogic Theology of the Book of Lamentations*. Atlanta: SBL, 2007.

Mankowski, P. V. *Akkadian Loanwords in Biblical Hebrew*. Harvard Semitic Studies 47. Winona Lake, IN: Eisenbrauns, 2000.

Marlow, Hilary. *Biblical Prophets: Contemporary Environmental Ethics*. Oxford: Oxford University Press, 2009.

Marshall, I. H. "Myth." In *New Dictionary of Theology*, edited by Sinclair B. Ferguson, and David F. Wright, 449–51. Leicester, UK: InterVarsity, 1988.

Bibliography

Marshall, John W. "Postcolonialism and the Practice of History." In *Her Masters Tools?: Feminist and Postcolonial Engagement of Historical-Critical Discourse,* edited by C. Vander Stichele, and T. Penner, 93–108. Atlanta: SBL, 2005.

Martin, Tony. "Rescuing Fanon From the Critics." In *Rethinking Fanon: The Continuing Dialogue,* edited by Nigel C. Gibson, 83–102. Amherst, NY: Humanity, 1999.

Maynard, J. A. "The Home of Deutero-Isaiah." *Journal of Biblical Literature* 36 (1917) 213–24.

Mazar, B., Y. Shiloh, and H. Geva. "Jerusalem: The Early Periods and the First Temple Period." In *The New Encyclopedia of Archaeological Excavations in the Holy Land,* 5 vols., edited by E. Stern, 2:698–716. Jerusalem: Israel Exploration Society and Carta, 1993.

McCarthy, Dennis J. "Creation Motifs in Ancient Hebrew Poetry." In *Creation in the Old Testament,* edited by Bernhard W. Anderson, 74–89. Philadelphia: Fortress, 1984.

McConville, Gordon. "Pilgrimage and 'Place': An Old Testament View." In *Explorations in a Christian Theology of Pilgrimage,* edited by Craig Bartholomew and Fred Hughes, 17–28. Aldershot, UK: Ashgate, 2004.

McEvenue, Sean. "Who Was Second-Isaiah?" In *Studies in the Book of Isaiah: Festschrift Willem A. M. Beuken,* edited by J. van Ruiten, and M. Vervenne, 213–22. Leuven: Leuven University Press, 1997.

McFague, Sallie. *The Body of God: An Ecological Theology.* London: SCM, 1993.

Meadowcroft, T. J. "Between Authorial Intent and Indeterminacy: The Incarnation as an Invitation to Human-Divine Discourse." *Scottish Journal of Theology* 58 (2005) 199–218.

———. *The Message of the Word of God: The Glory of God Made Known.* Leicester, UK: InterVarsity, 2011.

Melugin, Roy F. "Figurative Speech and the Reading of Isaiah 1 as Scripture." In *New Visions of Isaiah,* 281–305. Sheffield, UK: Sheffield Academic Press, 1996.

Memmi, Albert. *The Colonizer and the Colonized.* Exp. ed. Boston: Beacon, 1991.

Merendino, R. P. *Der Erste und der Letzte.* Leiden: Brill, 1981.

Mieroop, M. van de. *A History of the Ancient Near East: ca. 3000–323 BC.* Oxford: Blackwell, 2004.

Milgrom, Jacob. *Leviticus 1–16.* Garden City, NY: Doubleday, 1991.

Millard, A. "Early Aramaic." In *Languages of Iraq, Ancient and Modern,* edited by J. N. Postgate, 85–94. Baghdad: The British School of Archaeology in Iraq, 2007.

Miller, Daniel J. "The Shadow or the Overlord: Revisiting the Question of Neo-Assyrian Imposition on the Judaean Cult during the Eighth–Seventh Centuries B.C.E.?" In *From Babel to Babylon: Essays on Biblical History and Literature in Honour of Brian Peckham,* edited by Brian Peckham, Joyce Louise Rilett Wood, and John E. Harvey, 146–68. London: T. & T. Clark, 2006.

Moltmann, Jürgen. *Der Geist des Lebens.* Munich: Kaiser, 1991. ET *The Spirit of Life.* Minneapolis: Fortress, 1992.

Moore, Stephen D. *Empire and Apocalypse: Postcolonialism and the New Testament.* Sheffield, UK: Sheffield Phoenix, 2006.

Morrow, William. "'To Set the Name' in the Deuteronomic Centralization Formula: A Case of Cultural Hybridity." *Journal of Semitic Studies* 55 (2010) 365–83.

Motyer, J. A. *The Prophecy of Isaiah: An Introduction and Commentary.* Downers Grove, IL: InterVarsity, 1993.

Muilenburg, J. "The Book of Isaiah Chapters 40–66." In *Interpreters' Bible*. Vol V, 381–773. New York: Abingdon, 1956.

Myers, Norman. "The Biodiversity Crisis and the Future of Evolution." *The Environmentalist* 16 (1996) 37–47.

Newsom, Carol A. "Response to Norman K. Gottwald, 'Social Class and Ideology in Isaiah 40–55." *Semeia* 59 (1992) 75–78.

Ngugi wa Thiong'o. *Decolonizing the Mind: The Politics of Language in African Literature.* Oxford: Currey, 1986.

Niehr, Herbert. "The Changed Status of the Dead in Yehud." In *Yahwism after the Exile: Perspectives on Israelite Religion in the Persian Era*, edited by R. Albertz, and B. Becking, 136–55. Assen: Van Gorcum, 2003.

Nihan, Christophe. *From Priestly Torah to Pentateuch.* Tübingen: Mohr Siebeck, 2007.

Nissinen, M. "Die Relevanz der neuassyrischen Prophetie für die alttestamentliche Forschung." In *Mesopotamica—Ugaritica—Biblica*, FS Kurt Bergerhof, edited by M. Dietrich, and O. Loretz, 217–58. Kevelaer: Butzon & Bercker, 1993.

Nissinen, M., and S. Parpola, "Marduk's Return and Reconciliation in a Prophetic Letter from Arbela." In *Verbum et Calamus*. FS Tapani Harviainen, edited by H. Juusola, J. Laulainen, and H. Palva, 199–219. Helsinki: Vammanlan Kirjapaino Oy, 2004.

Northcott, Michael S. *The Environment and Christian Ethics.* Cambridge: Cambridge University Press, 1996.

O'Brien, Julia M. *Challenging Prophetic Metaphor: Theology and Ideology in the Prophets.* Louisville, KY: Westminster John Knox, 2008.

O'Connor, Kathleen M. "'Speak Tenderly to Jerusalem': Second Isaiah's Reception and Use of Daughter Zion." *Princeton Seminary Bulletin* 20 (1999) 281–94.

Ollenburger, Ben. *Zion, the City of the Great King: A Theological Symbol of the Jerusalem Cult.* Sheffield, UK: JSOT, 1987.

Olyan, Saul. "Exodus 31:12–17: The Sabbath according to H, the Sabbath according to P and H." *Journal of Biblical Literature* 124 (2005) 201–9.

———. *Rites and Rank: Hierarchy in Biblical Representations of Cult.* Princeton: Princeton University Press, 2000.

Oorschot, Jürgen van. *Von Babel zum Zion: Eine literarkritische und redaktiongeschtliche Untersuchung.* Berlin: de Gruyter, 1993.

Orlinsky, Harry. "Nationalism-Universalism and Internationalism in Ancient Israel." In *Translating and Understanding the Old Testament*, edited by H. T. Frank, and W. L. Reed, 206–36. Nashville TN: Abingdon, 1970.

Oswalt, John. *The Bible among the Myths: Unique Revelation or Just Ancient Literature?* Grand Rapids: Zondervan, 2009.

———. *The Book of Isaiah: Chapters 1–39.* Grand Rapids: Eerdmans, 1986.

———. *The Book of Isaiah Chapters 40–66.* Grand Rapids: Eerdmans, 1998.

Otzen, Benedikt. "The Concept of Myth." In *Myths in the Old Testament*, edited by Benedikt Otzen, Hans Gottlieb, and Knud Jeppesen, 1–21. London: SCM, 1980.

Overholt, Thomas. *Channels of Prophecy: The Social Dynamics of Prophetic Activity.* Minneapolis: Fortress, 1989.

———. *Cultural Anthropology and the Old Testament.* Minneapolis: Fortress, 1996.

———. *Prophecy in Cross Cultural Perspective: A Sourcebook for Biblical Researchers.* Atlanta: Scholars, 1986.

Paganini, Simone. "Who Speaks in Isaiah 55.1? Notes on the Communicative Structure in Isaiah 55." *Journal for the Study of the Old Testament* 30 (2005) 83–92.

Parpola, S. "Assyria's Expansion in the 8th and 7th Centuries and Its Long-Term Repercussions in the West." In *Symbiosis, Symbolism, and the Power of the Past: Canaan, Ancient Israel, and Their Neighbors—From the Late Bronze Age through Roman Palaestina*, edited by W. G. Dever, and S. Gitin, 99–112. Winona Lake, IN: Eisenbrauns, 2003.

Parpola, S., and K. Watanabe, editors. *Neo-Assyrian Treaties and Loyalty Oaths*. State Archives of Assyria 2. Helsinki: Helsinki University Press, 1988.

Paul, S. M. *Amos*. Hermeneia. Minneapolis: Fortress, 1991.

———. "Deutero-Isaiah and Cuneiform Royal Inscriptions." *Journal of American Oriental Studies* 88 (1968) 180–86.

Penchansky, David. "Up for Grabs: A Tentative Proposal for Doing Ideological Criticism." *Semeia* 59 (1992) 35–41.

———. *Twilight of the Gods: Polytheism in the Hebrew Bible*. Westminster: John Knox, 2005.

Perinbam, B. Marie. *Holy Violence: The Revolutionary Thought of Frantz Fanon, An Intellectual Biography*. Washington, DC: Three Continents, 1982.

Pinnock, Clark. *Most Moved Mover: A Theology of God's Openness*. The Didsbury Lectures. Carlisle, UK: Paternoster, 2001.

Porter, Barbara N. *Images, Power, and Politics: Figurative Aspects of Esarhaddon's Babylonian Policy*. Philadelphia: American Philosophical Society, 1993.

Portier-Young, Anathea E. *Apocalypse Against Empire: Theologies of Resistance in Early Judaism*. Grand Rapids: Eerdmans, 2011.

Postgate, J. N. "The Ownership and Exploitation of Land in Assyria in the 1st Millennium BC." In *Reflets des deux fleuves*, 141–52. Leuven: Peeters, 1989.

Purcell, Nicholas. "Colonization and Mediterranean History." In *Ancient Colonizations: Analogy, Similarity & Difference*, edited by Henry Hurst, and Sara Owen, 115–40. London: Duckworth, 2005.

Pury, Albert de. "Abraham: The Priestly Writer's 'Ecumenical' Ancestor." In *Rethinking the Foundations: Historiography in the Ancient World and in the Bible. Essays in Honour of John Van Seters*, edited by S. L. McKenzie, and T. Römer, 163–81. Berlin: de Gruyter, 2000.

Quinn-Miscall, Peter D. *Reading Isaiah: Poetry and Vision*. Louisville, KY: Westminster John Knox, 2001.

Reich, R. *Excavating the City of David: Where Jerusalem's History Began*. Jerusalem: Israel Exploration Society, 2011.

Rendtorff, Rolf. "Jesaja 56,1 als Schlüssel für die Komposition des Buches Jesaja." In Rendtorff, *Kanon und Theologie*, 172–79. Neukirchen: Neukirchener, 1991. ET *Canon and Theology*, 181–89. Minneapolis: Fortress, 1993.

Rice, Gene. "Dining with Deutero-Isaiah." *Journal of Religious Thought* 37 (1980) 23–30.

Richter, Sandra. *The Deuteronomistic History and the Name Theology*. Berlin: de Gruyter, 2002.

Roberts, J. J. M. "The Davidic Origin of the Zion Tradition." *Journal of Biblical Literature* 92 (1973) 329–40.

———. "The End of War in the Zion Tradition: The Imperialistic Background of an Old Testament Vision of Worldwide Peace." In *Character Ethics and the Old Testament*, edited by M. D. Carroll R., and J. E. Lapsley, 119–28. Louisville: Westminster John Knox, 2007.

Rogerson, J. W. *Myth in Old Testament Interpretation*. Berlin: de Gruyter, 1974.

Römer, Thomas. "Abraham Traditions in the Hebrew Bible outside the Book of Genesis." In *The Book of Genesis: Composition, Reception, and Interpretation*, edited by C. A. Evans, J. N. Lohr, and D. L. Petersen, 159–80. Leiden: Brill, 2012.

Ryken, Leland, James C. Wilhoit, and Tremper Longman, editors. *Dictionary of Biblical Imagery*. Downers Grove, IL: InterVarsity, 1998.

Said, Edward. *Culture and Imperialism*. London: Chatto & Windsor, 1993.

Sanders, Seth L. *The Invention of Hebrew*. Urbana, IL: University of Illinois Press, 2009.

Sawyer, John F. A. "Daughter of Zion and Servant of the Lord in Isaiah: A Comparison." *Journal for the Study of the Old Testament* 44 (1989) 89–107.

Schaudig, H. "'Bēl Bows, Nabu Stoops!' The Prophecy of Isaiah xlvi 1–2 as a Reflection of Babylonian 'Processional Omens.'" *Vetus Testamentum* 58 (2008) 557–72.

———. *Die Inschriften Nabonids von Babylon und Kyros' des Großen, samt den in ihrem Umfeld entstandenen Tendenzschriften. Textausgabe und Grammatik*. Münster: Ugarit-Verlag, 2001.

Schmid, H. H. "Creation, Righteousness and Salvation." In *Creation in the Old Testament*, edited by Bernhard W. Anderson, 102–17. Philadelphia: Fortress, 1984.

Schramm, Brooks. *The Opponents of Third Isaiah: Reconstructing the Cultic History of the Restoration*. Sheffield, UK: Sheffield Academic Press, 1995.

Schwartz, Baruch J. "Reexamining the Fate of the 'Canaanites' in the Torah Traditions." In *Sefer Moshe: The Moshe Weinfeld Jubilee Volume*, 151–70. Winona Lake, IN: Eisenbrauns, 2004.

Scott, James C. *Domination and the Arts of Resistance: Hidden Transcripts*. New Haven, CT: Yale University Press, 1990.

Segovia, Fernando F. "Mapping the Postcolonial Optic in Biblical Criticism: Meaning and Scope." In *Postcolonial Biblical Criticism: Interdisciplinary Intersections*, edited by Stephen D. Moore, and Fernando F. Segovia, 23–78. London: T. & T. Clark International, 2005.

Seitz, Christopher R. *Isaiah 1–39*. Interpretation. Louisville, KY: Westminster John Knox, 1993.

———. *Zion's Final Destiny: The Development of the Book of Isaiah: A Reassessment of Isaiah 36–39*. Minneapolis: Fortress, 1991.

Shanks, H. *Jerusalem: An Archaeological Biography*. New York: Random House, 1995.

Simons, J. *Jerusalem in the Old Testament: Researches and Theories*. Leiden: Brill, 1952.

Skjoldal, Neil O. "The Function of Isaiah 24–27." *Journal for the Evangelical Theological Society* 36 (1993) 163–72.

Smelik, K. A. D. "Distortion of Old Testament Prophecy: The Purpose of Isaiah XXXVI–XXXVII." In *Crises and Perspectives*, edited by A. S. van der Woude, 70–93. Leiden: OTS, 1986.

Smith, Anthony D. *Chosen Peoples: Sacred Sources of National Identity*. Oxford: Oxford University Press, 2003.

Smith, D. E. "Messianic Banquet." In *Anchor Bible Dictionary*, edited by D. N. Freedman, 4:788–91. New York: Doubleday, 1992.

Smith, Gary V. *Isaiah 1–39*. NAC. Nashville, TN: Broadman & Holman, 2007.

Smith, M. S. *God in Translation: Deities in Cross-Cultural Discourse in the Biblical World*. Forschungen zum Alten Testament 57. Tübingen: Mohr Siebeck, 2008.

———. *The Origins of Biblical Monotheism: Israel's Polytheistic Background and the Ugaritic Texts*. New York: Oxford University Press, 2001.

Bibliography

Smith, Morton. *Palestinian Politics and Parties that Shaped the Old Testament.* 1971. Reprint. London: SCM, 1987.

Smith-Christopher, Daniel. *A Biblical Theology of Exile.* Minneapolis: Fortress, 2002.

———. "The Book of Daniel" and "The Additions to Daniel." In *New Interpreters' Bible,* 7:19–194. Nashville, TN: Abingdon, 1996

———. "Ezekiel on Fanon's Couch: A Postcolonialist Dialogue with David Halperin's Seeking Ezekiel." In *Peace and Justice Shall Embrace: Power and Theopolitics in the Bible: Essays in Honor of Millard Lind,* edited by Ted Grimsrud, and Loren L. Johns, 108–44. Telford, PA: Pandora, 1999.

———. "Reading Jeremiah as Frantz Fanon." In *Jeremiah (Dis)placed: New Directions in Writing/Reading Jeremiah,* edited by A. R. Pete Diamond, and Louis Stulman, 115–24. London: T. & T. Clark, 2011.

Sommer, Benjamin. *A Prophet Reads Scripture: Allusion in Isaiah 40–66.* Stanford: Stanford University Press, 1998.

Soskice, Janet Martin. *Metaphor and Religious Language.* Oxford: Clarendon, 1985.

Southwood, Katherine E. *Ethnicity and the Mixed Marriage Crisis in Ezra 9–10: An Anthropological Approach.* Oxford: Oxford University Press, 2012.

Sparks, Kenton L. "*Enuma Elish* and Priestly Mimesis: Elite Emulation in Nascent Judaism." *Journal of Biblical Literature* 126 (2007) 625–48.

Spivak, Gayatri. *Critique of Postcolonial Reason: Toward a History of the Vanishing Present.* Cambridge: Harvard University Press, 1999.

Stavrakopoulou, Francesca. *Land of Our Fathers: The Roles of Ancestor Veneration in Biblical Land Claims.* London: T. & T. Clark, 2010.

Stinson, Michelle. "A Triptych of the Table: Rebellious, Judgment and Restoration in the Book of Isaiah." Unpublished paper, Old Testament Meals Consultation, SBL Conference, Atlanta, 2010.

Strawn, Brent. "'A World under Control': Isaiah 60 and the Apadana Reliefs from Persepolis." In *Approaching Yehud,* edited by J. L. Berquist, 85–116. Atlanta: SBL, 2006.

Stromberg, J. *An Introduction to the Study of Isaiah.* London: T. & T. Clark, 2011.

Stuhlmueller, Carroll. *Creative Redemption in Deutero-Isaiah.* Rome: Biblical Institute Press, 1970.

Stummer, F. "Einige keilschriftliche Parallelen zu Jes. 40–55." *Journal of Biblical LIterature* 45 (1926) 171–89.

Sugirtharajah, R. S. *Postcolonial Criticism and Biblical Interpretation.* Oxford: Oxford University Press, 2002.

Sweeney, Marvin A. *Form and Intertextuality in Prophetic and Apocalyptic Literature.* Tübingen: Mohr Siebeck, 2005.

———. *Isaiah 1–4 and the Post-Exilic Understanding of the Isaianic Tradition.* Beiheft zur ZAW. Berlin: de Gruyter, 1988.

———. *Isaiah 1–39: With an Introduction to Prophetic Literature.* Grand Rapids: Eerdmans, 1996.

———. "Re-evaluating Isaiah 1–39 in Recent Critical Research." In *Recent Research on the Major Prophets,* edited by Alan J. Hauser, 93–117. Sheffield, UK: Sheffield Phoenix, 2008.

———. "Sargon's Threat against Jerusalem in Isaiah 10,27–32." *Biblica* 75 (1994) 457–70.

————. "Textual Citations in Isaiah 24–27: Toward an Understanding of the Redactional Function of Chapters 24–27 in the Book of Isaiah." *Journal of Biblical Literature* 107 (1988) 39–52.

Tadmor, H. "The Aramaization of Assyria: Aspects of Western Impact." In *Mesopotamien und seine Nachbarn: politische und kulturelle Wechselbeziehungen im Alten Vorderasien vom 4. bis 1. Jahrtausend v. Chr.* Rencontre assyriologique internationale Berlin, 3. bis 7. Juli 1978, edited by H.-J. Nissen, and J. Renger, 449–70. Berlin: Reimer, 1982.

Talmon, S."The 'Comparative Method' in Biblical Interpretation—Principles and Problems." In *Congress Volume: Göttingen, 1977*, edited by J. A. Emerton, 320–56. Leiden: Brill, 1978.

Thiselton, Anthony C. *Thiselton on Hermeneutics.* Grand Rapids: Eerdmans, 2006.

Tiemeyer, Lena-Sofia. *For the Comfort of Zion: The Geographical and Theological Location of Isaiah 40–55.* Leiden: Brill, 2011.

————. "Geography and Textual Allusions: Interpreting Isaiah xl–lv and Lamentations as Judahite Texts." *Vetus Testamentum* 57 (2007) 367–85.

————. *Priestly Rites and Prophetic Rage: Post-Exilic Prophetic Critique of the Priesthood.* Tübingen: Mohr Siebeck, 2006.

Tomasino, Anthony J. "The Babylonian New Year Festival: New Insights from the Cuneiform Texts and Their Bearing on Old Testament Study." In *Congress Volume: Leuven, 1989*, edited by J. A. Emerton, 331–44. Leiden: Brill, 1991.

————. "Isaiah 1:1—2:4 and 63–66, and the Composition of the Isaianic Corpus." *Journal for the Study of the Old Testament* 57 (1993) 81–98.

Toorn, K. van der. *Scribal Culture and the Making of the Hebrew Bible.* Cambridge: Harvard University Press, 2007.

Tufnell, O. et al. *Lachish IV: The Bronze Age.* London: Oxford University Press, 1958.

Tufnell, O., C. H. Inge, and G. L. Harding. *Lachish II: The Fosse Temple.* London: Oxford University Press, 1940.

Tufnell, O. *Lachish III: The Iron Age.* London: Oxford University Press, 1953.

Tull, Patricia K. "Persistent Vegetative States: People as Plants and Plants as People in Isaiah." In *The Desert Will Bloom: Poetic Visions in Isaiah*, edited by A. Joseph Everson, and Hyun Chul Paul Kim, 17–34. Atlanta: SBL, 2009.

Tull Willey, Patricia. *Remember the Former Things: The Recollection of Previous Texts in Second Isaiah.* Atlanta: Scholars, 1997.

————. "The Servant of YHWH and Daughter Zion: Alternating Visions of YHWH's Community." In *SBL 1995 Seminar Papers*, 267–303. Atlanta: Scholars, 1995.

Uehlinger, C. "Clio in a World of Pictures—Another Look at the Lachish Reliefs from Sennacherib's Southwest Palace at Nineveh." In *"Shut Up like a Bird in a Cage": The Invasion of Sennacherib in 701 B.C.E.*, edited by L. L. Grabbe, 221–305. Sheffield, UK: Sheffield Academic Press, 2003.

Ussishkin, D. "The Assyrian Attack on Lachish: The Archaeological Evidence from the Southwest Corner of the Site." *Tel Aviv* 17 (1990) 53–86.

————. *The Conquest of Lachish by Sennacherib.* Tel Aviv: Tel Aviv University, Institute of Archaeology, 1982.

————. "Lachish." In *The New Encyclopedia of Archaeological Excavations in the Holy Land*, 5 vols., edited by E. Stern, 3:897–911. Jerusalem: Carta, 1993.

————. "The 'Lachish Reliefs' and the City of Lachish." *Israel Exploration Journal* 30 (1980) 174–95.

Bibliography

———. *The Renewed Archaeological Excavations at Lachish (1973–1994)*. 5 vols. Tel Aviv: Institute of Archaeology, Tel Aviv, 2004.

Van Winkle, Dwight W. "The Meaning of *yad wašem* in Isaiah LVI 5." *Vetus Testamentum* 47 (1997) 378–85.

Vanderhooft, D. S. *The Neo-Babylonian Empire and Babylon in the Latter Prophets*. Atlanta: Scholars, 1999.

Vanhoozer, K. J. "From Speech Acts to Scripture Acts: The Covenant of Discourse and the Discourse of Covenant." In *After Pentecost: Language and Biblical Interpretation*, edited by Craig Bartholomew, Colin Greene, and Karl Möller, 1–49. Scripture and Hermeneutics vol. 2. Carlisle, UK: Paternoster, 2001.

Vaughn, A. G., and A. E. Killebrew, editors. *Jerusalem in Bible and Archaeology*. Atlanta: SBL, 2003.

Veyne, Paul. "Y a-til eu un impérialisme romain?" *Mélanges d'archéologie et d'histoire de l'école français de Rome* 87 (1975) 793–855.

Volf, Miroslav. *Exclusion and Embrace: A Theological Exploration of Identity, Otherness, and Reconciliation*. Nashville, TN: Abingdon, 1996.

Von Rad, Gerhard. "The Theological Problem of the O.T. Doctrine of Creation." In *Creation in the Old Testament*, edited by Bernhard W. Anderson, 53–64. Philadelphia: Fortress, 1984.

Vriezen, K. J. H. "Archaeological Traces of Cult in Ancient Israel." In *Only One God? Monotheism in Ancient Israel and the Veneration of the Goddess Asherah*, edited by B. Becking, M. Dijkstra, M. C. A. Korpel, and K. J. H. Vriezen, 45–80. Sheffield, UK: Continuum, 2001.

Waltke Bruce K., and M. O'Connor. *An Introduction to Biblical Hebrew Syntax*. Winona Lake, IN: Eisenbrauns, 1990.

Walton, John H. *The Lost World of Genesis One: Ancient Cosmology and the Origins Debate*. Downers Grove, IL: InterVarsity, 2009.

Watts, John D. W. *Isaiah 1–33*. Rev. ed. Nashville, TN: Nelson, 2005.

———. *Isaiah 34–66*. Nashville, TN: Thomas Nelson, 2000.

———. "Jerusalem: An Example of War in a Walled City (Isaiah 3–4)." In *"Every City Shall be Forsaken": Urbanism and Prophecy in Ancient Israel and the Near East*, edited by Lester L. Grabbe, and Robert D. Haak, 210–15. Sheffield, UK: Sheffield Academic Press, 2001.

Webb, Barry G. "Zion in Transformation: A Literary Approach to Isaiah." In *Bible in Three Dimensions*, edited by David J. A. Clines, Stephen E. Fowl, and Stanley E. Porter, 65–84. Sheffield, UK: JSOT, 1990.

Weinfeld, Moshe. *Social Justice in Ancient Israel and in the Ancient Near East*. Jerusalem: Magnes, 1995.

Weippert, M. "'Ich bin Jahwe'—'Ich bin Ištar von Arbela': Deuterojesaja im Lichte der neuassyrischen Prophetie." In *Prophetie und Psalmen*. FS Klaus Seybold, edited by B. Huwyler, H.-P. Mathys, and B. Weber, 42–58. Münster: Ugarit-Verlag, 2001.

Wessels, Wilhelm J. "Nahum." *Old Testament Essays* 11 (1998) 615–28.

Westermann, Claus. *Isaiah 40–66*. London: SCM, 1969.

Whybray, Norman. *Isaiah 40–66*. London: Marshall, Morgan & Scott, 1975.

Wightman, G. J. *The Walls of Jerusalem from the Canaanites to the Mamluks*. Sydney: Meditarch, 1993.

Wildberger, Hans. *Isaiah 1–12*, translated by Thomas H. Trapp. Minneapolis: Fortress, 1991

———. *Isaiah 13–27*, translated by Thomas H. Trapp. Minneapolis: Fortress, 1997.

———. *Isaiah 28–39*, translated by Thomas H. Trapp. Minneapolis: Fortress, 2002.

Wilken, Robert Louis, translator and editor. *Isaiah Interpreted by Early Christian and Medieval Commentators.* Grand Rapids: Eerdmans, 2007.

Williams, Michael A. "Variety in Gnostic Perspectives on Gender." In *Images of the Feminine in Gnosticism,* edited by Karen L. King, 2–22. Philadelphia: Fortress, 1988.

Williamson, H. G. M. *The Book Called Isaiah: Deutero-Isaiah's Role in Composition and Redaction.* Oxford: Clarendon, 1994.

———. *A Critical and Exegetical Commentary on Isaiah 1–5.* London: T. & T. Clark, 2006.

———. *Variations on a Theme: King, Messiah and Servant in the Book of Isaiah.* Carlisle, UK: Paternoster, 1998.

Willis, John T. "An Important Passage for Determining the Historical Setting of a Prophetic Oracle: Isaiah 1:7–8." *Studia Theologica* 39 (1985) 151–69.

Wilson, Robert. *Prophecy and Society in Ancient Israel.* Philadelphia: Fortress, 1980.

———. *Sociological Approaches to the Old Testament.* Philadelphia: Fortress, 1984.

Wöhrle, Jakob. *Fremdlinge im eigenen Land: Zur Entstehung und Intention der priesterlichen Passagen der Vätergeschichte.* Göttingen : Vandenhoek & Ruprecht, 2012.

———. "The Integrative Function of the Law of Circumcision." In *The Foreigner and the Law: Perspectives from the Hebrew Bible and the Ancient Near East,* edited by R. Achenbach, R. Albertz, and J. Wöhrle, 71–87. Wiesbaden: Harrassowitz, 2011.

———. "The Un-Empty Land: The Concept of Exile and Land in P." In *The Concept of Exile in Ancient Israel and Its Historical Contexts,* edited by Ehud Ben Zvi and Christoph Levin, 189–206. Berlin: de Gruyter, 2010.

Wright, C. J. H. *The Mission of God: Unlocking the Bible's Grand Narrative.* Downers Grove, IL: InterVarsity, 2006.

Wright, Jacob L. "Continuing these Conversations." In *Historiography and Identity (Re)formulation in Second Temple Historiographical Literature,* edited by L. Jonker, 149–67. London: T. & T. Clark, 2010.

Wright, Jacob, and Michael Chan. "King and Eunuch: Isaiah 56:1–8 in Light of Honorific Royal Burial Practices." *Journal of Biblical Literature* 131 (2012) 99–119.

Yee, Gale A. "The Anatomy of Biblical Parody: The Dirge Form in 2 Samuel 1 and Isaiah 14." *Catholic Biblical Quarterly* 50 (1988) 565–86.

Younger, K. Lawson. *Ancient Conquest Accounts: A Study in Ancient Near Eastern and Biblical History Writing.* Sheffield, UK: JSOT, 1990.

———. "'Give Us Our Daily Bread.' Everyday Life for the Israelite Deportees." In *Life and Culture in the Ancient Near East,* edited by Richard E. Averbeck, Mark W. Chavalas, and David B. Weisberg, 269–88. Potomac, MD: CDL, 2003.

———. "Sargon's Campaign against Jerusalem—A Further Note." *Biblica* 77 (1996) 108–10.

Zimmerli, W. "Ich bin Jahwe," in *Geschichte und Altes Testament.* FS Albrecht Alt, edited by W. F. Albright, 186–92. Tübingen: Mohr Siebeck, 1953.

Scripture Index

Author Index

Author Index

Author Index